NON AD PERNI-CIEM

In Memory Of

Janet Wright Devine 1948

Dedicated by the
Carleton College
Alumni Association

The Transformation of the North Atlantic World, 1492–1763

Recent Titles in Studies in Military History and International Affairs
Jeremy Black, Series Editor

When Reason Fails: Portraits of Armies at War: America, Britain, Israel and the Future
Michael Goodspeed

A History of Modern Wars of Attrition
Carter Malkasian

When Men Lost Faith in Reason: Reflections on War and Society in the Twentieth Century
H. P. Willmott

Between the Lines: Banditti of the American Revolution
Harry M. Ward

America as a Military Power: From the American Revolution to the Civil War
Jeremy Black

British Strategy and Politics during the Phony War: Before the Balloon Went Up
Nick Smart

War in the Age of the Enlightenment, 1700–1789
Armstrong Starkey

Turning the World Upside Down: The War of American Independence and the Problem of Empire
Neil Longley York

The Transformation of the North Atlantic World, 1492–1763

An Introduction

M. J. SEYMOUR

Studies in Military History and International Affairs
Jeremy Black, Series Editor

Westport, Connecticut
London

Library of Congress Cataloging-in-Publication Data

Seymour, M. J. (Michael J.)
   The transformation of the North Atlantic world, 1492–1763 : an introduction / M.J.
Seymour.
      p. cm. — (Studies in military history and international affairs, ISSN 1537–4432)
   Includes bibliographical references and index.
   ISBN 0–275–97380–8
      1. Europe—Territorial expansion.   2. America—Discovery and exploration.
   3. Europe—Colonies—History.   4. Discoveries in geography.   I. Title.   II. Series.

D210.S43 2004
909.08—dc22   2004014020

British Library Cataloguing in Publication Data is available.

Library of Congress Catalog Card Number: 2004014020

ISBN: 0–275–97380–8
ISSN: 1537–4432

First published in 2004

Praeger Publishers, 88 Post Road West, Westport, CT 06881
An imprint of Greenwood Publishing Group, Inc.
www.praeger.com

Printed in the United States of America

∞™

The paper used in this book complies with the
Permanent Paper Standard issued by the National
Information Standards Organization (Z39.48–1984).

10   9   8   7   6   5   4   3   2   1

The author asserts his right to be identified as the author of this work.

Contents

Acknowledgments

In any project within the academic community, a great many and varied influences contribute to the eventual outcome, even if only one name appears as the author. One way of expressing the thanks due to those who have contributed to the project is to list them here.

First and foremost, for the inspiration to identify and undertake the project, and for his constant advice as it has developed, I am greatly indebted to Professor Michael Mullett. For his early enthusiasm and support for the project, I thank the series editor, Professor Jeremy Black. Once commissioned, the project has been greatly aided by the comments and suggestions at various stages by Dr. Steve Constantine, Professor Peter Harman, Professor John MacKenzie, Mary Mutton, Dr. Moira Peelo, Ken Robertson and Frank Wareing. I am also very grateful for the technical support and guidance of the publishing team.

The prize for endless patience and unfailing confidence in me to see the project to completion goes to Terry, to whom I dedicate this book.

Introduction:
Framing the Questions

. . . I went ashore in a boat with armed men, taking Martín Alonso Pinzón and his brother Vicente Yáñez, captain of the *Niña*. I took the royal standard, and the captains each took a banner with the Green Cross which each of my ships carries as a device, with the letters F and Y, surmounted by a crown, at each end of the cross.
. . . [I]n the presence of them all I was taking possession of this island for their Lord and Lady the King and Queen, . . . [1]

When, in the Course of human events, it becomes necessary for one people to dissolve the political bands which have connected them with another, and to assume, among the Powers of the earth, the separate and equal station to which the Laws of Nature and of Nature's God entitle them, a decent respect to the opinions of mankind requires that they should declare the causes which impel them to the separation.[2]

Less than three hundred years separate the events commemorated in these words, which exemplify the transformation in the early modern period of the relationships amongst the societies inhabiting the Atlantic littoral between 10°S and 60°N. In the years between an underresourced, largely speculative venture sponsored almost on a whim by a minor monarch on the edge of Europe—Queen Isabel of Castilla—and the proclamation of a new republic self-consciously asserting universal and eternal principles of representative government—the United States—there lies a literal reorientation of the early modern European world from its classical Mediterranean–Indian Ocean axis, to the "Atlantic Rim." The North Atlantic was not, of course, the only region of the globe to experience new interactions between societies during this period, and in particular there was contemporaneously substantial growth in the volume and value of commerce between western Europe and Asia. When measured by the numbers of lives directly affected, however, by far the greatest movements of peoples and transformation of societies occurred around the North Atlantic, with the destruction of indigenous social forms, unrestrained competition for political and economic pre-eminence, and the enforced migration of millions condemned to slavery.

By convention, Columbus—as good a name as any by which to call the *genovese* Cristoforo Colombo and *castellano* Cristóbal Colón—"discovered" the lands of the western Atlantic by mistake, intent as he was on finding an alternative, shorter route to the riches of the Orient.[3] His immediate successors launched a conquest and settlement on a geographical scale vastly greater than any Iberian societies had previously undertaken, drawing inspiration from the experience of the Iberian *Reconquista* for spiritual succour, intellectual justification, and practical models for the subjugation of non-Christian peoples.[4] Whatever Columbus may have believed he was doing when he waded ashore and proclaimed to his tiny company the seizure of Guanahani,[5] the very different societies of late-fifteenth-century western Europe, North and West Africa, Amazonia, the Caribbean, central and eastern America, were none of them obviously poised to take advantage of any redefined understanding of their geography of commerce, politics, and settlement. Over the succeeding three centuries, all of these societies contributed to the transformation of the North Atlantic from impermeable obstacle to essential highway, from new frontier of the *Reconquista* to Anglophone lake, achieved only after a thitherto-unprecedented scale of transplantation of peoples and *matériel*. Most remarkable of all, this period of encounters between societies previously unaware of each other's existence concluded with the North Atlantic dominated by West Europeans,[6] even though for most of this period the Europeans collectively were neither the most numerous nor the most militarily powerful of the societies engaged in the region.

By 1763 and the Peace of Paris that concluded what was perhaps the Europeans' first world war, the Atlantic between the Equator and Iceland had become in large measure an Anglophone "interior ocean,"[7] equivalent to the Roman imperial characterisation of the Mediterranean as *mare nostrum*, of a kind that only 130 years earlier the English jurist Selden[8] at his most expansive had dared to advocate only for the Channel separating England and France. Dominated by the naval forces and commercial strength of the British Empire of King George III, the Atlantic and its littoral between 1763 and 1776 was the fulfilment of an imperial vision which began to have meaning during the War of the League of Augsburg/King William's War (1689–97) and the War of the Spanish Succession/Queen Anne's War (1702–13) with Louis XIV's France, but was given real substance only in the British perspective on the French and Indian War

(1754–63), called in Europe the Seven Years War. British prime minister Pitt "the Elder" may have said that in this war, North America could be won in battles in Europe, but in reality Continental European—Hanoverian— interests were progressively subordinated to those of the new king's English-speaking subjects on both sides of the Atlantic.

Why write this book? In many respects, the subject of European "discoveries" and empires is already well served by historians, for students and general readers alike, as the Note on Bibliography at the end of this introduction indicates. The growth in numbers of professional historians in the English-speaking world, quite apart from elsewhere, has encouraged a substantial growth in published materials of great ingenuity and sophistication, covering almost all aspects of this subject. Conventionally, the subject has been approached through national histories—for example, the rise and decline of Spain, the Anglo-French struggle for ascendancy, the growth of the British Empire, the colonial origins of the United States, or the study of non-European societies through their interactions with "the West." Recently, however, historians have been returning to consideration of transnational perspectives, to the truly "big picture" of Atlantic studies.[9] Nevertheless, the challenge to our understanding remains why, and why in that era, was the North Atlantic transformed: first, from diverse and separate societies into any kind of empire; second, into an empire dominated by West Europeans; and third, from a Hispanic into an Anglophone empire? Furthermore, why were these transformations characterised by violence, suffering, slavery, and exploitation, and why not by peaceful coexistence and fruitful cooperation?

The purpose of this book is by no means necessarily to provide all or even part of the answers. It is, however, through a series of essays—chapters—on aspects of themes within the subject, to encourage further and wider questions and debate about changes that were, if neither inevitable nor predictable during this period, then at least potentially may be revised or even reversed in the future. The essay format is intended to make the themes of the book more accessible to students seeking to develop their own ideas on particular aspects of the period, and thus the chapters may be read independently of one another or in a sequence other than that in which they appear in the book. Within the essays, the topics of discussion have been grouped under headings that invite readers to contextualise their particular interests in wider frameworks, whilst offering "shorthand" entries to other aspects. Inevitably, there is some proliferation of subheadings, but these should not prove too distracting to those general readers new to the subject who are invited to consider the work as a whole, as an introduction to issues that may continue to stretch the minds of historians engaged in original research on primary sources.

In this study, we shall remind ourselves that the transformations that brought the peoples of the North Atlantic to where they stood by 1763 was not the only possible destination of a journey begun in 1492. We will reflect on some of the avenues and turnings on the journey which were not followed, of alternative outcomes that were ignored or missed, by posing again some of the questions that are so difficult yet so interesting to consider, if we hope to understand our present world and the morality of our positions in it. Why were pre-Columbian peoples throughout the Americas swept aside and condemned to the margins of land, status, and power? What are the consequences of our answer for our response to the revolt in our own time of the Maya in the Mexican state of Chiapas?[10] Why did no African peoples seize for themselves a part of the American territorial and economic bounty? Is Africa's modern impoverishment a consequence of an habitual stripping of its human and material assets begun in the creation of Atlantic empires? Did West Europeans seize the North Atlantic, or did other indigenous peoples relinquish it? Why was an Iberian imperialist Catholic agrarian aristocracy superseded by an Anglophone constitutionalist Protestant capitalist republic, as the dominant force in the Western Hemisphere? Why is the American Declaration of Independence written in the language of William Shakespeare, and not in the language of Miguel de Cervantes?

Competing by war, trade, and settlement to exploit the ocean and its littoral, the indigenous peoples of America, Africa, and Europe also contributed to the subsequent emergence of self-consciously new cultural and national identities in the Western Hemisphere. These identities were and have remained significantly at odds with those of the original protagonists, such that the transformation of the North Atlantic world in early modern times prompts further questions about why this particular outcome has been sustained into our own day. If it was by no means self-evident that Europe's first modern contact with the Americas would lead to the creation of a single global superpower—Anglophone, capitalist, and rooted in the Western Hemisphere—what is there to suggest that further transformation from the present may not be yet to come, perhaps to a Latino-Asian cultural leadership in American societies further orientated to the Pacific?

As the twenty-first-century global experience develops around the Pacific Rim, so the Atlantic Rim set its precedent, starting in the early modern period. In 1492, no conscious global economy existed, and most societies across the world still only imagined each other's existence, despite centuries of contact through intermediaries in pursuit of luxuries. By 1763, not only the geographic and political but perhaps more profoundly the mental and economic maps of the world had been redrawn, as the "classic" Mediterranean-Indian Ocean axis was forcibly displaced by the Atlantic and its littoral as the nexus of global power.[11] The "world" of Cosimo de' Medici was superseded by that of Thomas Jefferson, so how did Braudel's "Mediterranean in the Age of Philip II"[12] become the "North Atlantic of George III"?

Whilst much scholarly effort has been and is devoted to describing these enormous changes in greater or lesser detail, there is always a challenge to explain them in ways that are at once recognisable to their participants and meaningful to modern readers. As observed long ago by A. J. P. Taylor, "Every historian tries to be accurate, though none succeeds as he would like to."[13] In my exploration of possible explanations and suggestions of further questions, this book necessarily relies on the scholarship of many others to whom in gratitude I hope to have done justice and to have given due acknowledgement, but the interpretations and gloss put on their works are my own, as also are the faults. Inevitably, my thinking has drawn on substantial and diverse bodies of scholarship, many of which contribute important details to the understanding of the themes I am exploring. Equally inevitably, some major work or works of scholarship are not given as full or as explicit recognition as they deserve, for which neglect I invite correction by experts on those particular topics within my general subject.

"Standing on the shoulders of giants," however, I may suggest that there may yet be a little farther to see, whilst leaning heavily on their guidance and scholarly foundations. I do not propose to commend to the reader any particular school of general historical explanation with which to structure the discussion—although acknowledging all the while the inspiration of the *annalistes* and particularly of Braudel—so to that extent this is an old-fashioned, naïve empiricist's approach to the subject, which I believe will best suit students or new readers in this subject. There are, however, certain propositions which throughout this work inform my discussion of events and developments, which deserve now to be declared, because they are by no means shared by all those scholars pursuing this subject.

The chief of these propositions is that, in exploring the transformation of the early modern North Atlantic world, we may legitimately seek to ascribe some sense of motive to participants, even though for the most part they did not record their views about their actions or situation. Whilst we should acknowledge the importance of the emotional or irrational in the choices individuals make in respect of the particular actions that made events, our understanding of any historical period is surely impoverished if we presume that events were purely contingent.[14] In this account, in our post-Marxist and post-Freudian world, I pursue the proposition a priori that for all those actors who had any choice about their part in the drama through the three or so centuries of our period, principally men and mostly of West European origin, the common characteristic in their decisions seems to me to be explicable in terms of the deliberate choices of participants, and these choices depended on self-conscious and usually rational calculation of advantage, through exercises in the arithmetic of probable outcomes expected to arise from their choice of action. That arithmetic was not necessarily or solely materialistic, for there were also ethical equations to be worked through, and across the whole period we see examples of individuals making more or less selfless calculations. Notwithstanding modern marketing's understanding of consumer behaviour, I presume—with old-style economists—that most actors, most of the time, were conscious of their own preferences and undertook the rational pursuit of the best interests of those preferences, even if we may now in hindsight find difficulty in recognising their definition of self-interest.[15] Some events in the drama were, of course, contingent, and not infrequently outcomes were wildly different from those intended, but a broad consistency with which choices made by individuals seem to imply that they believed themselves to be likely to profit—materially or morally—by their choices, for me strongly suggests calculation.

Is calculation embedded in the early modern western European mind, perhaps as a consequence of a popular mediaeval Christian concern with the balance sheet of sin as the test for entry to heaven?[16] Certainly, it contrasts with a Stoic or an Epicurean concern with living a virtuous life, or with a Buddhist wish to avoid causing suffering, or with a Jewish concern to live according to the ancient laws. For early modern Europe, although we may be tempted to render calculation as capitalism, famously portrayed as Europe's special contribution to human civilisation,[17] we yet recall that capitalism was neither a Protestant nor even a Christian speciality, as the flourishing of commerce and enterprise in Indian[18] and Chinese[19] societies before the arrival of early modern West Europeans, for example, demonstrates.[20] I leave it to my readers, however, to ponder how far this habit of calculation still dominates the thinking of some or other of us now living around the North Atlantic.

Calculation was, I suggest, necessary but not sufficient to explain choices and outcomes in this Atlantic story: it was coupled with determination to seize the day. Is it perhaps in this combination that we may identify an explanation for the peculiar success of West Europeans in dominating the North Atlantic, and amongst those of West European origin, the success of some rather than others of those societies? Was there—is there—innate in these societies a will to dominate, exploit, or profit, sustained by calculation of the odds of achieving those ends? Time and again during this period, West Europeans were outnumbered when they encountered other societies, so was violence a response to numerical inferiority? Was it fear of opposing numbers that ensured the experience of transformation was characterised by conflict? As with capitalism, so neither is a predatory urge unique to West European societies, and this point is illustrated by the achievements of the Mongols in the thirteenth century[21] or of Russians' eastward expansion in central Asia from the sixteenth to the eighteenth centuries.[22] It is perhaps significant, however, that West European urges to dominate extra-European societies in the early modern world inaugurated a period of sustained success that climaxed in the European imperialism of the years before 1914.[23]

I further contend that arising from calculations of advantage, the significant technologies to make the outcomes possible were deployed as and when the perceived needs arose. Technology provided means to pursue ends that had already been willed, but the creation of these technologies was not contingent on the needs of the imperialists; their widespread and practical application, however, were. By this account, so-called scientific and technological advances in the early modern period were distributed according to the random genius of individuals, and seldom on cue to solve pressing problems. For example, despite the evident needs for them, medical advances played virtually no part in the development of the early modern North Atlantic,[24] and most of the important developments in maritime transport arose either before or after this period.[25]

Last but not least of the propositions informing this account is my use of analytical categories that are convenient for viewing developments in retrospect but that were not necessarily recognised by the actors at the time—imperialism, colonialism, mercantilism, globalisation. The absence of evidence of self-consciousness of all relevant factors amongst the actors need not undermine or deny the possibility that the actors participated for motives or were influenced by forces which we may characterise clearly only in retrospect. These concepts nevertheless have value for an historian who wishes to make sense of complex developments that lie between one perceived reality and another, later one that is demonstrably different: they help us to explore the question, how did we get from there to here?

I may, for example, propose that in pursuing their personal enrichment through plunder, the conquistadores drew resolve from their society's tradition of struggle with their Islamic neighbours, whilst their achievements also strengthened the development of a bureaucratised military-imperial state later based in Madrid, which exploited the capitalist potential of the New World. Although Cortés did not write using terms like these, my proposition may nevertheless be the meaning for us of the following:

There is a certain tribe called the Chichimeca. . . . I have given my men instruction that if they discover in these people some aptitude or ability to live as the others do and to be instructed in the knowledge of Our Holy Faith and to recognize the service which they owe to Your Majesty, they are to make every effort to pacify them and bring them under Your Majesty's Yoke; . . . If, however, they find that they . . . refuse to be obedient, the Spaniards are to make war on them and reduce them to slavery; so that there may be no part of all this land which does not serve and acknowledge Your Majesty. By making slaves of this barbarous people, who are almost savages, Your Majesty will be served and the Spaniards will benefit greatly, as they will work in the gold mines, and perhaps by living among us some of them may even be saved.[26]

The structure of this book is intended to allow the reader to explore the transformation by working through a priori or intuitive possibilities to see whether or how far they fit or provide insight into causality. In the early chapters, there is a consideration of structural ingredients contributing to the processes of Atlantic occupation and settlement, put forth to ponder the availability and influence of these factors within early modern European societies, with some comment on their significance amongst other societies of the littoral. The factors at work include technical prerequisites and technological innovation; modes and means of exploitation, including some social and economic circumstances as well as religious and other ideological factors; the availability or absence of alternatives to Atlantic expansion; and favourable environmental factors. These will be explored for their relative significance to try to distinguish between the profound and the immediate causes, and between the necessary and the sufficient conditions for the transformation. My discussion of these elements has an unavoidably taxonomic character in the representation of complex experience in patterns and connections, to explore conceptions and preconceptions, to distinguish tools of analysis or lines of enquiry, to try to propose the relative weight and subtle interplay of forces and features only imperfectly captured in our sources and perceptions. I have sought to identify points of reference and observation from which readers may draw their own comments and conclusions, so that my lists may provide anchors or starting points for further discussion of possible interpretations of why the world of 1763 was different to that of 1492.

Subsequently, this book pursues a chronological survey aiming to remind the reader to ask about why the outcomes were as they were and not otherwise; what role to ascribe to key decisions and decision makers. There is a broad chronological sequence, within which themes of particular interest are considered, as 1492–1607: the long sixteenth century of first contacts and Iberian pre-eminence; 1607–1697: the era of opportunity; and 1697–1763: the struggle for imperial mastery. Although the periodisations are largely conventional, they nevertheless provide convenient reference points for readers less familiar with some of the material who may wish subsequently to pursue their own connections with contemporaneous events elsewhere.

Throughout the study, I stress transformation—how much the societies and circumstances of the North Atlantic changed and, from the perspectives of the peoples living through the period and despite the elements of calculation, how unpredictably. By considering a variety of the *possible* explanations for the transformation, the book fulfils, in the manner of an interpretative essay, the purpose of posing questions whilst not necessarily conclusively answering them. There is, however, one interpretative proposition to which this book is attached: that at the heart of the transformation of the North Atlantic to a region dominated by Europeans, lies a succession of coalitions, of exploitative and asymmetrical alliances with indigenous peoples from which those of European origin, and particularly those of English origin, emerged as chief beneficiaries.[27] The events of October 1492[28] neither predestined nor inspired those of July 1776: why the Atlantic Rim changed the way it did is central to understanding this period.

Men make their own lives, but they do not make them just as they please, they do not make them under circumstances chosen by themselves, but under circumstances directly encountered, given and transmitted from the past.[29]

A NOTE ON PROPER NOUNS

Throughout the book, I have employed where possible the form of proper nouns that is closest to the original usage; hence *Isabel of Castilla*, for example, is used in preference to *Isabella of Castile*. When there may be doubt about the person or place referred to, I have indicated a common, Anglophone variant of the name. I have consistently used *conquistadores* as the collective noun for the early Iberian invaders of the New World, in preference to the strict English equivalent. I hope in these small ways to remind readers of the extent of the linguistic transformation of our understanding of the early modern North Atlantic.

A NOTE ON BIBLIOGRAPHY

With a subject as immense and complex as that proclaimed in the title of this book, it is inevitable that academic endeavour continues to advance our understanding and to render outdated any attempt to give comprehensive guidance to the scholarly literature. For the reader new to this subject, therefore, I offer in the references, whenever possible, a pointer to further materials on particular topics, a pointer that I hope will stimulate interest whilst providing more detailed guidance to recent scholarship. My choice of such pointers is driven by a judgement about which are most likely to be accessible—physically as well as intellectually—to lead the reader in and to be useful points of departure into the more detailed debates.

Amongst a wealth of possible recommendations for analytical accounts within a broadly narrative framework, new readers may find much of interest in the following.

Fage, J. D. *A History of Africa*. 4th ed. London and New York, 2001. A concise introduction to more specialist works by Fage and other authors.

Kamen, H. *Spain's Road to Empire: The Making of a World Power, 1492–1763*. London, 2002. The work of one of the most eminent of the Anglophone scholars of Iberia.

Taylor, A. *American Colonies*. The Penguin History of the United States, Vol. 1. New York, 2001. A lively and geographically wide-ranging account, covering European incomers' and colonials' activity generally, including the Caribbean, central America, and the Pacific coast, in some areas to 1800.

Wilson, J. *The Earth Shall Weep. A History of Native America*. London, 1998. The (generally tragic) story of interaction between indigenous peoples of North America and incomers is told with regard to the interpretations of indigenous peoples themselves, and in a less polemical style than that of some accounts.

Because it is the work of a single author, each of these accounts has a consistency of style and coherence of interpretation that may make them more accessible.

Multivolume, multiauthor works allow for more sense of unfolding debate and differences of interpretation, amongst which are the following.

Canny, N. P., ed. *The Origins of Empire*. Vol. 1 of *The Oxford History of the British Empire*, edited by W. R. Louis. Oxford and New York, 1998.

Forster, R., ed. *European and Non-European Societies, 1450–1800*. Vol. 27 of *An Expanding World. The European Impact on World History, 1450–1800*, edited by A. J. R. Russell-Wood. Aldershot and Brookfield, Vt., 1997. At the time of writing incomplete, in which extracts and articles are reproduced (rather than new writing commissioned) in thematic volumes edited by acknowledged experts, as introductions to established scholarly debates, and in which the range of articles encompasses European activities generally, with some regard to the experience of the other societies around the globe, particularly in the two parts of volume 27.

Louis, W. R., ed. in chief. *The Oxford History of the British Empire*. 5 vols. Oxford and New York, 1998–1999.

Marshall, P. J., ed. *The Eighteenth Century*. Vol. 2 of *The Oxford History of the British Empire*, edited by W. R. Louis. Oxford and New York, 1998.

Winks, R. W., ed. *Historiography*. Vol. 5 of *The Oxford History of the British Empire*, edited by W. R. Louis. Oxford and New York, 1999. Volumes 1 and 2 contain contributions by different authors at article length; each article presents a summary of scholarly understanding of its respective topic, but of course they generally confine themselves to a British perspective and the development of understanding of what became the British empire.

At the time of writing, materials on Web sites are both substantial and growing, with the expectation that they will become stable and available for the long term. Of particular interest, new readers may appreciate the following.

http://www.britac.ac.uk/portal/ is the British Academy's directory of online resources in the humanities and social sciences, "designed as an entry point to available resources for those working in higher education and research," although the materials on some related sites are also suitable as introductions for readers new to the subject and period. At the time of writing (August 2003), the site is still developing its range.

http://www.economics.utoronto.ca/munro5/EcoGradCourse.htm contains material supporting Prof. John H. Munro's graduate student seminar Topics in the Economic and Social History of Later Medieval and Renaissance Europe, 1250–1600 in the Department of Economics, University of Toronto; Prof. Munro's materials contain a wealth of thought-provoking ideas, with references, ranging widely over the early period of this present study (last accessed August 2003).

http://www.fas.harvard.edu/~atlantic/ is the site for the International Seminar on the History of the Atlantic World, 1500–1800, " . . . established at Harvard University in 1995 by Prof. Bernard Bailyn, under the auspices of the Charles Warren Center for Studies in American History and with the support of the Andrew W. Mellon Foundation. The aim is to advance the scholarship of young historians of many nations interested in aspects of Atlantic history in the formative years; to help create an international community of scholars familiar with approaches, archives, and intellectual traditions different from their own and ultimately to further international understanding." At the time of writing (August 2003), the site is still developing its range.

http://www.geocities.com/Athens/Styx/6497/ includes reference materials relating to the colonial endeavours of some the smaller West European societies: Danish, Swedish, Brandenburgers, as well as the more familiar Spanish, Portuguese, and Dutch (last accessed August 2003).

http://www.vlib.org/History.html is the History Network Central Catalog of the World Wide Virtual Library maintained at the University of Kansas (Lawrence, KS) and the European University Institute Library, which provides links to a wide variety of materials, including some primary sources relating to the Atlantic aspects of European and New World history, in the major European languages including English, Spanish, Italian, German, French, and Swedish; for Portuguese materials, readers may wish to consult Yale's http://www.library.yale.edu/rsc/history/porthist.html (last accessed August 2003).

http://www.historyworld.net is, at the time of writing (August 2003), planned to comprehend ready reference, introductory materials with timelines and brief supporting articles, with links to other sites, particularly of museums.

http://web.uccs.edu/~history/index/colonial.html is one amongst the several exciting sites hosted by university history departments, in this case the University of Colorado–Colorado Springs, which are welcoming to new readers to the subject and contain helpful links to a wide variety of other materials (last accessed August 2003).

For readers seeking more traditional forms of bibliography and with access to the facilities to pursue the references, I draw attention to the following.

Norton, M. B., gen. ed., and P. Gerardi, assoc. ed., *The American Historical Association's Guide to Historical Literature*. New York, and Oxford, 1995. Arranged topically, with cross-references, entries are for the most part monographs but there also items from specialist journals; acknowledged experts selected the items (most of them published in English between 1961 and 1992) for their contributions to scholarly understanding, and for each item there is a helpful brief outline of its content and significance.

Porter, A., ed. *Bibliography of Imperial, Colonial, and Commonwealth History Since 1600*. The Royal Historical Society Bibliography. Oxford, 2002. The items have been selected to provide starting points for further reading and research in all aspects of the history of British experiences of empire, by bringing together otherwise disparate or obscure references in a common format. Overwhelmingly, the items are in English, and most of them were published between 1945 and 2000. Whilst there is (as the editors admit) no attempt to evaluate them, the items included are themselves sources of further references, the format facilitates exploration of the comparative dimension, and the work includes references to the published versions of original sources.

For those pursuing the current scholarly debates in detail, amongst the most fruitful sources are the specialist journals, in particular:

American Historical Review for its wide-ranging coverage of historical topics both general and particular, as a venue for current controversies and debates

English Historical Review for its learned reviews of new publications and its annual compendium of scholarly articles published in European journals

Hispanic American Historical Review for its scholarly articles and its engagement with scholarship other than that in English, across the Western Hemisphere

William & Mary Quarterly as a showcase for careful scholarship on the colonial experience in North America.

At the time of writing, the publication of a new journal, *Atlantic Studies: Literary, Historical, and Cultural Perspectives* is awaited in 2004.

CHAPTER 1

Setting the Scene

Unlike the great empires of antiquity, those that developed around the North Atlantic in the early modern period were to an unprecedented and overwhelming extent dependent on sea travel. Within the European experience, although Periclean Athens had been a seaborne empire, it had relied on relatively short journeys within the Mediterranean basins, and subsequent European empires before c. 1500 were almost entirely land-based, if not always landlocked. The significance of this, possibly obvious, point about the ocean is thrown into relief when we recall that the technical capacity for transatlantic sea travel existed at least in western Europe, for perhaps five hundred years before Columbus's first voyage. The ability to conduct transoceanic voyages repeatedly and within acceptable margins of safety and reliability need not have been first exploited only by West Europeans, nor commenced on a significant scale only in the mid to late fifteenth century C.E. The technology of ocean travel is the subject of the next chapter, but the recognition of its existence in Europe by at least the tenth century prompts at least three questions that this chapter addresses: why did such a long period elapse between the first development of the minimum of necessary technology and the Columbus expeditions; why was such technology not developed in other societies around the Atlantic littoral; and why was it that Europeans made the first contact between western Europe and the Americas?

THE "LEGACY" OF ST. BRENDAN AND LEIV EIRIKSON

Regardless of whether an Irish monk or a Viking adventurer did or did not first cross the Atlantic in the Dark Ages, stories that the journey had been successfully made were in circulation, amongst Irish monastic communities and later in Norse sagas from the twelfth century, even if our surviving texts of the latter were not captured in writing until the fourteenth century. Cunliffe has argued that contact across the seas provided the means by which Celtic societies in western Europe were able to sustain a distinctive maritime culture and identity until c. 1500.[1] Modern reconstructive marine archaeology demonstrated in the last century that boats of the type believed to have been available to a Brendan were capable of making the Atlantic crossing in northern latitudes.[2] Nevertheless, it has yet to be substantiated that the Celts' far-flung maritime trading contacts extended to lasting settlement in the Western Hemisphere. On the other hand, the evidence for Norse transatlantic travel and settlement has been better attested—not only by seafaring experiments in imitation of Leiv Eirikson but also in the interpretation of archaeological finds, most famously in Newfoundland, as being of Norse origin around the year 1000, together with the evidence that Norse settlement in Greenland survived, if not always flourished, between the late tenth century and c. 1400. It is, therefore, reasonable to conclude that for mediaeval Europe, at least, the availability of the means to reach the Americas was not itself sufficient to encourage such enterprise. What, then, restrained West Europeans from following the examples of Brendan or Leiv Eirikson?

At this point it may be tempting to resurrect as an explanation a lack of an enquiring mind, and a convention of some histories of European settlement across the Atlantic was to point to a purported mediaeval European resistance to "new" knowledge or contact with alien cultures, as one of the impediments to exploration. A corollary of this argument would be that until the advent of the cultural phenomenon called the Renaissance, itself inspired by the combination of a revival of classical culture and the advent of new learning, European societies were unwilling or unable to contemplate the kind of experimental enterprise needed to reach across the North Atlantic. At best, mediaeval obscurantism would be held responsible for inhibiting enterprise; at worst, the intellectual tyranny of the Roman Catholic church had first to be challenged before exploration could begin.

Such a caricature of mediaeval thinking is readily exposed by reference to the examples within the Middle Ages of contact between West Europeans and, to them, alien societies equipped with "new" knowledge. It may with justice be argued that the most common form of these contacts was crusade, the quintessentially antagonistic approach to other so-called alien cultures. It should, however, also be acknowledged that crusades were launched within western Europe against people of (at least some) shared culture—for example, against heretical Cathars in Provence (particularly ruthlessly between 1209 and 1229) and as the cover story for ruthless assault and expropriation, as in the Fourth Crusade's sack of Constantinople/Byzantium (1204).

Western Europe was, in fact, recurrently exposed to new cultural and intellectual contacts, particularly from the Islamic, Orthodox Christian, and Jewish worlds during the period c. 1100 to c. 1450, even if its reaction to these contacts was as often as not destructive. Although their responses were expressed in very different forms and generating diverse outcomes, western European societies interacted with others around the Mediterranean as in the creation and maintenance of the Latin states of *Outremer* (on the Palestinian mainland, 1099–1291); the *convivencia* of Christian, Jewish, and Islamic peoples in Andalusía (perhaps most celebrated in the lives of Averroës [ibn Rushd] and Maimonides in late twelfth-century Córdoba); and the Sicilian court of *stupor mundi*, the emperor Friedrich II Hohenstaufen (r. 1220–50). Further afield, the Baltic crusader state of the Teutonic Knights (fl. 1226–1410) and the travels, amongst others, of Marco Polo (his account is of experiences in 1271–95), exposed European societies to novelty and challenges, not all of which could be or were dismissed as irrelevant merely because they were not Christian.

These direct experiences of other societies occurred in intellectual climates which were, up to a point, prepared to contemplate change and exploration and possessed mental furniture within which to accommodate novelty. Intellectual developments within western Europe itself, with practical as well as theological aspirations and implications, were exemplified by but not confined to the writings of such as the neo-Aristotelian Thomas Aquinas, the mathematicians and optical experimentalists Robert Grosseteste and Roger Bacon, and the logicians Duns Scotus and William of Ockham, to name only some of the most well-known thinkers of the thirteenth and fourteenth centuries, all of whom acquired European-wide reputations—and equally, attracted violent criticism. Thus, there were examples of enquiring minds and of intellectual frameworks within which to set the results of exploration.

It should also be recalled that by no means were the Middle Ages in western Europe a period of stagnation. Indeed, there were significant technological innovations in the period, widely disseminated, such as the harnessing of forces of nature to create powered machinery, exemplified by the watermill's adaptation beyond grinding flour to industrial processes such as those in metallurgy, textiles, or brewing. Engineering developments permitted the construction of huge buildings—gothic cathedrals as well as castles. Agricultural productivity developed sufficiently quickly to sustain population growth, at least until the fourteenth century (aided by favourable climatic conditions[3]) that to some extent undermined incentives to seek "virgin" lands beyond Europe to colonise for cultivation. For the purposes of marine navigation, perhaps the most significant development was the adoption and dissemination of the magnetic compass.

It cannot be denied, however, that from the perspective of Atlantic travel, the mediaeval period was remarkable for the lack of initiatives, but the explanation perhaps lies less in the lack of an enquiring mindset and more in the lack of information in western Europe that there was a destination worth seeking on the other side of the Atlantic ocean. As will be explored further in this book, exploration and settlement by West Europeans depended crucially on a plausible outcome from a calculation of the likely return on the investment necessary to undertake the enterprise, and amongst key elements in the arithmetic was knowledge, real or imagined but nonetheless believed, about the destinations. What was lacking in mediaeval Europe was a convincing answer to the question of where and how much would be the benefit in sailing west.

Norsemen of Leiv Eirikson's ilk would seem to have been prepared to presume, unusually in western European experience in the absence of explicit information, that there was a sufficiently high probability of an attractive landfall within the endurance of ships and crews of tenth- to twelfth-century Viking Europe, to make the undertaking of voyages of exploration more attractive than staying within the confines of their known world. Armed reconnaissance was, it may be supposed, an essential part of their maritime routine; were it otherwise, they should never have undertaken first raiding and then invasion across modern-day Scotland, England, Ireland, and France, for example, beginning in the late eighth century. Where quick returns could be obtained, plunder was the method; against militarily more robust societies, trade was the key. Targets for invasion and settlement were identified amongst those lands the Norsemen encountered where indigenous settlement was either thin or relatively poorly defended, into which categories North America fell, as did Iceland or Greenland.

Norse maritime enterprise was progressively superseded by some measure of integration or accommodation with the peoples amongst whom the Norsemen chose to settle, for which a number of examples may be cited. In England, the creation of the Danelaw (from the peace of Wedmore, 878) acknowledged the division of the Anglo-Saxons' territory between different cultural groups as defined by their customary justice; the presence of Norsemen or so-called Normans in ninth-century Novgorod and Kiev may have contributed to the development of early monarchy amongst Russian tribes; in return for acknowledging the suzerainty of the Frankish kings (formalised by Charles the Simple in 911), Norsemen became the ruling élite in Normandie; their recruitment as mercenaries by the emperor in Byzantium (formalised from the treaty of 912) created the Varangian guards. Across Europe, therefore, Norsemen became, from the tenth century, if not domesticated then to some degree acculturated and certainly rewarded with higher standards of material culture than those enjoyed by their forebears.

After the Viking period, West Europeans had by the twelfth century in effect abandoned speculative armed reconnaissance in favour of assault on known targets, usually but not exclusively on the contiguous Eurasian landmass or accessible within the Mediterranean. The Normans, themselves the heirs of Viking settlers, pursued the conquest of societies in the southern Italian peninsula and Sicilia (from c. 1030), England (from 1066), and Wales (from 1068), whilst their Iberian contemporaries pursued the *Reconquista*, and increasingly sought to exploit for their campaigns the objectives of the Roman Catholic church. The ultimate collaboration was already achieved by the end of the eleventh century: from 1098 for almost four hundred years, crusade provided an ideological engine for plunder and conquest of societies alien to West Europeans (just as it would do later for the Atlantic conquistadores) without recourse to speculative reconnaissance.

Amongst mediaeval West European societies, conflict was not only the normative condition of contacts between neighbours but there continued to be a belief that military success would bring prompt, material rewards. Within western Europe, the outcomes of these conflicts were seldom conclusive or particularly long-lived, in contrast to the victories of the Mongols in the thirteenth century and Timur Leng (Tamerlane) in the fourteenth, which threatened but did not overwhelm West European societies. To sustain military endeavour, however, west European societies had to mobilise significant proportions of their material resources, so that successful prosecution of conflict against neighbours from the twelfth century increasingly relied in part on some measure of restraint of violence within a society to secure domestic peace for tax collection. An early exemplar of this was the imposition of the king's justice in the Angevin Empire of Henry II Plantagenet (r. 1142–89), the success of which enabled his son Richard I (r. 1189–99) to pursue even unsuccessful campaigns in the eastern Mediterranean and in France. Such incremental enlargement of the jurisdiction and competence of governments was again pursued with the collaboration of the Roman Catholic church, not least as an important source of technically trained bureaucratic personnel, so the Church in return retained a pre-eminent role in the mediaeval transmutation of European cultures and societies.

The West European focus on the attempted conquest and exploitation of neighbours, and by extension the attempts to create so-called crusader states, persisted until the late fifteenth century, when the balance of military advantage was perceived to have swung so decisively in favour of another Eurasian military power that West Europeans began to consider alternatives to their mediaeval strategies for conflict and conquest. The Viking arithmetic of speculative reconnaissance once again became attractive amongst West Europeans because not only was access to the known, desirable destinations by the traditional routes under new rulers but also much of western Europe was itself again threatened, now by the Ottomans.

MARITIME ENTERPRISE BEYOND WESTERN EUROPE

If Columbus "discovered" the New World as an accidental consequence of his search for a direct sea route to "the Indies," what was the state of geographical knowledge around the world on the eve of his first transatlantic voyage? Why was Columbus not pre-empted, for example, by the peoples his contemporaries saw as so menacing, the Ottomans?

The Ottoman Empire that confronted West European societies from c. 1475 pursued expansion that was itself neither unidirectional nor unmindful of a wider strategic perspective, as the conquest of Egypt (1517), wars with Safavid Iran (1530s), and a naval expedition to Gujerat (1538) later demonstrated. Although the empire of the Gazis did not in the event project its power across the Atlantic Ocean, it nonetheless possessed the technologies and resources potentially to do so. The Topkapi palace received diplomatic representatives from kings and courts in western Europe, and the empire was connected to the west (through the merchant communities and networks of Sephardic Jews) and to the north and east (through those of Armenians). Indeed, Ottoman firearms experts gave assistance to Islamic rulers as far afield as Sumatra and Malindi,[4] from whom the empire could add to its geographical information about much of the globe between longitude 10°W and 105°E. Geographical knowledge and interest were expressed through such compendia as the map of the world (1513) and the *Kitab-i Bahriye* (1521) by Piri Reis, sometime admiral of the Red Sea fleet.

The Ottoman state also demonstrated a readiness to adopt technologies and techniques developed elsewhere, so its artillery and shipbuilding benefited from the work of individual West European craftsmen, whilst seafarers from the Arabian Gulf and the Indian Ocean provided expertise for naval enterprise. In addition, sultans retained the services of naval adventurers—whether pirates or corsairs, depended on the prevailing political and military climate—such as Kemal Reis in the late 1490s, and the Algiers-based Hayruddin Barbarossa from 1534, whose fleets included craft easily the equal of their West European contemporaries, and significant numbers of mariners and fighters who, because by origin they were West Europeans, were styled renegades. Thus, the allied states of North Africa and the determination of a Barbarossa gave the Ottoman Empire a putative slipway to the Atlantic world. Time and again during the whole period of this study, and in the sixteenth century particularly, the Ottomans reminded their contemporaries that West Europeans did not possess a pre-eminent power—or destiny—to shape the early modern world.

Nevertheless, no sultan attempted during the early modern period to compete with West Europeans in their Atlantic enterprises, although a fleet was sent east to assist the Islamic rulers of Sumatra against the Portuguese in 1568. Internal political strife was neither more nor less signifi-cant of an impediment than amongst West European states, and lack of resources did not itself deter enterprise. What was missing, however, was a clear profit to be derived from such Atlantic enterprise, either in re-sources to be gained by the Ottoman state or to be denied to its enemies, when contrasted with the immediate and constant rewards of controlling the overland trade routes for the bulk of commodities traded from the orient to Europe until the later seventeenth century.

If Africa north of the Sahara was already within the Ottoman sphere of influence in the early 1500s, West African societies, in the vast territories between the mouths of the rivers Senegal and Kongo/Zaire, were not predestined to become satellites of the Portuguese or other Europeans. The great kingdoms of the interior, Songhai and Kanuri, or those of the coast, such as Oyo and Benin, were for longer-range cultural and com-mercial contacts largely orientated to the Islamic societies to their east and north-east. Trade rather than plunder characterised fifteenth-century con-tacts as peoples of the West African coasts sought European trade goods—fabrics, ironware, firearms—and the Europeans sought gold and pepper, in sufficient quantities for the contacts to be viewed as mutually beneficial. Trade in slaves was already established amongst West African societies, to which a demand amongst Iberian settlers of the Atlantic islands of the Açores, Madeira, and the Canarias constituted by 1500 only a modest additional fraction of the human trade.

Prior to contact with West Europeans, some West African societies al-ready possessed the social and political structures to mobilise resources—construction materials, food and water storage, if not navigation and ocean sailing techniques—to make maritime enterprise at least theoreti-cally possible. Yet even if indigenous boat designs were not capable of producing ocean-going craft, when these designs are compared with the contemporaneous designs and sizes of vessels that West Europeans used for their ocean crossings (to which European weapons technology and east African seafaring expertise[5] might perhaps have been added), West African societies might have been capable of pursuing Atlantic enterprise. Certainly, not all stretches of Africa's long Atlantic coastline were blessed with easy anchorages for larger vessels, but at least from the Gulf of Guinea, seasonally prevailing currents and wind systems—north- and westward—did not prevent transatlantic ventures. Before the arrival of the Portuguese, trade with the interior took precedence over maritime enterprise for West Africans. Enterprise off the eastern shores, by contrast, exploited the monsoon system with considerable success both in alliance and competition with merchants and marauders from the Red Sea, Ara-bian Gulf, and Indian Ocean. Great Zimbabwe (fl. c. 1200–1450?) dem-onstrated the capacity of societies of the interior to mobilise personnel and resources for long-distance trade, particularly in gold, without such commerce having to be the preserve of outsiders. As with the Ottoman Empire, then, on the eve of Columbus's voyages, the societies of West Africa that might have possessed the means seem to have lacked the incentive to undertake Atlantic exploration.

Societies on the western side of the Atlantic, however, did not pursue the technologies needed for oceanic enterprise so that Native Americans at this date were unable to "discover" Europe, rather than the other way around. That some pre-Columbian Mesoamerican societies undertook highly complex projects (amongst the principal monuments of which are the architectural remains of Yucatán and the central highlands of Mexico) evidences a sophisticated command of methods for exploitation and management of manpower and resources, based on a substantial agrarian economy trading in surplus, sustained by ruthless application of military force over tributary societies and substantial geographical extent. As far as may now be determined, mainland societies did not attempt to extend their *imperia* to the islands of the Caribbean, notwithstanding that none of their indigenous peoples were likely to have provided any serious resistance to determined invaders from the mainland.

Mesoamerican societies had, by the eve of Columbus's voyages, developed complex systems of measurement of time and space derived from extensive astronomical observations, but these values were not applied by them to questions of ocean navigation. That Mesoamerican societies lacked significant maritime technologies was apparent to the earliest European arrivals: roadways within the interior rendered sea travel less attractive for communication, and local intensive agricultural productivity made redundant a marine trade in bulk goods. Above all, Mesoamerican societies were not troubled by a belief that they lacked commodities that could be obtained only by crossing the seas. Mexica (Aztec)[6] contact with other indigenous societies comprehended trade but also a knowledge that there were potential rivals to be confronted and subjugated. In the absence of significant population pressure or scarcity of resources, Mesoamerican societies vied for a predominance from which to expropriate the products, labour, and human sacrifice of their neighbours. The conquistadores would be welcomed by Totonacs and Tlaxcalans to supplant the Mexica, with the prospective benefit to these indigenous allies of the ending of expropriation.

The societies to the east of the Ottomans, in which originated the luxury trade goods so much desired by West Europeans, were at least as aware of their goods' ultimate destinations in the West, as were Westerners aware of the East. In the early Middle Ages, Arabic-speaking travellers and geographers had ranged as far as Hedeby in northwest Europe and Guangzhou (Canton) in east Asia. In the aftermath of the thirteenth-century conquests of Genghis Khan, Italian merchants and missionaries were able to trek across central Asia to report firsthand on China, so that Marco Polo was not the only source of intelligence about "the West." Whilst there survive for modern readers accounts of the spectacular journeys of Ibn Batuta in the mid–fourteenth century, from his home in Morocco as far afield as East Africa, India, and China, and across the Sahara to Timbuktu,[7] by the mid–fifteenth century, Islam still connected co-religionists in Granada, Baghdad, Malacca, and Mindanao, as it also did in Mombasa.

There was but little, however, to attract traders from India (despite their extensive maritime trade connections around the Indian Ocean throughout our period), China or south-east Asia to seek to deal directly with West European societies. Late-fifteenth-century Europe had no monopoly of any commodity in demand in the societies of Asia, and what was known of Europe's intellectual, artistic, and material culture compared poorly with those of the peoples of the Eastern Hemisphere. Nor was it yet the case that the Europeans were clearly pre-eminent in the technologies of building, travel, or warfare. The terms of trade were clear: oriental goods were provided to Europe through intermediaries as a by-product of more profitable trade links from the South China Sea and around the Indian Ocean; Europeans paid in bullion for these goods because they had no other commodities for which there was a market in Asia.

Yet well before West Europeans identified a sea route to India and further east, China possessed the means to make the journey from east to west. Ming emperors of China after 1388 promoted enterprise aimed primarily at supporting the defence of the empire and the restoration of its internal peace and prosperity following the final defeat of the Mongols. The early fifteenth century, however, saw an expansionist phase in which the Chinese imperial state demonstrated that it could mobilise the technical resources and political will to project its power across the hemisphere. Seven expeditions led by the Muslim admiral Cheng Ho between 1405 and 1433 ranged as far as Jeddah and Mogadishu and included an attempted invasion of what is now Sri Lanka. These fleets, probably equipped with naval artillery,[8] sought to suppress piracy, to establish trade and political relations, and to enhance the security of China's existing international trade.

If these expeditions are characterised as reconnaissance in force, the motives may have been a wish to project Chinese state power to catch up with the informal commercial power of its merchants: had these reconnaissances been followed up with garrisons, a formal Chinese maritime empire in the hemisphere would have pre-empted that of Portugal by a century. The missions were not continued, however, possibly because of their cost to the imperial treasury;[9] complex internal trade and political ties combined with, to all intents and purposes, autarky, encouraged the Asian superpower to focus on domestic and near-neighbour issues, even whilst its peoples pursued commercial enterprises across and beyond the region.

Cheng Ho presumably went where he already had reason to believe that the journey was worth making, to those places of which he already had some knowledge, so his missions were not likely to have extended to pure exploration.[10] Japan, and further south the Philippines, stood at the limit of the explorers' eastern horizon for fifteenth-century China, which had no particular need of a direct route to western Europe and no cultural tradition of conquest and proselytism such as motivated Iberian or some Islamic societies. Thus, sailing eastward over the Pacific held no particular appeal other than the pursuit of knowledge of the world outside the Middle Kingdom, for which knowledge there was apparently no very great appetite.

WHY COLUMBUS? WHY 1492?

Given that Columbus's stated objective was to reach the orient, the so-called discovery of the New World might be characterised as an example of unintended consequences, a serendipitous turn of events that might—probably would—have befallen anyone travelling vaguely westward across the Atlantic between the equator and 60°N. This history-as-accident approach would allow us to conclude that contact was inevitable as soon as the resources and incentives to undertake the voyage were conjoined, and that the credit for the discovery might just as easily have fallen to any one of a number of voyagers known to have been undertaking expeditions around the 1490s, from any one of a number of West European societies that were equally poised and equally competent to undertake it. This model may presume that there was some, perhaps only implicit, competition to be first to cross the Atlantic (almost as a parallel to the 1960s "race to the moon") and that, as was sometimes suggested by early modern casuists seeking to discredit the case that she had by reason of first contact a pre-eminent domain in the New World, Castilla[11] had won by pure chance. In its presumption that all or most West Europeans were engaged in similar endeavours, such a model leaves unexplored why Castilla in particular engaged in the race and leaves unrecognised the extent to which this win by Columbus and Castilla ran against the form book of fifteenth-century West European enterprise.

Having pondered how and why West Europeans did not bridge the Atlantic earlier than the end of the fifteenth century and were not pre-empted by other societies, we should now reflect on how and why this so-called first contact was undertaken by a lonely, obsessive exile backed by an emergent Castilian crusading state, rather than by one of the more obvious European candidates. From the perspective of the later fifteenth century, the pre-eminent promoter of maritime exploration was the Portuguese crown. In the same period, the societies then best equipped with technical skill and capital to undertake the project and which should have been expected to produce a consortium of enterprising navigators and merchant capitalists to do so were Italian.

The geographical and mercantile orientation of Europeans and their long-time, long-range trading partners in Asia were conditioned by their centuries of contacts across the contiguous Eurasian landmass. Because sea travel was quicker, cheaper, and, for bulk carriage, easier than land travel anywhere in Europe after the fall of the Roman Empire, the search for maritime routes to the orient was attractive, not least because it would eliminate some of the intermediaries in the trade who added to the expense of goods for their West European consumers. The terms of this existing trade were particularly poor for Europeans because they lacked any significant commodities to offer in exchange for the Eastern luxuries, leading to a constant drain of bullion from Europe to the East. Whilst traded volumes remained relatively small, the loss of bullion was offset to some extent by inflows from Africa, but any increase in demand for bullion within Europe was bound to compromise the availability of precious metals with which to pay for Oriental imports. If more of the costs of transport could be serviced from within European economies—by letters of credit, for example—and either the volumes of bullion exported declined or larger volumes of goods were obtained for the same volume of exported bullion, the relative elasticity of Oriental supply could be made to feed a growth in European demand.

It was the Portuguese who first attempted seriously to exploit this equation. Portugal's wars of independence from Islamic rulers were concluded by the mid–thirteenth century and from Castilian attempts at domination by the early fifteenth century (although the temptation subsequently remained strong for Portuguese kings to intervene in Castilian affairs). Military success in the Maghreb, however well begun in the seizure of Ceuta in 1415, proved difficult to sustain and was catastrophically reversed at Tangier in 1437. Although the development of maritime enterprise might, in retrospect, seem natural for Portugal—the difficulty of land and river transportation, the limited agricultural productivity of the interior, the absence of indigenous precious commodities all provided spurs—the launch of enterprise associated particularly, but not originating,[12] with Dom Henrique, "Henry the Navigator,"[13] from 1418 arose as much from that prince's commitment to the spread of his model of Christianity as it was about taking financial risks beyond the confidence of his Portuguese merchant contemporaries. The successes, relative to the size of investment, in Madeira and the Açores allowed for further positive spin on the modest returns from the expeditions down the West African coast to 17°N. That from the 1460s there were some early returns, in the form of small quantities of precious metals and semiprecious stones from Sierra Leone and poor-quality substitutes for Asian spices—*malagueta*—from what is now Liberia was hugely significant in terms of Portugal's economy; yet at the same time, they were not likely to undermine either the volume or the value of the established trade between East and West through the Levant. Thereafter, the Portuguese crown's commitment was intermittent because its modest resources could not support both military enterprise in North Africa and the exploration of Africa's Atlantic coastline. Instead, exploration and the pursuit of trade proceeded in alliance but was always dependent on actual or projected commercial viability.

If the Portuguese sought more profitable, because more direct, contact with the sources of the trade in Oriental luxuries, why did they follow the African seaboard southward, instead of taking the well-known sea route across the Mediterranean to the Levant *entrepôts*? Certainly, Levantine merchants were not restricted by their Ottoman overlords from trading with any particular group amongst the so-called Franks, but Italian interests, especially, worked hard to exclude West European rivals from the trade, as they continued to do into the 1600s. The other major West European force in the eastern Mediterranean basin, the Knights of St. John, pursued a combination of enforced trade and piracy, from their island base of Rodos until 1522 and thereafter from Malta. Outgunned and outnumbered for Mediterranean piracy to be an easy option, Portuguese maritime enterprise sought to out-think the traditional trades by exploring alternative routes to the same destinations.

If the existence of a continent on the western side of the Atlantic was to be a huge surprise, so, too, and to the same extent was the discovery by Portuguese navigators that Africa extended almost as far as 35°S, particularly with so little commercial return south of 5°S, in the vicinity of the mouth of the Kongo/Zaire. Only in the Indian Ocean did the venture and investment promise to deliver sizeable returns. To reach the Oriental sources of commodities was a major achievement of exploration and navigation, but once in contact, the Portuguese had almost nothing with which to trade, for they lacked not only goods in demand but also the bullion that was the usual alternative medium for exchange. Consequently, trade with Portuguese merchants was enforced on Asian societies by military and naval power, secured in the most spectacular manner under the leadership of Francisco de Almeida and Afonso de Albuquerque, successively viceroy and governor of Portuguese India between 1505 and 1515. Presumably unaware of their emulation of the technique, the Portuguese from c. 1500 became the Vikings of the Indian Ocean, stealing what they could not buy and holding the existing trading networks to ransom. These achievements, less than two decades after Columbus's first contact with the Americas, even with all their inherent risks, nevertheless offered better and more consistent returns on the investment than did anything by then reported from the western side of the Atlantic. From the Portuguese perspective, Castilla had drawn the short straw.

Italian entrepreneurs, meanwhile, were able to draw on western Europe's richest sources of venture capital (available through banks and bonds), which they could more readily secure against disaster (by joint stock and marine insurance underwriting). To these commercial advantages, they added geographical knowledge accumulated from revived classical and more recent Islamic scholarship, combined with extensive practical experience of oceanic seafaring beyond the Straits of Gibraltar, for example, from the (by the mid–fifteenth century) regular seaborne traffic from Genova and Venezia to Southampton and Antwerpen. The wars between the Italian states during the fifteenth century up until 1464 stretched the resources but did not fatally damage the commerce of the Italian peninsula, so at least until the French king Charles VIII's invasion (1494–95), individual Italian adventurer-entrepreneurs should have been able to find sponsors for long-range maritime enterprise.

That Caboto (Cabot) and Columbus searched for other patrons, however, symbolised the unwillingness of Italian merchants or rulers to divert resources from the established profits of the Mediterranean trades, even when those trades were threatened by an Ottoman expansion of the later 1400s so militarily effective that even the Venetian Empire was at risk. This risk was acknowledged in *La Serenissima*'s treaty with Mehmet II in 1479, and reiterated in the siege of Otranto (1480–81). Imagined sea routes from Europe to the West should have become attractive because their prospective journey times and costs were possibly so much shorter than those of the routes via the Cape of Good Hope to India and south Asia.

The measurable profit on the Italians' doorstep, however, remained sufficiently attractive to outweigh the appeal of new routes. Exploration on the off chance of finding rewards was a consequence of Columbus's experiences, not a cause. With as yet no recognised motive of pure science[14] to sustain maritime exploration, only the promise of profit could prompt the provision of even such modest resources as those given to Columbus, just as they had been given to Dias to allow him to round the Cape of Good Hope in 1488. Late-fifteenth-century indicators for Italian enterprise suggested that the existing networks of trade, with the commercially (relatively) sophisticated Italian peninsula as the intermediary for consumers across the rest of Europe, would remain those most likely to return consistent profits. Otherwise, the best prospects for state and personal enrichment, and for asserting political and military superiority over Europe's most aggressive neighbours, lay to the east of Suez. In any case, from 1499 rampaging French and Imperial forces within, and Ottoman expansion without, so disrupted the peninsula that only individual Italian entrepreneurs, such as Vespucci and Verrazano, continued to participate in the Western adventures.

If Christians and spices—allies and riches—were what Europeans were seeking, no one would sensibly have contemplated a journey beyond the familiar other than on the calculation that the destination was already known to be worth the effort of going. Columbus's own motives for his proposed expedition may have been as venal as personal enrichment with which to establish or even re-establish himself as a person of worth and status (following his failure and impoverishment as a merchant) and as vainglorious as the desire to be famous as the man who proved the viability of the shortest sea route to the Orient. His motives certainly did not encompass a wish for immortality as a navigator and explorer of unknown lands, for otherwise he would surely have embraced what others accepted before his death—that he had opened the way to a new world. Lacking the personal wealth to fund his expedition (or to indulge himself in it as a whim), Columbus sought financial backing in the form of venture capital. Then, as now, venture capital was available to those who could persuade backers that a significant financial return was to be expected from a successful enterprise. He seems to have concluded relatively early in his search for backing that only a royal sponsor would be willing to risk the capital necessary to launch his expedition. If all he had sought was a royal warrant or licence, comparable to a patent of monopoly or to letters of marque, such documents were obtainable in almost any European court for a relatively modest fee, promising as they did to bestow titles and riches over which the licensor had no jurisdiction. Columbus's dedication to his proposal led him to spend the best part of a decade touring the courts of Europe seeking a royal sponsor, but did his search take so long because he was an unrecognised genius, or was it perhaps that his proposal was, to most hearers, not commercially viable?

When the financial return on an expedition was particularly in doubt or when the objectives of an expedition were not primarily commercial, royal sponsorship might be obtained. Thus, João II offered a bounty to captains who sailed farther south each year, presumably because the prospects of a commercial return were thought uncertain. On the other hand, a consortium of Bristol merchants backed Caboto, although a royal warrant was also obtained. What was it, then, that made Columbus's proposal so unattractive to possible sponsors? It is unlikely that it was because he was not a denizen: the Italian Caboto worked from England, and the Portuguese Magalhães (Magellan) was commissioned by Castilla. It was not necessarily that his proposal was particularly outrageous; at one time or another, most European monarchs also funded, for example, someone to turn base metal into gold. More likely, it is that Columbus was simply incapable of inspiring confidence in himself as the leader of his proposed expedition, on which status he insisted. His later recorded feuds with his officers, and the indignity of his being returned to Europe in chains in 1500, strikingly demonstrate how difficult a person he could be, even by the standards of his era—arrogant, secretive, jealous of his standing—and this may explain why he was for so long unable to persuade either merchants or monarchs to invest in his scheme.

Los reyes católicos, Fernando and Isabel, were not given to gambling with their crowns' limited resources. Their political objectives had at first been the preservation of their personal union of the crowns against challenges by overmighty nobles and particularist cities, and thereafter to complete the sanctified task of liberating Iberia from the last vestige of the Islamic "occupation" whilst also extending their direct territorial dominion. These territorial ambitions, particularly of Fernando, led to dynastic alliances with England, Portugal, and the Burgundian dynasts of the Holy Roman Empire, as well as imperialist war in the Italian peninsula, all of which seemed aimed primarily at the containment of France. Endeavour beyond Iberia might have led perhaps to North Africa or, via Aragón's Neapolitan kingdom, to the Levant. Transoceanic enterprise, from the perspective of 1492, appeared to make no sense whatever.

Although economically modest, Castilla in the late fifteenth century had a tradition of maritime enterprise, principally for trade and fishing, and the conquest of the Canarias, led initially by a Norman adventurer, demonstrated a capacity for colonial enterprise. Castilla's commerce was dominated by the trade in wool through the great fairs at Burgos and the port of Bilbao, with resident merchants in what is now Belgium. Cádiz and Sevilla, later to be so prominent in the Atlantic commerce in people and goods, were at this stage still engaged primarily in serving the fishing industry in the case of the former, and an agricultural hinterland in the case of the latter. Palos de la Frontera was not an obvious starting place for major oceanic travel—then as now, the harbour at nearby Huelva was superior—and Palos was chosen as the starting point for Columbus's first voyage in order to provide ships and men as a penalty imposed by the crown for the community's default in some way now obscure. Marine and colonial expertise there certainly was, but no special experience of commercially sponsored maritime exploration.

The Castilian crown emerged from civil war (1462–72) heavily in debt and with limited opportunities to enrich itself or fund enterprise. Much capital and entrepreneurial resource lay within the kingdom of Aragón, where royal opportunities to exploit it for the needs of war were, however, heavily restricted by the *fueros*, in particular of the merchant cities in Catalunya and Valencia. The war with Granada (1481–92) was largely paid for by the *hermandades* and the papacy. What, then, prompted Isabel to authorise royal sponsorship of and payment for an enterprise so apparently at variance with the immediate best interests of Castilla in the 1490s?

Much more so than her husband, the queen was apparently personally committed to the religious aims of the Reconquest that were fulfilled at the fall of Granada. Columbus had for several years practised his appeal to the Catholic monarchs for support for his proposed expedition and had received encouragement in his approaches to Isabel from the treasurer of the *hermandad*, the *converso* Luis de Santángel. It may therefore have seemed only common sense for Columbus to stress in his latest proposals the potential advantages to Castilla of contacts with societies that could become at once sources of income, through the taxation on trade goods and potential allies in the struggle with Islam. Like Vasco da Gama, Columbus sought Christians and spices, but at a time when Isabel may have been particularly anxious to find ways to offset the self-inflicted social and economic damage arising from the persecution (particularly from 1480) and (in 1492) the expulsion of the Jews.

Thus, Isabel took a gamble with relatively modest resources whilst offering Columbus largely unspecified rewards, to be gained only if he were successful in terms that the queen could define later. For Isabel a successful expedition would have been one from which flowed only a fraction of the income already received by the Portuguese crown as its share of the West Africa trade; any strategic alliance would have been a bonus. If sailing west were the novel component and his having command the major drawback of Columbus's proposal, its stated objective of contact with the orient was unexceptional in western Europe by the 1490s. Had other proposals been made that offered more certain rewards than those imagined for her by Columbus, Isabel may have yet again declined to support him. The Columbus plan, however, had the advantage, regardless of its success or failure, of not bringing Castilla directly into competition with the established European participants in prospective or actual trade with the orient, mostly Portuguese and Italians, precisely because of its novel proposal to voyage westward.

FIRST CONTACT

Because we now know that Columbus's first contact with Western Hemisphere societies was followed in only a few decades by the virtual extinction of the peoples of the islands and the conquest of the civilisations of the mainland, it is perhaps difficult to address the question of whether these outcomes were inevitable. Was there some characteristic innate to the people involved or to the circumstances prevailing at the time that made the outcomes inescapable, irrespective of what may have been the wishes of individual actors in the drama? Would the outcomes have been different, if the lasting European bridge across the Atlantic had been established by others, for example, by a Brendan or a Leiv Eirikson?

As we have already noted, Columbus undertook his westward voyage expecting to make landfall in a part of the world about which he believed he already knew, the Orient. Consequently, in what he actually found he strove to identify peoples, cultures, and artefacts that he could claim to recognise, and he chose to characterise what he encountered in the terms for which he had been prepared—hence "Indians." Just like the amateur lost whilst orienteering, he persuaded himself that what he saw fit where he thought his map showed him he should be. He was, however, both shocked and disappointed at what he perceived as the primitive societies of the islands, and he attempted to mitigate this setback by claiming that he had landed amongst outlying (primitive) islands of the (sophisticated) Oriental mainland.[15]

The contrast between what Columbus had persuaded himself, his backers, and his crews to expect—the fabulous wealth and cultural sophistication of the peoples such as described by Marco Polo—and the actuality of hunter-gatherer peoples of limited material culture, did not prompt Columbus to a massive reappraisal of the expedition's purposes or a re-evaluation of its mission parameters. The objectives remained to secure commodities tradable in the European economies as low bulk–high value, to maximise the return on the investment in the voyage. Clutching at straws, Columbus endeavoured to secure specimens of whatever could be even vaguely described as spices, and to pursue any traces of artefacts of gold. As his journal reveals, Columbus was particularly anxious to be told about sources of gold that were farther to the west of his landfall. It is, however, hard to imagine how, in these first contacts, it was possible for his Taínos interlocutors to provide the kind of confirmation of his theories he so desperately wanted. More likely, surely, was that Columbus glossed any sort of response from the inhabitants as the answers he needed.

In reality, the expedition was confronted by much that was strange, thitherto unknown to West Europeans, amongst both flora and fauna. Some efforts were made to gather samples as physical evidence of the adventure, but novelties, whether human or animal, were poor substitutes for the proof Columbus desired to confirm the claims he had made to Isabel about reaching the Orient. Vasco da Gama, in striking contrast, later returned to Portugal from India with cargo of precisely the commodities he had been sent to find,[16] at a profit estimated at 600 percent.[17] Despite the lack of convincing evidence that Columbus had fulfilled his mission, Isabel and her advisors were sufficiently impressed with what he *had* found to be willing to confirm her sponsorship and risk further, expensive resources in a second expedition on a significantly larger scale.[18] This was improvised and dispatched to the west only six months after Columbus returned to Iberia.

As subsequent expeditions even within Isabel's lifetime soon revealed, Columbus had not reached the sources of Eastern trade goods, but instead had reached a new world. Did this realisation make a difference to the attitudes of Iberian explorers and their rulers, towards these Western territories in which they very quickly began to settle?

Perhaps only Columbus had truly expected to reach the orient. The other participants, by contrast, may have expected to reach new and "primitive" lands. By the 1490s, amongst Iberian seamen experience of the Atlantic was that island groups had been discovered (and rediscovered) for about 150 years past. It was conceivable that more such islands remained to be found. If a route to the orient were to be viable, it was both reasonable and practical for it to be found by island hopping across the Atlantic. If such islands were found, Iberian societies were already equipped to deal with them because Castilla had sponsored the successful invasion and settlement of near-tropical lands with what they considered primitive inhabitants, in the Canarias. The Guanche people had been "discovered" c. 1400, and although they were promptly overcome in Lanzarote and Fuerteventura and their culture largely extinguished by Norman adventurers and colonists from Iberia, the conquest of Gran Canaria and of Tenerife were roughly contemporaneous with Columbus's expeditions. Thus, at her disposal Isabel had expertise in the settlement, exploitation, and government of colonies that could be matched at this date in few other West European societies, outside of Iberia: principally the English in Ireland and Swedes in Finland.

Portuguese explorers and traders by the 1490s likewise had experience of "first contact" with "primitive" peoples along the West African littoral, but the response to these encounters characteristic of the Portuguese was to establish forts and factories, not to attempt colonisation. Where the Portuguese did have experience of colonisation was in the Atlantic islands of the Madeira group, the Açores, and the Cape Verde group, but these were uninhabited when the Portuguese first settled them. In competition with Castilla for the Canarias, Portuguese attempts to conquer Gran Canaria were repelled by its Guanche inhabitants. Castilian experience of the Portuguese was that disputed claims to first discovery might be referred to the papacy for arbitration, but prior possession was by far the best position to hold—hence the size of Columbus's second expedition and its determination to plant settlements. In sum, there were Portuguese who knew how to explore and how to force trade with the peoples they encountered, and there were Castilians who knew how to colonise territories at the expense of their existing inhabitants.

An assumption that Castilian, Hispanic, European, Christian culture was superior to anything encountered in the Western Hemisphere, was a learned response to first contact, and not one simply exported from Iberia. Although the fall of Granada was the climax of the *Reconquista*, that triumph was not the end of the early modern struggle between Christian Iberia and Islam, and for West Europeans of the 1490s there was abundant evidence of the power of non-Christian societies and cultures. What Columbus and his immediate successors learned quickly, however, was that Taínos and Arawak societies lacked almost all the trappings of "civilised" communities previously encountered—no monuments, no cities, no economy much beyond subsistence. Even the Guanches had built pyramids, of sorts, and had, for example, complex funerary customs that Canarian colonists and priests recorded without comprehending them. Indigenous peoples of the Caribbean, however, could be likened to beasts of the field, endowed with an understanding of little more than how to exist. Not until the great debate between Las Casas and Sepúlveda did the Castilian crown fully resolve that, as if they were children, the indigenous peoples should be taught about Christian civilisation, rather than that, as if they were cattle, they should be exploited and enslaved.

The Castilian response to first contact in the western islands was thus consistent with their experience of earlier, similar encounters in the Canarias. Columbus's objectives were quickly superseded by the implementation of a colonial project which, under royal patronage, began the settlement and exploitation of both lands and peoples. In these vital early years, Taínos and Arawak societies proved unable either by force or ideology to resist Castilla's project, and Iberians quickly acquired the habit of contempt for, and the expectation of military superiority over, the peoples and cultures they encountered.

If instead of Taínos or Arawaks Columbus had first made contact with Mexica (Aztecs) or Maya, Castilla's response might perhaps have been more like that of the Portuguese in southeast Asia. There, the evident social and political sophistication of the peoples encountered encouraged the Portuguese to seek alliances to compensate for their disadvantage in manpower, which could only partly be offset with superior naval and firearms technology. Strategically significant outposts were seized by daring feats of arms but the complete overthrow of indigenous ruling systems in favour of a colonial regime was not, for the Portuguese, a realistic prospect. Confronted by Taínos and Arawaks, however, Columbus's immediate successors quickly enforced the *encomienda*, as they did in the Canarias and would later do on the Mesoamerican mainland. The consistent inability of the island peoples to mount prolonged or effective resistance to the Iberian invaders promoted an expectation that indigenous peoples would never seriously resist or impede the colonial project. Interest in finding a route to the Orient persisted, but not at the expense of the exploitation of the lands and peoples already discovered.

Was this exploitation essentially racist? Already by the 1490s, parts of Iberian society had evidenced its intolerance for those who could be portrayed as different, but *marranos* and *moriscos* were despised because they were perceived as enemies within Hispanic society, agents of what in a later century in Spain would be called a fifth column. The racism of *limpieza de sangre* may have provided a vocabulary with which to express discrimination based on differences of culture, but in Iberia the differences of race were largely cultural, rather than physiological. By contrast, the indigenous peoples of the Americas were immediately distinguishable by physiognomy, and their paganism could justify their subordination, but they were neither invited nor expected to become Spaniards.

In this, the Castilian project rejected one, highly effective model of imperialism: the classical Roman Empire had achieved considerable success in winning the allegiance of political élites amongst the peoples it conquered by offering them access to the benefits of the empire. The Ottoman Turks contrived a modus vivendi with their non-Islamic subject peoples—whether Jews or Orthodox, Roman, or Coptic Christian. In contrast, only briefly did conquistadores seek to come to terms with indigenous élites—for example, in the short-term alliances of Cortés with the Mexicas' enemies. Instead, as soon as possible, indigenous élites were swept aside to become to the incomers' eyes indistinguishable from their former subjects and equally liable to exploitation.

Would these outcomes have been any different had the discoverers come from somewhere other than Iberia? Amongst West Europeans, Portuguese or English explorers of the 1490s would probably have subscribed to the same model as that of Columbus's successors: as soon as it became apparent that the indigenous peoples were little able to defend themselves, a project for conquest and colonisation would likely have been pursued, on lines similar to those in the Atlantic islands and Ireland. Amongst Islamic societies, there was by this time a long track record of converting, often by force, infidel peoples to the faith, and thereafter offering access to the fruits of Islamic civilisation—learning, law codes, trade, and technology—as demonstrated in central and east Africa. Had first contact been made by people from West Africa, they might have tried to replicate their domestic economy of trade in precious commodities and slaves. Thus, it is difficult not to conclude that for the Taínos and Arawak, as soon as "discovery" occurred resistance was futile: they would be assimilated.

FURTHER READING

For: an accessible account of voyaging for trade and settlement that helps to set the Atlantic developments in their mediaeval context of marine endeavour in the seas around Europe, see G. V. Scammell, *The World Encompassed. The First European Maritime Empires, c. 800–1650* (London and New York, 1981), and for an account that synthesises much other literature, see F. Fernández-Armesto, *Before Columbus: Exploration and Colonization From the Mediterranean to the Atlantic, 1229–1492* (Philadelphia, 1987); a lively, scholarly, one volume introduction to Scandinavia's early mediaeval interaction with the wider world, see E. Christiansen, *The Norsemen in the Viking Age* (Oxford and Malden, MA, 2002); a gorgeously illustrated and scholarly introduction to the subject of Norse settlement in North America, see the catalogue of the millennium exhibit at the Smithsonian, W. F. Fitzhugh and E. I. Ward, eds., *Vikings: The North Atlantic Saga* (Washington, D.C., 2000); a detailed appraisal of the evidence for how far Norse exploration may have reached at its furthest extent, see

A. Næss, *Hvor lå Vinland?* (Oslo, 1954), in which the "Eyktarstad Problem" is pursued to argue that Chesapeake Bay was probably the northernmost limit of Vinland; a readable, recent, synoptic, one-volume introduction to major themes and developments in the West European Middle Ages, see C. R. Backman, *The Worlds of Medieval Europe* (New York and Oxford, 2003), although unfortunately its guides to further reading are brief; a scholarly, one-volume analytical narrative, see S. J. Shaw, *Empire of the Gazis: The Rise and Decline of the Ottoman Empire, 1280–1808*, vol. 1, *History of the Ottoman Empire and Modern Turkey* (1976; reprint, New York and Cambridge, 1985); and for a recent readable account of the interplay between the Ottoman Empire and western societies, see D. Goffman, *The Ottoman Empire and Early Modern Europe* (Cambridge, 2002); careful introductory material by region, for fifteenth century Africa, see R. Oliver, ed., *From c. 1050–1600*, vol. 3, *The Cambridge History of Africa* (New York and Cambridge, 1986); a scholarly account of the pre-Columbian economy of Mexico, see R. Hassig, *Trade, Tribute, and Transportation. The Sixteenth-Century Political Economy of the Valley of Mexico* (Norman, OK, 1985), and C. R. Edwards, "Nautical Technology and Maritime Routes in Mesoamerica," *Atti del XL Congresso Internazionale degli Americanisti* 4 (1972): pp. 199–202; a scholarly account of Chinese maritime enterprise, see L. Levathes, *When China Ruled the Seas: The Treasure Fleet of the Dragon Throne 1405–1433* (Oxford, 1994), and for a popular account with challenging propositions about the extent of Chinese explorations, see G. Menzies, *1421: The Year China Discovered the World* (London, 2002), published in the United States as *1421: The Year China Discovered America* (New York, 2003); an account of late mediaeval Portugal, as well as the era of discovery, see for example J. M. Garcia, *Breve História dos Descobrimentos e Expansão de Portugal* (Lisboa, 1999); whereas an authoritative and accessible anglophone account of Portuguese maritime empire remains C. R. Boxer, *The Portuguese Seaborne Empire, 1415–1825* (London, 1969), a text commended by history textbooks currently used in Portugal; a concise summary account of fifteenth century Italian economy and society, notwithstanding the recent publication of three English-language social histories of early modern Italy, see P. Burke, *The Italian Renaissance: Culture and Society in Italy,* 2nd ed. (Princeton, NJ, 1999) pp. 181–256; a modern life account (amongst the many) of Columbus, see F. Fernández-Armesto, *Columbus and the Conquest of the Impossible,* rev. ed. (London, 2000), which is suitably sceptical of some of the grander claims made for the man whilst acknowledging his extraordinary drive; a useful, summary account of late fifteenth century Iberia, see H. Kamen, *Spain, 1469–1714* (New York and Harlow, England, 1983); a useful work of general reference on the early discoveries, see S. A. Bedini, ed., *Christopher Columbus and the Age of Exploration: An Encyclopedia* (1992; abridged and reprinted, New York, 1998).

CHAPTER 2

Going There and Getting Back: Technological and Technical Prerequisites and Developments in Travel

It is remarkable that, although European societies deployed across the region only small fractions of their available human and material resources, West Europeans emerged as politically and economically preeminent around the North Atlantic during the early modern period. Notwithstanding the enormous difficulty in suggesting any reliable figures for this period, by c. 1750, the combined homeland populations of the leading West European imperial powers—the French, the British, the Irish, Iberians, the Dutch, and the Swedish—totalled perhaps 45.5 million.[1] By comparison, even after some 250 years or more of West European settlement in the New World, the combined populations of those of European culture in the Caribbean and mainland North America c. 1750, was perhaps less than 1.2 million,[2] with relatively few others settled on the Atlantic islands and the West African littoral.

This West European pre-eminence, however, is not to be explained simply as the consequence of technological superiority, of the possession of knowledge applied to sustaining improved performance of devices or machines to achieve effects disproportionate to their human inputs. Technological developments made some of the going easier: they did not of themselves determine outcomes. The technologies of firearms or of sailing ships—perhaps the two conventionally regarded as of most significance—do not, by themselves, explain either the West European settlement of the North Atlantic or the later Anglophone domination of much of the region. Firearms technology, for example, as discussed in the next chapter, was a valuable but never entirely sufficient ingredient in the emergence of European domination over indigenous peoples. Furthermore, it is perhaps surprising to recall that, relative to the centuries immediately preceding and succeeding our period, although there was incremental development there was comparatively little fundamental advance in either the technologies of travel and communication or for the exploitation of natural resources, both areas we might suppose would have been valuable aids to early modern empire-building. Certainly, there were incremental improvements in the details of construction and operationalising of these activities, but as I have already remarked in chapter 1, the ability of West Europeans to cross the ocean predated by several centuries a determination to make the passage routine. Thus, the early modern period for Europeans saw the deployment of means that were instruments of transformation but which means were not themselves transformed.

We may propose that there were no hugely significant or uniquely favourable technological circumstances that prompted West European settlement in the North Atlantic, or the collapse of indigenous resistance, or the later Anglophone ascendancy over that part of the hemisphere. On the other hand, the early modern period did see significant developments in European technical and managerial capacity—the ability to perform and repeat complex tasks with reasonable probability of achieving predicted outcomes—which were significant in the history of early modern societies in western Europe, and for their projection around the North Atlantic. The ability to exploit raw materials, to mobilise surplus money, personnel, transport, and military power, we may suggest were prerequisites for the creation and maintenance of empire in any age, and indeed may also be observed in the empires indigenous to the Western Hemisphere, such as that of the Inca. Yet in the story of early modern competition amongst Europeans for domination of the North Atlantic, the facts of technical capacity do not seem in themselves to have been sufficient to inspire the adventurers, to provoke attempts at empire-building, or, crucially, to determine outcomes. Nevertheless, they were the means by which the domination of the hemisphere was achieved. In this and the next chapter, we survey technological and technical developments under the headings of travel and of warfare.

TRAVEL

It is perhaps an obvious but nonetheless essential characteristic of the development of the early modern Atlantic that all the participating European societies relied on a capacity to maintain routine contact across the ocean. In contrast with current or prospective travel through outer space, early modern journeys across the ocean did not require that generations of voyagers live, reproduce, and die before their vessel reached its destination. Instead, transatlantic journey times could compare favourably with those across continental Europe. As noted by modern authors, "the voyage from Spain varied between 39 and 175 days, the route back from 70 to 298 days";[3] and

Over the sixteenth century and the first half of the seventeenth, the average length of a voyage from San Lúcar to Veracruz was ninety-one days in convoy. From Cadiz to the same destination took only seventy-five days on average, because there was no sand bar of the sort which guarded San Lúcar, but a hundred and one days was a journey time within normal limits. The return voyage from Mexico to Andalusia never took less than seventy days and could be much prolonged.[4]

For journeys within Europe, for example, "in 1567 it took the duke of Alba four and a half months to move his personnel from Spain to the Netherlands,"[5] taking the core of his staff by sea to the Italian peninsula and then the army overland to establish the Spanish Road. For most of the Road's period in use (1567–1620), "thousands of men at a time were able to travel the 700 or so miles between Milan and Brussels in five to seven weeks."[6] For journeys by sea, from the Levant to Venice "about seventy days was normal,"[7] and between northern Europe and the central Mediterranean, voyages might reasonably take three months.[8] We should note that it took much longer to establish routine crossing of the Pacific than of the Atlantic because of issues of landfall, endurance, and sailing conditions.[9]

Furthermore, European contact across the Atlantic was characterised by the transportation of commodities—and people—in bulk. Although the commodities shipped east across the ocean were most famously the gold and silver bullion obtained through plunder and then mining, there was from the middle of our period a growth in volume transportation of agricultural commodities such as tobacco and sugar, which, although generating considerable profit for the merchant wholesalers, over time fell in unit price as the quantities reaching European consumers steadily increased.[10] Long-range trade in both luxuries and staples was not unique to the Europeans' approach to the New World's commodities; it was also a feature of the Mexica empire and was therein similarly characterised by duress and exploitation.[11]

Although it may again seem obvious, it is perhaps also worth restating that their lack of significant maritime forces put the indigenous peoples of the Western Hemisphere at a powerful disadvantage in their encounters with Europeans. At the time of first contact, Mesoamerican societies lacked the technology to pose a serious challenge to Europeans on the ocean; rafts and canoes, for example, even with sails,[12] were no match for even the modest vessels of the early European incomers. Nevertheless, native craftsmen under the direction of López quickly mastered the skills to build a flotilla of brigantines, equipped with artillery, with which Cortés blockaded Tenochtitlán in 1521.[13] Although these vessels were crewed by, in effect, press-ganged Iberians,[14] given the perennial shortages of skilled manpower amongst the conquistadores, we may surmise that amongst their indigenous allies some subsequently learned not only to build but also to crew such vessels. Thus, maritime expertise was not innately the preserve of Europeans. The story of the North Atlantic would have unfolded differently had Mesoamerican societies been able to threaten the maintenance of maritime communications between the small and scattered forces of the Europeans, either in the New World or between the western and eastern sides of the ocean.

On the eastern littoral of the Atlantic, West African coastal peoples deployed large (but not ocean-going) boats to move troops along rivers and the coastal channels[15] and perhaps were recruited to crews of European sailing vessels, including those which transported slaves.[16] As in Mesoamerica, although there may initially have been a technology gap between West Africa and western Europe, there were opportunities to copy European maritime designs and sailing techniques to augment indigenous capabilities, but these were not apparently exploited to the level of ocean-going craft. Thus, Europeans were not challenged for control of the transoceanic trade in humans or the shipment of goods, notwithstanding West African interest in profiting from the commerce. Only the corsairs based in North Africa might threaten Europeans at sea, interdicting transatlantic traffic from time to time, but never with sufficient determination or numbers to cut the Europeans' communications for any significant length of time, because of the corsairs' preference for Mediterranean action.[17]

Travel technology was vital because it was also, to a large extent, coterminous with communication. Early modern Europeans had technology for communication little better and in several respects worse than that of the Romans, 1,500 years before them: signal beacons, semaphore paddles, and carrier pigeons could speed simple messages over relatively short distances, but not until the nineteenth-century invention of the electric telegraph would European empires benefit from rapid communication. Elsewhere in the early modern world, travel by land or sea was at least as effective as amongst Europeans, and in some respects superior. In early-sixteenth-century South America, for example, the Inca road network allowed relays of messengers to cover perhaps "50 leagues a day,"[18] even without horses. In southern China throughout this period, rivers were used extensively for trade and communications,[19] and chapter 1 noted that imperial China had, by the early 1400s, already demonstrated the capability to project military and political power across the seas. Around the Indian Ocean, notwithstanding the considerable amount of time that might elapse before the completion of a trading voyage, there were nevertheless significant maritime trading connections maintained not only around the littoral but also connected with the interiors of African, Arabian, and Indian lands, centuries before the direct intrusion of West Europeans.[20]

The technology of transatlantic travel we may for convenience characterise as having four constituents: shipbuilding, navigation/cartography, endurance, and sailing technique. Notwithstanding their vital significance in the history of this period, it is striking that in the early modern Europeans' domination of the North Atlantic, there were virtually no dramatically significant developments or innovations in any of these four constituents. The technology of travel employed by, for example, Admiral Anson in his circumnavigation of the 1740s,[21] would have been readily comprehended by Magalhães (Magellan) in 1519. The technologies that existed in Columbus's days were incrementally refined and in their application pushed to the limits, but no major technological breakthrough was made to assist the development of reliable sea transport to strengthen the sinews of the Europeans' maritime empires, before Harrison's chronometers, successive models of which were tested from 1736.[22] Indeed, Harrison's achievement—the widespread adoption of chronometers, based on Harrison's inventions but manufactured in volume and much more cheaply, began in the 1780s—marked only the beginning of the period in which successful technological innovation managed to meet long-recognised needs. Advances in the technology of travel neither caused the development of European empires in the Atlantic, nor were advances consequences of those empires: rather, the available technologies were simply good enough for those empires to develop and then maintain adequate economic, political, and cultural links across the ocean.

Shipbuilding

Shipbuilding effectively comprehended ship design in the early modern period, and, for the historian J. H. Parry, the most important developments for Europeans occurred during the mid–fifteenth century, in a combining of characteristics drawn from Atlantic and Mediterranean ship designs: the Atlantic square-rig and the Mediterranean lateen sails, and in hull designs between that of the capacious northern cog and the slender southern galley, with a straight keel and stern-post rudder:[23] "This was the development which made the Reconnaissance physically possible."[24] Indeed, barely thirty years after Columbus's first Atlantic crossing, a ship of a similar design—the *Victoria*—completed the first European circumnavigation of the globe (1519–22). For Parry, the carvel was the distinctive archetype of the ships of the Reconnaissance, and was a prerequisite technological development. Recent reflection upon the findings of marine archaeology, however, may extend Parry's periodisation of this development in design. Instead of in the mid-1400s, the emergence of the carvel design may be placed much earlier, in perhaps the 1200s in the harbours of northern Portugal.[25] Thus, Parry's prerequisite technology was available for perhaps two hundred years or more before Columbus's first Atlantic crossing. In any case, as already noted in chapter 1, oars and sails had been successfully combined to allow northern European Vikings to cross the North Atlantic in the tenth century, and oar-powered vessels remained important in the Mediterranean through the early modern period. Why, then, did early modern Atlantic shipping abandon oars in favour of sails?

Since classical times, the galley, particularly for war, had dominated the Mediterranean. The galley's prominence at the battle of Lepanto (1571) underlined this point, and it remained in French Mediterranean war fleets into the mid–eighteenth century (if only as a means to punish the likes of Jean Valjean) and in the navies of Italian states into the time of Lord Nelson. Although impractical in the early modern period for unescorted transoceanic voyages because the size of its crew exceeded its capacity for stores for long journeys, the galley was nevertheless the only vessel that could operate independently of the wind. It should have been ideal for rapid transits amongst the islands of the Caribbean and for short-range defence within harbours. Two war galleys were sent from Iberia to the Caribbean in 1582, and thereafter small numbers of them operated from Santo Domingo and Cartagena, but the provision was never extensive,[26] even though possible labour shortages could be remedied with slaves from Africa. The explanation for this abandonment of the galley may lie not in a growing conviction of the innate technical superiority of sail,[27] but in the difference in prevailing sea conditions between the Mediterranean and the western Atlantic and Caribbean.[28]

In a comparison between the mid–fifteenth century and the late eighteenth century, no profound innovation in shipbuilding arose from an urge to discover. Rather, the practical challenges of transatlantic travel reinforced the emergent superiority of sails over oars, arising from the relatively smaller crew sizes and consequent improvements in endurance. There were only incremental developments of maritime technology, but these were to refine what was already possible. Attempts to innovate by flouting the custom and practice of shipwrights could lead to such tragedies as the loss of the *Vasa* in 1628, to the ultimate benefit of twentieth-century marine archaeology.[29] Effective innovation was based on limited experimentation, but within the parameters of early modern West European ship design there emerged sufficient variations to allow for some specialisation of function, chiefly between shipping in the Mediterranean and the Atlantic, and between the activities of fishing, commerce, and warfare.

For fishing and trade, other than those that were strictly subsistence and coastal, the emphasis in design was necessarily on providing for oceanic seaworthiness without inhibiting access to most harbours; a small crew to allow for maximum carrying capacity (and endurance); and means to preserve cargo in as good a condition as possible. The optimum designs were eventually developed by the Dutch, in the fishing buss (equipped to preserve the catch—particularly herring—on board) and the trading *fluit*, yet these vessels did not dominate the North Atlantic to the same extent that they dominated the North Sea and Baltic.[30] Instead, the long-range commercial fishing fleets of Bilbao, St. Malo, and Bristol that were prominent in the Grand Banks and Iceland fisheries relied on designs somewhat smaller than the buss that sought to facilitate the line fishing used for cod, whereas the merchantmen of Sevilla and London tended to rely on more heavily armed vessels than the *fluit*. If there was, to some extent, a kind of nationalism in naval architecture, this reflected traditional designs and available materials and different priorities in performance that inhibited the adoption of optimum, Dutch forms with their small crews, broad beams, and shallow drafts. On this point, it is worth noting that, notwithstanding post-1707 Britain's later superiority in naval and mercantile shipping numbers, in the early modern period, there were no innate advantages of trading vessel design or sailing technology enjoyed by English-speaking societies. Indeed, the English Navigation Act of 1651—the only piece of English republican legislation substantially reenacted by the restored Stuart monarchy and arguably the starting point of the growth of English mercantile power—was made effective largely by success in redeploying Dutch merchant bottoms captured during the First Anglo-Dutch War (1652–54).

The requirements of naval warfare, particularly with the widespread adoption of naval artillery, equally reflected the different circumstances of competing European societies. Most famously, perhaps, Felipe II's 1588 Armada for the invasion of England contained many vessels heavily manned with soldiers rather than sailors, often carrying land artillery ill adapted to maritime use.[31] Its English opponents, in contrast, were often better handled, mounted guns with higher rates of fire and were crewed by fighting sailors.[32] Despite its potential as the definitive clash of alternative naval designs, however, the running fight up the Channel led to the sinking of only one vessel by gunfire, and the decisive event in the battle was probably the English attack by fireships on the Armada hoveto at Gravelines. That so many units of the 1588 Armada fled without their anchors was to be as important in the subsequent losses of men and ships, as were the spoiling of stores for the long voyage back to Iberia (itself a consequence of Drake's raids on Cádiz and Sagres and their local shipping in 1587).[33] Far more telling, in terms of competing warship designs and naval technique, was the Dutch victory over another Armada at the Downs in 1639,[34] which in Parker's view established the role of the frigate as a design more generally serviceable than the galleon.[35] From the middle of the seventeenth century, English naval vessels appeared to enjoy advantages of design over their Dutch opponents, through weight of firepower and heavier displacement made possible by the deeper waters of the English navy's harbours.[36] In the 1690s, however, French naval architecture responded to the strategic stalemate with the Anglo-Dutch battle fleets by deploying commerce raiders of the frigate type.[37] The possession of a powerful navy, capable of operating around the globe and equipped with a mix of units ranging from the heaviest ships of the line to the medium-sized cruisers to the smaller convoy escorts, by c. 1700 had become the hallmark of the most energetic European imperial powers.[38]

Well-found vessels capable of successful transatlantic crossing could be as small as the 8 tons of the *Squirrel*, the frigate in which Sir Humfrey Gilbert was lost in 1583,[39] whereas the galleons employed in the flota could range in size between 300 and 1,000 tons,[40] and at the extreme, the Portuguese *Madre de Deus*, deployed in the Asian trade, was said in 1592 to be of 1,600 tons. Size alone, as modern experience of transatlantic yachting underlines, was not determinative of success, either in making the oceanic crossing or in exploration of the Atlantic littoral. Indeed, European explorers valued the presence in their flotillas of smaller craft to facilitate inshore and estuarine reconnaissance. Such craft, however, were bound to have more limited endurance and thus could be more vulnerable to the effects of unduly prolonged journeys arising from, for example, adverse weather conditions (or poor navigation). Thus, for practical purposes, the minimum specifications within the existing performance envelope of European shipping for the types of vessels employed reflected in part the differentiation in function between exploration, transplantation, and commerce.

The building of ocean-going shipping was neither of necessity nor need have remained, a West European monopoly. Other societies around the littoral possessed the necessary raw materials and could acquire the technical skills to build ocean-going vessels, even if only in imitation of European designs. The essential maintenance of careening and replacing worn or damaged masts and sailing gear readily broadened into construction de novo, for which a further spur was the relatively short working life of wooden vessels, particularly in the tropics—five to ten years was not unusual,[41] although some considerably older vessels served in the English fleet against the Armada, and beyond.[42] A number of attributes assisted the development of European-style shipbuilding in the New World in particular, notwithstanding the potential monopoly of communications that a mother country could enjoy by banning naval construction in the colonies.

First and foremost, even by the standards of the period, shipbuilding was what we may characterise as an intermediate technology. Unlike present-day marine engineering, whether civil or military, the techniques of (and tools required for) early modern European ship construction were not unduly specialised and the necessary skills were transferable to experienced woodworkers, even if such craftsmen were reduced to the expedient of copying an existing—or wrecked—vessel. The performance—in terms of carrying capacity and speed—of West European vessels was also so evidently superior to any indigenous designs[43] that these latter tended to survive only in the specialised roles of river traffic and local fishing, for which Europeans adopted various forms of the canoe. In contrast, Arab and Asian ship designs remained distinctive into the modern era, typified by the *bagla*[44] and the so-called junk, reflecting the persistence of the marine conditions that had prompted the evolution of their designs. Thus, despite the limited numbers of European shipwrights in the New World, shipbuilding—to a serviceable standard if not of the highest quality—was technically feasible from early on in our period.

Second, basic raw materials were also available in the Western Hemisphere, even if only in the form of substitutes for those familiar to shipbuilders in western Europe, such as timber, linen sailcloth, hemp for rigging, and pitch for caulking. Iberia was in any case chronically short of shipbuilding timber, as also was the Dutch republic, so that their raw materials were generally imported, for which the main European sources were in the Baltic. In some cases, the resources of the New World were superior to those of western Europe, and indeed, by the mid–seventeenth century, the New England region was viewed by the English as a vital strategic reserve of shipbuilding raw materials, particularly timber for construction and pine for pitch. For some time, however, there could be shortages of nautical metalware—iron, brass or bronze fixings and fittings—and quality sailcloth, but these items could be recycled from wrecked or unseaworthy vessels. Over time, colonial manufactures proved able to meet some of the requirements of volume and quality, thus easing a dependence on the skilled production of Europe. Gun-founding, on the other hand, particularly for the manufacture of dependable naval artillery, required considerable material resources and skills which encouraged colonial societies to remain dependent on established European sources.

Third, the growth in demand for shipping between the areas of European settlement in the Western Hemisphere early exceeded the capacity of the mother countries to supply it. From the 1540s, shipbuilding developed on the Pacific coast of Mexico to meet a shortage of vessels with which to service a trade in luxuries and bullion with the conquistadores of Peru.[45] This was but an early example of the development of patterns of shipping traffic to meet the market demands between European settlements in the Western Hemisphere, rather than simply to service contact between colony and mother country. In the earlier seventeenth century, Dutch merchant ships played a vital role in maintaining trade between

English-speaking colonies, and between these colonies and Europe, until the expansion of the English merchant marine in the later 1600s.[46] By the latter part of the century, trade between the Caribbean islands and New England was serviced by New England seamen and shipping.[47] For the Luso-Hispanic world, this trend towards colonial seafaring was intensified by shipbuilding to mitigate a decline in the numbers of ocean-going vessels built in Iberia, so that by 1650 about a third (by number rather than tonnage) of the transatlantic fleets were American-built.[48]

A further limiting factor was a chronic shortage of skilled marine personnel for which a capacity to build ships could not compensate.[49] One way of compensating for a shortage of skilled manpower was to employ fewer, larger vessels, which approach was adopted by the Iberian states in the sixteenth century. An alternative was to try to encourage recruitment and training of crews, but because those societies with large merchant fleets were not necessarily the same societies as the colonisers, there was a risk of becoming dependent on foreigners. Rather like a modern state-sponsored airline in a developing country, high wages might attract skilled personnel if there was otherwise open competition, but in the case of the early modern shipping, those career sailors who chose to base themselves in the West might also be tempted to take up piracy.

Given the importance of Atlantic shipping, we might expect that West African societies would have participated. West Africa in this period possessed all of the attributes we have already identified as contributing to the development of oceanic shipbuilding in the New World. In some respects, West African societies were even better endowed because they were geographically and culturally well placed to develop superior marine technologies by drawing on the technical resources of Islamic societies as well as those of West Europeans. Appropriate or adaptable raw materials were available, along with numerous craftsmen to undertake construction, in societies rich enough to deploy the requisite labour and materials. Commercial incentives existed in the shape of a commodity trade—in slaves—for which a high level of demand should have encouraged (in a European model of capitalism) progressive expansion of African ownership, from the sources of supply to comprehend the means of transportation to the markets. Over this period as a whole, West Europeans on the West African littoral were neither numerous nor possessed of overwhelming firepower, and although they competed with one another,[50] Europeans would not have been able to protect their commerce if seriously challenged by the indigenous peoples. Yet no sustained efforts were made by West Africans to extend their command and control to the carrying trade in their chief commodity.

Why this was so may be explained in the terms of trade which prevailed in West Africa. Amongst indigenous societies in which the economy had developed beyond subsistence, commerce in the commodities in greatest demand—salt, livestock, iron, labour—produced more than adequate returns. For those goods that Europeans supplied, such as firearms, small manufactures, and textiles, demand remained good but not such to encourage direct access to the sources of these goods to improve volumes or reduce prices. There was not a sufficiently powerful incentive for West Africans to enter the maritime trades on a significant scale, relative to the value of the trade, because their returns from coastal trade remained strong.[51] Nor were there considerations of defence or security sufficient to encourage the development of indigenous deep-sea naval power.[52] West African societies were not seriously threatened in our period with invasion and occupation by Europeans, not only because of the hostility for Europeans of the natural environment but also because the level of cooperation that West Africans offered to Europeans was sufficient to meet the outsiders' demands. Until the nineteenth century, the European presence could be tolerated without risk, because it serviced particular needs of the domestic African economies.

Shipbuilding was not only vital for trade and communications around the North Atlantic, it was also one of the most important of the small number of early modern industrial activities. The acme of that activity in the fifteenth and sixteenth centuries was the Venetian Arsenal, where a veritable production line fitted out galleys for *La Serenissima*'s war fleet.[53] At the other end of our period, by the end of the eighteenth century, the British naval dockyards of Portsmouth and Chatham were models of industrialised manufacture of standardised components required for complex warships. Even in an already industrialising age, the Royal Navy's dockyards reached new levels of sophistication and scale in the organisation of labour and raw materials.[54] Both in the sixteenth-century Venetian republic and in eighteenth-century Britain, a state bureaucracy mobilised money, men, and materials on a scale otherwise uncharacteristic of the period. Although possessed of the raw materials and the technical skills, however, apart from New England and Bermuda, the North Atlantic colonies in the early modern period did not achieve complete self-sufficiency in shipbuilding. It might be tempting to suggest that the limiting factor in Western Hemisphere shipbuilding activity was a chronic shortage of skilled marine personnel for which a capacity to build ships could not compensate. As we have already observed, however, crews could be recruited from amongst the indigenous populations.[55] Instead, that colonial construction was not undertaken on the industrial scale of the Arsenal or Portsmouth reflected the lack of a sufficiently powerful incentive—the absence, for the most part, of an imminent threat of invasion by another European power for which powerful naval forces were required as a deterrent.[56]

Navigation and Cartography

Put crudely, navigation and cartography were the techniques by which to ensure that journeys ended at the intended places. Incremental improvements in the technologies of navigation and cartography during our period were as much consequences of as spurs to exploration, occupation, and settlement of the Atlantic littoral. Thus, years before the first Columbus voyage, Venetian maps in the mid–fifteenth century already attempted to portray possible destinations to the west of mainland Europe, based on speculation rather than on even fragmentary hard evidence, and consequently were useless for the practical purposes of mariners. In contrast with the relatively limited achievements of the mapmakers, practical oceanic navigation was developing amongst the fishing fleets of western Europe, and it was likely these skills, rather than scientific navigation, that allowed Sebastián del Cano to complete Magalhães's circumnavigation of the globe barely 30 years after Columbus's first American voyage. Indeed, we have already remarked that the lack of means to determine longitude until the celebrated achievements of Harrison did *not* prevent three hundred years of successful transatlantic navigation.

Successful navigation for commerce relied heavily on the knowledge and skills of the pilot.[57] Vasco da Gama reached Calicut in 1498, guided by Ibn Majid. Early modern Arab and Indian pilots in the Indian Ocean were family members who kept closely guarded their knowledge of the particular locality in which they worked,[58] more as a way of preserving their income and status rather than as a quality control mechanism over the technical proficiency of pilots (running aground would do that). In the (for them, unfamiliar) waters of the Orient, therefore, West Europeans were, at least initially, dependent for navigation upon the cooperation and skills of indigenous peoples. In the Western Hemisphere, of course, in the absence of indigenous knowledge of the performance envelope of European sailing vessels, there were no reliable maritime native guides, so that West Europeans had quickly to become their own pilots. This challenge enhanced the premium on the skills of acute observation and recollection of details of the sea and land—of currents, bottom conditions, weather, and topography. The net effect was to raise the minimum level of competence needed by any navigator seeking to operate in the Western Hemisphere within the safety limits considered reasonable in the period. Practice made perfect, and such important knowledge had, within limits, to be shared if the volume of transatlantic traffic were to expand. In this period, for the practical navigator, charts came second to the observations of pilots.

Only the bravest adventurers, such as Henry Hudson, were willing to head westward and gamble on where they might arrive; in contrast, Columbus thought he knew where he was going.[59] The development and maintenance of political and commercial contacts across the ocean depended on the ability to replicate journeys, achieved most consistently in the annual cycle of convoys, the flotas and *galeones*, which from the sixteenth century linked Iberia, the Atlantic and Caribbean islands, and Mesoamerica. The institution of a formal convoy system from Sevilla, beginning in the 1520s and perfected in the 1560s, however, in part reflected the relative shortage of experienced pilots and the difficulties to be confronted in making landfall at or near the target after a transatlantic voyage.[60] Transatlantic routes became established as experience taught the optimum headings—and seasons—for completing the journey between specified points, to which the most important ingredients were the annual movements of winds and currents that initially advantaged voyagers from east to west starting from Iberia, and which periodically isolated voyagers originating in West Africa or Central America. This was not to deny the role of accident or contingency; to quote only two examples, Cabral's so-called discovery of Brasil may only have formalised the sightings consequent on earlier explorers' prolonged beating to windward to regain the shore of Namibia, and the Pilgrim Fathers' landing at Plymouth Rock was after the *Mayflower*'s captain Christopher Jones got lost and missed his target at the mouth of the Hudson River. Consequently, shipping in the North Atlantic, perhaps to a greater extent than in waters close to Europe or coasting West Africa, relied on the firsthand experience of masters and their pilots to make landfalls in the general vicinity of their chosen destinations. Seafarers might share their experience through written portolani, routiers, or rutters,[61] but throughout this period practical navigation relied on the magnetic compass, a limited range of direct observations, dead reckoning and applied meteorology. These were but poor aids to first-timers and even to experienced seafarers—as late as 1707, miscalculation of its location led a British navy fleet commanded by Sir Clowdisley Shovell to disastrous shipwreck in the Scilly Isles.

Ideas of geography around the Atlantic littoral in the late fifteenth century did not in themselves determine that potential explorers either would or would not contemplate sea journeys of long duration. Falling off the edge of the world has been whimsically cited as the major deterrent to ocean travel in the period before Columbus, whereas sailing out of sight of land, over the horizon and for several days, was possibly practised from prehistoric times and probably in the early mediaeval period.[62] Admittedly, it is only in retrospect that certain classical and mediaeval European and Islamic thinkers, for example, can be identified as correct in their calculations of the size of the globe or the extent of the Eurasian landmass, but none of the ideas competing for the attention of early modern contemporaries would have necessarily been relevant to seafarers. Columbus was perhaps unique in basing his arguments for westward voyaging on a particular set of calculations about the size of the globe that he illustrated with a map, in contrast with the more empiricist approach of men like Caboto.[63]

Such empiricism was reflected only partly in the maps and globes devised to portray the world, to show in some kind of relative space where places are. To be of wide practical use, such illustrations needed to be to a scale and accuracy achieved only as a consequence of the explorations, and initially at the behest of a market of armchair explorers. Practical cartography emerged to meet the political and bureaucratic needs of states competing to define their boundaries,[64] as much as to service the needs of seafarers. Charts were created to assist voyagers who had not personally been to their chosen, known destinations, which was why Columbus referred to a chart as he approached his first landfall in the West.[65]

Notwithstanding the interest of the Columbus family in the making of practical charts, the science of cartography began to catch up with the practice of travel in the era of improved observational techniques, only from the later 1600s. Efforts to make maps useful to seafarers benefited from incremental improvements in surveying but, as with ship design, for much of this period the available techniques were enough to be useful adjuncts to direct experience or shared sailing directions—for example, when seeking to identify a landfall or to enter a strange harbour unaided. Much more challenging—and of more immediate utility to seafarers— was the question of global position fixing, to which considerable intellectual effort was deployed, principally through celestial observation. A number of European states sponsored projects to create reliable timepieces and star charts[66] as the practical means to determine longitude, by analogy with the observations of the sun as the means to fix latitude. In mid-ocean, maps could be of help in determining the direction in which to travel only when the user already knew his location to plot it on the map.

Having made new landfalls, Europeans expressed claims of title to real estate through bestowal of their names for places already endowed by indigenous peoples, and thereafter Europeans advertised to one another their claims on maps and globes. From bold expressions of piety such as San Salvador,[67] to gross flattery such as Virginia, or the simplest deceit such as the Fortunate Isles or Greenland, naming conventions rendered a complex of services further to enrich the conquest of new lands in the imaginations of rulers and potential settlers. Why, then, did any indigenous names survive, such as Gananoque, Nantucket, or Okeechobee?

Columbus claimed he had reached the Indies, where there were places and peoples of which Europeans had some knowledge. Nevertheless, instead of attempting to ascribe the indigenous names, Columbus bestowed on the places he visited such names as San Salvador and Isla Española (Hispaniola), names expressive of a crusading spirit amongst newly united (in Christianity, if not unambiguously in politics) Hispanic societies. The adoption of Hispanic place names might seem justified whenever new, urban settlements were founded, and it might be argued that the peoples of the Caribbean islands had few places that could be recognised as significant from the perspective of the Iberian incomers. Nevertheless, names employed by indigenous peoples were cast aside almost wholesale, just as those people themselves disappeared. From the beginning, naming practices were not simply a consequence of an absence of indigenous signifiers; rather, naming was expressive of possession (irrespective of any existing occupants) and also aspirational, particularly the aspiration to see a lasting, united Hispanic Christian ideal of a state. This was reflected in Columbus's choice of Isla Española—"the Spanish island"—and Cortés's choice of Nueva España—"New Spain"—in which names "Spanish" and "Spain" were at best geographical terms in much the same way as the term "Italia" would remain until the 1860s.[68]

Some contrast was apparent in the naming of places on the mainland. Perhaps in a reaction against Columbus's assertions that he had reached the Indies, Iberian explorers tried at first to adopt names they thought to be in use amongst the peoples they encountered. The Franciscan, Diego de Landa, explained:

This province is called in the language of the Indians *Ulumil cuz yetel ceh,* meaning "the land of the turkey and the deer." . . . When Francisco Hernández de Córdoba came to this country and landed at the point he called Cape Cotoch, he met certain Indian fisherfolk whom he asked what country this was, and who answered *Cotoch,* which means "our houses, our homeland," for which reason he gave that name to the cape. When he then by signs asked them how the land was theirs, they replied *Ci uthan,* meaning "they say it," and from that the Spaniards gave the name Yucatan.[69]

More likely, perhaps, than simple misunderstandings was a combination of naming fatigue in the face of the sheer scale of the New World—how many Santiagos can a world have?—and an early, sharp awareness that the peoples of the mainland were more numerous and their societies more sophisticated than those of the islands. Their economic and political exploitation would therefore depend in part on some compromise with prevailing conditions, including some existing place names: thus, for example, the survival of Oaxaca or Tlaxcala, but the choice of Puebla de los Angeles (in its contracted form) for the new foundation in the valley of the Atoyac River.

Some names, however, possessed symbolic importance that could not be entirely discounted but nevertheless had to be revised as proof of the change of epoch. Perhaps the archetype of these was the name of the principal urban settlement of Mesoamerica. Although often called Tenochtitlán in the sixteenth century, the city was also called by its inhabitants and neighbours, *Mexico* or *Mexico Tenochtitlán*.[70] The physical destruction of the city in 1521 was accompanied by its nominal destruction, to be replaced by Ciudad de México. This change, however, represented a form of compromise, for the name *Mexico* was clearly feared amongst Cortés's indigenous allies,[71] and it was preserved in popular usage alongside Cortés's neologism of Nueva España.[72] In practice, the name was distinct in the respective languages: in *castellano*, it was rendered *Méjico*, whereas in Nahuatl, it was pronounced *Mesheeco*. Indeed, the imposition of Hispanic languages, particularly *castellano*, as a common tongue for government and law,[73] led to a greater standardisation of place names as recorded by bureaucrats and cartographers alike. Something of a pattern in naming conventions, however, was inaugurated and reflected in the common mix amongst European settlements of incomers' sentimental references to the places of their homelands—often but not always prefaced with the word "New"—and the adaptation, rather than adoption, of the names used by indigenous peoples.

For much of our period, the inexact techniques of navigation were sufficient, rather than determinative, for the establishment of routinised transatlantic travel. To say this, we might seem to liken the achievement to that of the early days of civil aviation, when in the 1930s it became practical for private travellers to cross the globe by commercial airline. Surely of greater significance, both in this period and subsequently, was the development of mass transit—to continue our analogy, the equivalent of the development of cheap air transport from the 1960s—that permitted the movement of millions of people across the North Atlantic. For this to have occurred in the absence of the means for rapid travel, the essential developments were in endurance.

Endurance

Crew and passenger endurance was determined by the ability, at a reasonable cost, to store sufficient food and potable fluids to last the expected duration of the ocean crossing. Cost was an inescapable factor in the calculation of endurance. In the case of a crossing intended to move commodities to market, whether to the New World or to Europe, there was the opportunity cost of allocating to rations a significant amount of the already limited cargo space. Something of the same arithmetic applied to the movement of people, but whereas voluntary migrants might have been willing to suffer the journey's poor diet and limited water in the hope of a better life in a new world, if slaves were to have any value on arrival, they had to be maintained at a minimum level of health. Although acknowledging the slave trade as morally repugnant, it is nevertheless the case that the trade would not have become established or been maintained for so long if it had not developed early on, techniques for the shipment of people in large numbers with calculable prospects of successful survival for onward sale: the commercial imperative of the trade was to keep the "cargo" *alive*. As recounted by one economic historian, losses amongst the slave cargo of 1 in 7 were acceptable, 1 in 3 or 1 in 4 possible, if disappointing; there were also losses amongst the crew.[74] Too lavish a provision of food and water would diminish profitability, just as much as would the deaths of too large a number of the cargo. Allocations per capita were determined by experience, a deadly trial and error, but one in which the profit motive led European slave traders, for example, to provision their vessels with a view to keep their cargoes healthy and to employ surgeons shipboard, who were paid a premium for the numbers of survivors delivered to the Western Hemisphere market places.[75] Mortality at sea could vary enormously, depending on the particular conditions of place of origin and duration of a voyage: an English Privy Council report on the 1680s slave trade suggested nearly a quarter, whereas one estimate for slave mortality generally in later-eighteenth-century British ships was approximately 10 percent.[76] In comparison, although catastrophic mortality through disease overtook some British naval expeditions, such as the 75 percent said to have been lost in Anson's circumnavigation (1740–44), amongst British naval crews serving in the West Indies in the 1740s it has been calculated that 6 percent of authorised complements were lost annually through death, from all causes.[77] Such figures compare favourably with early modern European urban mortality.

As well as cost, however, endurance depended on reliable methods for food preservation and above all, potable fluid storage. In the European experience, during the classical Athenian or Roman empires, food and drink in bulk were transported by sea stored in amphorae, usually ceramic and ranging in size, but for which the Attic standard was a capacity of 39 litres, whereas the Roman standard was just over 25 litres. By the early modern period, well-seasoned wooden barrels were preferred by West Europeans for preservation and storage, so that cooperage technology was a valuable ingredient of successful transatlantic travel.

The history of barrel-making may seem an obscure place in which to look for explanation of the European domination of the North Atlantic, but a brief comparison with storage methods employed elsewhere is instructive. Ubiquitous in Europe, cooperage was little used in other parts of the early modern world; in China, for example, long traditions of technical evolution had led to widespread use of glazed ceramic or cast metal containers, both for artistic and utilitarian purposes. In India, large metal containers were used for cooking, but earthenware was commonly used for storage and transportation.

Preservation by drying, smoking, or salting was practical for food solids, but the most precious supplies for ocean travel were potable fluids, whether water, beer, or wine—not only for drinking but also to allow for making dry-stored foodstuffs palatable. In emergency, rainwater might be collected, but such methods could not hope to meet the minimum daily requirements for survival of large numbers of passengers—whether free or enslaved—for the duration of a normal crossing. Indeed, as we have already remarked, one of the factors that delayed Europeans in the development of regular crossing of the Pacific was that the average journey time challenged the capacity of most vessels to store and maintain, in good condition, sufficient quantities of stores and particularly drinkable fluids.[78]

As with shipbuilding techniques, coopering[79] was a specialist, though transferable, intermediate skill, requiring tools and craftsmanship that were widely available amongst West Europeans and could be copied by others. Again like shipbuilding, the raw materials were available around the littoral and were exploited from the early sixteenth century. The finest barrels were traditionally said to be made from oak with iron hoops, but other types of wood in conjunction with linings such as tar could also be effective. West European settlers established local barrel-making, particularly in the timber-rich areas of North America where the forests also provided charcoal for smelting iron. A wooden barrel might be expected to have a working life of several years, and to some extent such barrels could be recycled or relined, or reused for commodities other than fluids. Certainly, they were not without their problems: the best barrels were made from timber which had been seasoned for 12 months or more, so they could be difficult to replace at short notice. Because they were made from organic material, rather than from inert substances such as glass or ceramic, they were vulnerable to extremes of temperature and humidity and to damage by parasites. Glass was, through most of this period, technically difficult—and hence expensive—to manufacture and, like ceramic storage containers, less able to withstand rough use or handling in transit. In addition, the capacity of the largest practical glass or ceramic containers in early modern Europe was a fraction of that which could be attained for the average wooden barrel, so that many more containers would be required for the same unit of volume. Other materials were used for short-term storage of fluids, such as leather for bottles or canvas for buckets, but these materials degraded too quickly to be practicable on transatlantic voyages. Pewter might have provided a reasonably practical alternative, particularly when sealed with lead, wax, or cork. As with glass, however, it was relatively expensive to manufacture large containers, and in any case pewter would taint water or other fluids stored in the material for any length of time. Although they were not necessarily the best means then known of preservation in storage, for the purposes of West Europeans in the early modern North Atlantic, wooden barrels were optimal, combining relative ease (and cheapness) of manufacture, with robustness and adaptability in use, with ease of storage and handling for transport.[80]

Lack of good barrels could have serious consequences: for example, as

I have already noted, much of the suffering amongst many of the crews who returned to Iberia from the 1588 Armada derived from the spoiling of their supplies of food and water. Yet despite its importance to travel and trade as well as warfare, cooperage technology did not significantly improve during the period. As with shipbuilding and navigation, an existing technology was exploited in support of the Atlantic endeavour, rather than a new technology devised to meet a clear need. It would be a large claim indeed, to try to assert that wooden barrels were the key to the European domination of the hemisphere, but it is surely important to recognise that without this cheap and plentiful means of storing drinking water, in particular, the slave trade and perhaps also European emigration to the New World might have been on a significantly smaller scale than that which actually occurred.

Sailing Technique

Routinised transatlantic crossings with commercially and socially acceptable levels of risk, necessarily relied on the development and dissemination of competent sailing technique, the ability to handle a sailing vessel. Early modern Europeans might distinguish this responsibility from both command and navigation through the practice of appointing to a larger vessel a sailing master who was not the captain, as well as the appointment of a pilot, who was responsible for navigation. Columbus, for example, on his first Atlantic crossing sailed with Juan de la Cosa as master and Peralonso Niño as pilot of the *Santa María*, and Columbus's journal reflects that decisions about navigation arose from conferences of men of the fleet. To some extent, this differentiation in role reflected the relatively low social status of seafarers, compared with the merchants or aristocrats who paid for and led expeditions. Safety at sea and hence the viability of the transatlantic link, however, always relied on the knowledge and experience of a corps of career mariners, the sailing masters.

Amongst other characteristics, the early modern period saw the publication of technical manuals on a wide variety of subjects, from agriculture to engineering, from medicine to astrology, from architecture to warfare. Seafaring was no exception, and how-to manuals were published in western Europe, appearing not only in the vernacular languages of their authors (rather than only in the language of learning, Latin), but also in translation, such as Pedro de Medina's *Arte de Navegar* (originally Valladolid, Spain, 1545), William Bourne's *Regiment for the Sea* (originally London, 1574) or Claes Hendricksz Gietermaker's *Vergulde Licht der Zeevaart* (originally Amsterdam, 1660). Whatever may be the reservations about how far, if at all, such manuals influenced practice, more so than many activities covered by these manuals, seafaring was and remained unforgiving of poor technique, such that a threshold of competence marked literally the difference between life and death. To become a ship's master, it was not sufficient to have been well born, rich, or educated at the university; sailing technique had to be learned from those who already possessed it, and demonstrated in practice. Thus, sailing masters were not only essential to the maintenance of transatlantic links by the exercise of their own skills, but they were also essential to the preservation of the links into the next generation by their willingness to impart their know-how to their successors.

Despite the attractiveness of the story, it is not true that Dom Henrique—Prince Henry the Navigator—established a maritime training academy at Sagres in the 1430s, a point reiterated by a recent biographer.[81] Equally romantic—and unlikely—is the notion that mariners had always to be bred to the sea. At the heart of each of these beliefs, however, was the idea that the skills and techniques needed for maritime travel had to be taught and that entry to the occupation had, in some sense, to be regulated. Trade and craft guilds, originating in mediaeval concern to maintain employment by limiting competition but also fulfilling social welfare functions, could be adapted to the testing of standards, but the sailing master's was an occupation ripe for professionalisation.

Perhaps unsurprisingly, some attempts were made in Iberia in the early years of transatlantic travel to introduce regulation and licensing, in support of minimum levels of competence. In 1500, by licence of Fernando the Catholic, there was created a Colegio de Pilotos Vizcaínos; in 1508, the post of pilot major was created to instruct and examine pilots on behalf of the Casa de la Contratación, the governing body of trade and communication with the New World; and in 1569, there was created a Universidad de Mareantes. England's King Henry VIII possibly modelled the Trinity House (chartered in 1512), with its branches in Deptford, Hull, and Newcastle, on the Iberian examples, and in 1564, a draft royal commission from Elizabeth I proposed the appointment of a chief pilot for England, responsible for examination and certification of all masters and pilots of ships of more than 40 tons burden.

In reality, most training was provided on the job to those willing to undergo its rigours, in the manner traditional to craft apprenticeship. Early modern West European governments lacked the bureaucratic resources to enforce strict regulation, and natural selection[82] ensured that the less competent would not thrive. A hierarchy of positions of responsibility afloat was broadly recognised amongst West European seafarers, so that to secure a berth as boatswain was regarded as a prerequisite to becoming a master's mate, preliminary to obtaining a master's ticket. Although family members might be given privileged access to the junior posts, the corps of sailing masters was to some extent characterised by free movement of labour of the demonstrably skilled. There was, indeed, some measure of internationalism of service, at least for the Castilian crown, illustrated by the careers of Columbus himself (a *genovese*), of the *fiorentino* Amerigo Vespucci's service as pilot major (1508–12), of the Portuguese Magalhães, of the Anglo-Italian Sebastiano Caboto as pilot major from 1516, after which appointment he returned to the service of the English crown.

Full professionalisation arose only as a side effect of the efforts of West European governments from the later 1600s to increase the numbers and quality of officers to serve in their expanded war fleets. Mercantilist thinking encouraged amongst West European governments the pursuit of larger shares of the world's maritime trade, which growth was thought to be obtained only at the expense of the share of another society. The acquisition of a larger share, or the protection of the existing share, required standing naval forces. Standing navies required larger numbers of trained personnel to be permanently available than were supplied by the merchant fleets, so that their officers could no longer be on temporary assignment from commercial sailing. Governments created naval academies to ensure a regular supply of professionalised cadres of ships' masters and navigators. In England, this transformation was exemplified in the work of Samuel Pepys to establish the formal examination of technical competence and promotion on professional merit, for lieutenant, in the career navy. Instead of sailing masters learning their skills in commerce and serving occasionally in war fleets, men trained by the governments' academies could set the standards of competence for careers in the merchant fleets.

Across the whole of our period, the principles of sailing technique remained more or less constant: running before a gale, avoiding shallows, beating to windward, avoiding damage to or loss of sailing gear because of carrying too much canvas. The extent to which these general rules should be applied or safely varied, developed over the period in step with the incremental improvement in the technologies of sailing ships. From the first crossings, however, neither the Atlantic Ocean nor the waters of the American or African coasts provided challenges sufficient to provoke significant improvements in sailing techniques. Sailing conditions were never so bad for so long as to isolate for any serious length of time, one part of the littoral from the others. If maritime communications were cut, this was more likely to be a consequence of human circumstances—economic, political, or military—than of marine or meteorological conditions. In general, the sailing challenges associated with transatlantic crossings were no different from those already experienced in European waters of the continental shelf: storms, shallows, dead calm.

These conditions were to some extent, however, different from those encountered in the Mediterranean or Baltic. The Mediterranean is, of course, effectively tideless, and the tidal ranges in the Baltic are relatively small. No point in the Mediterranean is more than 300 kilometres from land, and in the Baltic the distance is 150 kilometres. This is not to argue that Baltic or Mediterranean marine techniques were inferior or inadequate for transatlantic voyages. It is to say, however, that sailing techniques learned in the West European societies bordering the Atlantic, particularly around the Bay of Biscay, were more immediately applicable to transatlantic sailing than those acquired in the inland seas.

The skill required to cross an open ocean was in some respects less demanding than the ability to enter unknown coastal waters without running aground or being caught on a lee shore in a gale, cases of which regularly feature in narratives of exploration. Choosing a safe anchorage for a single vessel or a whole fleet was a task fraught with danger but judgements based on reasons other than marine safety could take precedence. Politics as much as practical concerns, for example, delayed the transfer of the bulk of the American trade from Sevilla to Cádiz, notwithstanding the difficulties in navigating the Guadalquivir River. Familiarity seems to have preserved the role of Vera Cruz on its original site as the flota's preferred point of transhipment on the Mexican Caribbean coast, despite being an open roadstead, vulnerable to storms. Much the same reasoning seems to have preserved the English interest in Roanoke, despite the relative proximity of Chesapeake Bay, although this also perhaps reflected security concerns, in a belief that Roanoke was hidden from Madrid.

For vessels of any size, effective sailing technique also relied on the performance of crews. This became particularly so as a consequence of the widespread adoption after c. 1500 of the classic, ship form of the square rig in which sails had literally to be manhandled aloft, rather than manipulated with rope—brails—from the deck.[83] The inherent dangers of working the sails aloft, particularly in foul weather, were generally discounted for crews in those early modern European vessels for which the square rig gave improvements in speed and handling (and consequently in the safety of vessels), notwithstanding the demands placed on crews at the standing yardarm by the requirements of the associated running rigging. Nevertheless, simple commercial considerations, if not humanity, dictated that casualties amongst mercantile crews were best kept to a minimum: every sailor to be fed and watered beyond the number absolutely essential to operate the vessel was a cost to be set against fee-paying cargo or passengers. The prosperity of the Dutch republic, particularly in the seventeenth century, was founded in part on the readiness of its seamen to undertake commercial voyages more frequently and with smaller crews than were the seamen of other West European societies, exemplified by the numbers of commercial trips per sailing season that Dutch vessels made through the Sound into the Baltic. For a crew to be kept as small as practical, therefore, each member had to be capable of performing the sailing duties with the minimum of risk, not only to his own life or limb but also to those of his shipmates. For this, cooperation and coordination amongst the crew were essential. Whereas slaves might be chained to oars and flogged into coordination because their task was narrowly repetitious, in a commercial sailing vessel relentless and harsh discipline could not effectively substitute for training and collaboration. Commercial pressure to keep crew sizes optimal therefore encouraged higher levels of skill amongst the sailors at work, particularly in deep-sea fishing and coastal trading vessels. Governments conventionally referred to these activities as the nurseries of sailors, and in Captain James Cook there was later a celebrated example of a man "bred to the sea," apprenticed in the unglamorous but commercially vital English east coast trade.

Warships, by contrast, were habitually overmanned—quite apart from the presence aboard of soldiers or marines—and this overmanning reflected the presumption that there would be losses—for example, through disease, accident, casualties in action, or the detachment of sailors for prize crews. Crucial to the performance of a warship were the skills of its key specialists: gunner, carpenter, sail-maker, master, pilot—not necessarily the same people as officers. For the majority of its crew, however, the minimum level of training necessary to complete their tasks was actually lower than that needed for merchant sailors. A surplus of manpower over the numbers essential to the sailing of a vessel need not produce efficiency gains; it might increase the speed with which some tasks could be completed, but such gains had to be set against the potential for greater idleness and possible indiscipline, arising from the same number of relatively low-skilled shipboard tasks being distributed amongst a larger group of men. Thus, losses or injuries amongst most of a naval crew were more easily accommodated—by redistributing the core duties amongst the rest of an already large watch—than was economical in commercial vessels. Navies were not immune from considerations of economy but in periods when these were important, warships could be "moth-balled,"[84] whereas a laid-up merchant vessel represented idle capital investment.

Although for much of our period, fighting navies were augmented by armed merchant vessels (and their crews) hired or requisitioned for the duration of a campaign, from the later 1600s, European states retained increasing numbers of standing naval units in peace as well as war. By the middle of the eighteenth century, West European navies had expanded to such an extent that their manpower needs exceeded the pool of volunteers, so that the press gang became a regular means of recruiting crews. In these cases, any men would do, and the shipboard regimes of brutal discipline and training sustained the fighting strength of the British navy, for example, very effectively. It should be noted, however, that the most skilled mariners were exempt from the press, at least in Britain, so that sea fishermen or the crewmen of East India Company ships were not to be found aboard Royal Navy vessels, unless otherwise guilty of some offence.

For most of the early modern period, however, crews for transatlantic voyages—whether commercial or military in objective—were recruited by the promise of rewards. These rewards were not of Aztec gold; sailors' wage rates and conditions of service made the job attractive. Marine employment stood comparison well with alternative, land-based occupations, and not only for the unskilled labourer. Having signed on, an ordinary seaman could generally expect regular rations, pay for the duration of his service, and probably no greater a risk of death at sea, whether from disease or accident, than that on land in many manual occupations. For those with higher levels of skill, their services could command a premium that likewise bore favourable comparison with land-based specialist occupations. In addition, the seasonality of sailing conditions meant that significant periods of time could be spent on-shore in any roundtrip voyage.

For most of its participants, commercial seafaring provided a reasonable living comparable to land-based occupations with occasional opportunities for profit by private trading, but by no means was it a fast track to prosperity. Maritime wage rates did not, in general, grow faster than those ashore, and there is little evidence that the development of merchant shipping in West European societies was inhibited by a shortage of personnel. Short-term challenges, principally war or piracy, could raise wage rates for voyages that were judged both commercially vital and time-critical, but it was rare for any merchant or trading company to be willing to take risks, with a ship and cargo, greater than those customarily encountered on the same route. Transatlantic voyages, if not risk free, over time attracted no greater risk to crews or cargoes than many other contemporaneous commercial activities.

CONCLUSION

That these transatlantic journeys could be undertaken by one person, more than once, made a vital difference to the character of the early modern empires. After the first exploratory crossings, transatlantic journeys ceased to be the exclusive preserve of career seafarers, for there were always some personnel—settlers, administrators, traders, and, significantly, their families—who crossed and recrossed the ocean, if not regularly then recurrently. To cross the Atlantic was, therefore, never, at least for reasons of technical necessity, a one-way journey into inescapable separation or oblivion. Social, cultural, and economic interrelationships, both interaction and interdependence, between mother country and new settlements were possible, and in these relationships, although colonial self-sufficiency might become desirable, it need not be imperative. Instead, the Europeans planted in the Atlantic were able throughout the period to draw on the technical, cultural, and subsistence resources of their homelands. In this context, the choice of those of European origins settled in the Western Hemisphere, in the later eighteenth and early nineteenth centuries, to divorce themselves from their cultural and political homelands, was truly revolutionary.

In summary, partly because the Atlantic could be crossed and recrossed, no persons of European heritage were obliged to adopt the lifestyle and culture of the indigenous people amongst whom they found themselves. The choices in this regard were illustrated early in the Iberian century, for of the two shipwrecked early explorers of Yucatán who survived until the Cortés expedition arrived, Aguilar preserved enough of his Iberian identity to rejoice at his rescue, whilst Guererro betrayed his to adopt the ways of his captors and die fighting at their side. Unlike the Mongol conquerors in China, Europeans did not "go native" in the Western Hemisphere but, more like the Romans, they attempted to establish in their settlements what they viewed as the essential characteristics of the culture and civilisation of Europe by constantly replenishing their stock of European cultural experience, based on the reliability of marine communications. They were thus further empowered in their campaigns everywhere to denigrate and in some instances eradicate, the cultures of the indigenous peoples. By the time of the nineteenth-century European imperialism in Asia and Africa, this Atlantic experience became the model and the norm.

A NOTE ON MEDICAL PRACTICE

Perhaps the most striking failure amongst West Europeans in either science or technology in our period, despite what seem in retrospect to have been powerful incentives to innovate, was in achieving substantial progress in medical practice and public health. Only from the later eighteenth century, was some effective remedy offered to scurvy, for example, a condition that adversely affected all those who undertook long-range maritime travel and which was eventually mitigated by remedies identified, in effect, by trial and error. Otherwise, across the whole early modern experience, the familiar European challenges of diseases associated with contaminated water, parasites, and dietary deficiency remained without effective prophylactic or therapeutic responses. Not until the nineteenth century would West European societies begin to reach the standards of preventative medicine and particularly public health, regarded as normative in much of the Roman Empire, 1,500 years before. Consequently, would-be colonists' physiological endurance of maritime, and particularly tropical, climate extremes remained as limited—if not in some respects worse—at the end of our period as at the beginning.

This is not to say that early modern intellectuals and scientists were not interested in the challenges of health care, nor in improving understanding of the workings of the human body. Such interest, however, was not increased by a particular desire to reduce death rates amongst colonists, and only later in our period by attempts to reduce the losses to, for example, naval manpower accounted for by disease. There remained for long in our period amongst professional health care practitioners a disdain for the lessons of traditional or folk remedies (even when these were more effective, such as those based on drugs derived from plants) whether these were practised by the so-called cunning folk of West European societies or amongst the indigenous peoples of the Atlantic littoral. On the other hand, consumption of the newly available and increasingly plentiful narcotics—sugar and tobacco—was advocated by some of the professionals for their supposed medicinal properties.

Yet the early modern period around the North Atlantic saw an explosion in levels of exposure to threats to health, and not only in the catastrophic impact of European diseases on the indigenous peoples of the Western Hemisphere. The disease ecology of the West African littoral, in particular, took a heavy toll on the Europeans who went there, and mortality amongst European settlers and African slaves in the Caribbean was also substantial. Whereas European diseases, often arising from humans' close proximity to domesticated animals over many centuries, wreaked havoc on the ecology of the Western Hemisphere, in reality no comparable challenge was exported from the New World to the Old, notwithstanding claims for the New World origins of syphilis.[85] West European societies had, it should be recalled, been devastated by the Black Death from the mid-1300s, and episodes of plague of one kind or another recurred across the whole of our period. Despite this cruel evidence of the risks of contagion, there was no disease barrier sufficient to deter West Europeans from transatlantic enterprise.

FURTHER READING

For: an interesting exploration of processes by which technological improvements come about, focusing particularly on the western experience but acknowledging the different trajectories in other cultures, see G. Basalla, *The Evolution of Technology* (New York and Cambridge, 1988); a classic expression of the "technological superiority" explanation of early modern West European imperialism, see C. M. Cipolla's 1965 essay "Guns and Sails," reprinted in his *European Culture and Overseas Expansion* (Harmondsworth, England, 1970), pp. 29–109; a thorough though concise reevaluation of the relationships (for early modern European societies) between overseas expansion, marine technology and state formation, see J. Glete, *Warfare at Sea, 1500–1650* (New York and London, 2000); a classic introduction to early modern marine travel, see J. H. Parry, *The Age of*

Reconnaissance (London, 1963), chapters 3–6; a useful, synoptic, technical account, see R. Gardiner, ed., *The Age of the Galley—Mediterranean Oared Vessels Since Pre-Classical Times* (1995; repr., London, 2000); an account that pursues in detail the technological development of European shipping into the early modern period, see R. Gardiner and R. W. Unger, eds., *Cogs, Caravels and Galleons: The Sailing Ship, 1000–1650* (London, 1994); a brief survey of seventeenth century North European shipbuilding, see B. Landström, *The Royal Warship* Vasa, trans. J. Franks (Stockholm, 1988); a convenient if dated summary account of fishing, see A. R. Mitchell, "The European Fisheries in Early Modern History," in *The Economic Organization of Early Modern Europe*, vol. 5, *The Cambridge Economic History of Europe*, eds. E. E. Rich and C. H. Wilson (New York and Cambridge, 1977) pp. 133–84; a convenient modern account of the naval campaign of 1588, see F. Fernández-Armesto, *The Spanish Armada. The Experience of War in 1588* (New York and Oxford, 1989); an introduction to the rich history of maps and map-making, see the illustrated, summary account by D. Buisseret, *The Mapmakers' Quest: Depicting New Worlds in Renaissance Europe* (New York and Oxford, 2003), or the more detailed accounts by J. N. Wilford, *The Mapmakers: The Story of the Great Pioneers in Cartography*, rev. ed. (New York, 2000), P. Whitfield, *New Found Lands. Maps in the History of Exploration*, catalogue of British Library exhibit (London, 1994), and J. Brotton, *Trading Territories: Mapping the Early Modern World* (London, 1997); accounts more specifically about the mapping of North America, see J. R. Short, *Representing the Republic: Mapping the United States, 1600–1900* (London, 2001); detailed engagement with the current scholarship concerning early modern cartography, see the journal *Imago Mundi: The International Journal for the History of Cartography*; discourse on some of the cultural complexities of naming, see S. Arias and M. Meléndez, eds., *Mapping Colonial Spanish America: Places and Commonplaces of Identity, Culture, and Experience* (Cranbury, NJ, and London, 2002); a volume of essays introducing major themes in early modern healthcare practice, see M. Pelling, *The Common Lot: Sickness, Medical Occupation and the Urban Poor in Early Modern England* (New York and London, 1998); a wealth of references at sites around the world, arranged principally around the major excavated wrecks of early modern vessels of European design, see the Texas A&M University Nautical Archaeology Program home page, http://nautarch.tamu.edu/nautbibl/postmed.htm; a great storehouse of scholarship on technical details as well as major themes in maritime history, see the periodical *The Mariner's Mirror: The International Journal of the Society for Nautical Research.*

CHAPTER 3

Conquest and Coercion: Technological and Technical Prerequisites and Developments in Warfare

We have now explored some issues surrounding the means of travel and communication, noting how essential this technology was to the transformation of the North Atlantic world. We have earlier noted, however, that the ability to cross the ocean predated Columbus's first voyage, by a substantial margin. Thus, travel technology was a necessary but not sufficient condition—and was not itself a cause—of the transformation. We also note that the transformation was characterised by violence, amongst Europeans as well as between Europeans and indigenous peoples. Exploring this, some historians have given prominence to the quality and availability of the means of violence, that is, the weapons and styles of warfare, in an extended debate on a so-called military revolution. We should therefore now ask, did Europeans develop a special kind of weaponry and warfare that gave them an intrinsic and unchallengeable advantage over the other indigenous peoples of the Atlantic? Or, in common with some other of their technologies, were the weapons already available to Europeans simply deployed to optimum effect?

However reassuring to the twenty-first-century Atlanticist mind it might be to try to ascribe military outcomes to superior firepower, particularly technologically superior firepower, even our most recent history does not conclusively demonstrate that the possession of more powerful weaponry ensures either security or victory. Nuclear weapons, to cite an extreme example, have not protected the United States from terrorism, nor did they secure victory in Vietnam. Similarly, I suggest that in the contacts between West Europeans and indigenous peoples around the

North Atlantic, weaponry and tactics were not themselves determinative of outcomes.

West Europeans crossed the North Atlantic in armed bands. This was not necessarily evidence of hostile intent: during the early modern period in Europe, the carrying by men in all social ranks of personal weapons was normative, both to symbolise status and for personal defence in societies only imperfectly policed. In such circumstances, however, disagreements might quickly become violent quarrels because deadly weapons were always ready to hand, whilst a resort to legal redress for personal grievances or slights was often deemed unworthy of "men of honour."[1] Notwithstanding the oft-repeated Christian injunction to peace and to "love thy neighbour," violence, we may suggest, was always available as an option in the vocabulary of early modern European social relations.

Violence was equally characteristic of some other societies around the littoral, but the readiness with which these societies had recourse to violence differed sharply, both amongst themselves and between these societies and the West Europeans they encountered. Certainly, a common human experience was of warfare as a means by which one society asserted control over another in order to exploit it. In Mexico, for example, warfare was a central feature of the pre-Columbian experience, only part of the significance of which was the ritualised murder of prisoners in mass human sacrifice.[2] In West Africa, war was pursued for control of resources and territory, which included the acquisition of slaves.[3] Thus, war and violence were not uniquely the attributes of West Europeans, nor were West Europeans necessarily more expert than other societies in the conduct of war. Why there was recourse to war rather than negotiation in the relations between these societies we shall consider in a later chapter. For now, however, we shall pursue the questions of means.

As soon as armed confrontations amongst West Europeans and between them and other societies of the littoral were initiated, we may perhaps speak of a combat equation, as a way by which we may summarise ex post facto the relative significance of key technical and technological[4] elements within and between the armed forces of opponents in war. We may describe the elements of the equation as perhaps those to be considered in respect of any armed conflict: manpower, training, morale, movement, firepower, command and control, and logistics. The relative significance of these elements varied with the details of each campaign and, to a degree, in response to changing priorities within the opposing forces. During the early modern period, the details of the elements changed slowly but in essentials they remained valid until the later eighteenth century, with the era of industrialised production and mass mobilisation. Weapons feature within a number of the elements, as we shall see.

MANPOWER

It should be recalled as an axiom of military theory that local superiority of numbers is a valuable element in securing victory, particularly in attack. That this proposition was understood in western Europe was evidenced in the dramatic growth in the size of armies across the continent and across the period, from the estimated 30,000 of the forces on the French side engaged at the battle of Pavia (1525) to the 60,000 of the French forces engaged at Blenheim (1704), both of which engagements ended uncharacteristically with crushing victories over the larger, French forces. In these conflicts on the European continent, however, the other elements in the combat equation of the forces on each side were often equivalent: comparable systems of training, types and amount of firepower, capacity for movement, command and control, and logistics. Thus, numbers of combatants was in large measure the only element in the equation that could be varied to any significant extent.[5]

Around the North Atlantic, in contrast, the size of European armies in the field meant that they were invariably outnumbered by their opponents amongst the indigenous peoples of Africa or the Western Hemisphere. From a crudely military viewpoint, for Europeans a number of propositions might flow from this chronic shortage of manpower. Tactically, in any engagement it would be essential to inflict significantly higher numbers of casualties than were sustained and important to ensure that the casualties inflicted on the enemy were fatal or incapacitating. Furthermore, it would be hazardous to take prisoners of war, because there would be insufficient forces to spare as guards for them. It rendered impractical the then-favourite European tactic of siege, or the possibility of maintaining an extensive occupation by garrison, or the protection of communications and supply routes by frequent patrols. This kind of military logic would lead to, amongst others, the following consequences: set-piece battles of the European kind were best avoided, in favour of careful targeting of key objectives; strategic bridgeheads had to be established and maintained as bases for other military operations, and communications by sea, between outposts as well as with the home country, were at a premium.

In fact, the principal European response to military manpower shortages was to recruit allies. First in numbers and significance were the allies amongst the indigenous peoples, recruited to fight and provide logistic support against those groups identified by the Europeans as their most powerful local opponents. Vital in this was the rapid accumulation of intelligence about the political and military circumstances prevailing in any given region, so that the Europeans could seek alliances with local partners who would rely on the Europeans and so be loyal, but were not so weak as to be ineffective against their local rivals. Such alliances had to promise the indigenous partners—at least initially—recognition and respect, and the real prospect of military advantages over their immediate rivals and enemies. For the incomers, recognition of indigenous peoples as in any sense partners posed twin challenges: on one hand, it might undermine Europeans' easy assumptions of cultural or racial superiority; on the other, it might reveal Europeans' weaknesses and undermine their potential to displace their allies as circumstances changed.

This approach lay at the heart of Cortés's campaigns in Mexico, in which tiny numbers of Europeans became the spearhead of native armies. Through the interpreters Aguilar and, particularly, Malintzin, renamed by the invaders Marina or la Malinche, Cortés first learned about, then exploited, the resentments between the subject peoples and their rulers in Tenochtitlán.[6] His limited Iberian forces successfully withstood attack by the Tlaxcalans who, despite their initial hostility, became convinced that the Iberians would prosecute war against the Mexicas to the benefit of Tlaxcala. In the military equation, the Tlaxcalans provided the bulk of Cortés's fighting manpower, facilitated his movement (as porters), and provided the logistics. Cortés and his Iberian troops' training and morale made them ruthless in applying their modest firepower to maximum effect. The alliance was cemented by joint prosecution of the massacre of the Cholulans and reinforced by the shared triumphant entry to Tenochtitlán. Perhaps strangely for a man so lacking in scruple and willing to betray others, once established inside the city and having coerced Motecuçoma into recognising him as the power behind the throne, Cortés did not abandon his Tlaxcalan allies in favour of some rapprochement with the Mexica élite. Instead, Cortés may have regarded the Tlaxcalans as the guarantors of his otherwise precarious military position: the Tlaxcalans shared the Iberians' desperate fight out of the city, their eventual destructive triumph over Tenochtitlán, and the spoils of that victory so that each received that which they prized most, with the gold going to the Iberians and the feathered cloaks to their allies. To the extent that the burden of the new, Iberian regime was at this time significantly lighter than that of the Mexica, the Tlaxcalans and other indigenous allies received the rewards they were promised by Cortés, even while they facilitated the destruction of native Mesoamerican cultures.

In West Africa, Mesoamerica, and the North American interior east of the Mississippi River, the Europeans' wars were conducted by proxy. Engagement with local allies initially to confront their indigenous rivals was a pattern repeated across the whole period and the whole hemisphere. Beyond Cortés, the examples range from the French support in 1609 and 1610 for the Hurons against their Mohawk enemies, to governor Andros's incitement of the Mohawks to go to war with Metacom—King Philip—in the 1670s, to the alliances with rival nations in the Ohio valley in the 1750s. From the European point of view, however, these alliances were worth-

while only if the indigenous allies could deliver effective military cooperation. Although some European weapons were provided, the structures
of military organisation, movement, logistics, command, and control remained those of the indigenous societies. The capacity to negotiate for the
purported advantages of alliance with the Europeans and to mobilise the
armed forces to prosecute their objectives, relied in turn on a minimum
threshold of political and social organisation within the indigenous societies. The Taínos, for example, did not reach this threshold of organisation
and therefore were not courted as potential allies: instead, they were condemned to slavery as inferior, primitive peoples.

The second group of allies were the settlers from Europe or of European
culture. In ways reminiscent of the mediaeval host or *posse comitatus*, settled
civilian populations could be liable for defensive military service at a moment's notice, subject sometimes to tests of ethnicity or legal status. In these
circumstances, European precedents might have suggested a neo-feudal
regime, in which land (and its servile population) was held in return for
military service. The *encomienda* was, in part, such a regime, but two vital
factors undermined such a system: for the Europeans there was practically
limitless availability of land, and the swift collapse of indigenous populations undermined the traditional agrarian prosperity. Instead, whether deployed against indigenous raiders from beyond the frontier of European
settlement, against interlopers from other European societies, or against
rebellious slaves, citizen militias became essential components of colonial
military establishments in the North Atlantic world. As such, militias represented a departure from the contemporaneous trend of armies in western
Europe, which was towards forms of military professionalisation and continuous service through peacetime as well as war—standing armies—maintained through taxation.[7]

Theoretically, the manpower needs of effective military establishments
could have been met by the permanent deployment of larger forces from
Europe. By this means, colonies might have expected to benefit in two
ways. First of all, in an early modern version of deterrence, standing forces
might be a protective shield of military and naval power that each mother
country extended to her dependencies around the littoral. Secondly, in an
environment of colonial competition, armed forces on station might en-
dow colonies with a ready capacity to expand their territory when favourable opportunities arose. Although specialist forces were from time
to time deployed across the Atlantic by European governments, these efforts were generally for short-term campaigns. In practice, few substantial
military or naval units were permanently stationed around the Atlantic
during our period, and the modest size of permanent military establishments demonstrated the relative lack of commitment of colonial governments to maintaining even minimum levels of professional military force.
This choice, however, reflected a realistic calculation of the costs and bene-

fits of other kinds of provision. On one hand, sizeable garrisons could be wasteful of cash and lives, as the inexperienced English discovered in the early years after their conquest of Jamaica (1655). On the other, for much of the period the most likely military threat was in the form of raids, rather than invasions,[8] against which the civilian population could be mobilised for the relatively small cost only of arms and equipment. Thus, militias could represent a rational and cost-effective solution to the manpower problem, which it was safe to arm for as long as the colonists did not rebel or seek independence, or, put another way, as long as their fear of enemies was greater than any distaste for their home governments.

TRAINING

It might be said that training is what distinguishes an army from an armed mob, and for early modern European armies, training meant drill. If we confine our discussion to the three principal specialisms within early modern West European armies—infantry, cavalry, and artillery—their military effectiveness was a direct function of proficiency at drill because these armies deployed in massed formations and generally fought in close order, chiefly as a means of compensating for the limitations of their weapons. Although tactics altered in detail over the early modern period, the need for drill to maximise the effectiveness of those tactics remained a constant, whether it was to achieve coordination between arquebusiers/musketeers and pikemen;[9] or to maintain firing by volley, whether by platoon or by line; or to deliver the shock of a charge or to weaken opposing forces through bombardment. From the late 1500s, manuals of drill were published in several European languages, codifying practices developed over the previous century in tandem with some developing standardisation of equipment and weapons. Drill coordinated the fighting effort of soldiers whose individual initiatives in combat weakened the formation.

Around the Atlantic, early modern Europeans made few attempts to train their indigenous allies in the drill and tactics of European-style warfare. Equally, although they quickly learned to use European weapons, the indigenous opponents of the Europeans made few attempts to adopt the drills of the invaders. This is in striking contrast with, for example, the experience in the Indian subcontinent, where from the mid–eighteenth century, European-style armies were recruited from amongst indigenous societies by the English East India Company and its European competitors and which were in some respects mimicked by indigenous rulers seeking to oppose the European infiltration. That neither of these developments arose around the Atlantic may perhaps be explained by a different calculation on the part of the colonial settlers and of their indigenous opponents than that made in India. On one hand, western colonial militias sought to retain a monopoly of skill in the most effective use of European weapons technology, building on their real monopoly of the manufacture of firearms and ammunition (which the Europeans did not enjoy in Asia), because it was their sole bargaining chip in the negotiation of any alliance with indigenous peoples. On the other hand, their indigenous opponents saw no innate superiority in European tactics for the deployment of fire-arms, when the circumstances of battle with which they were familiar were, in general, dominated by considerations of numbers of soldiers de-ployed and almost limitless space for manoeuvre.

To be in any way militarily effective, citizens of the militia had to have ready access to appropriate weapons and some familiarity with their use. Such familiarity could often be acquired through the practice of hunting game, not only augmenting food supplies but also protecting crops. These practices, however, placed a premium on the use of firearms, rather than on the use of the sword or pike, whereas some competence with these bladed weapons remained essential to European-style combat until around 1700. Use of firearms in hunting also relied on an individual acquiring some degree of accuracy, the independent identification of a target and choosing the optimum position and moment for firing. None of these individualistic skills was consistent with the battlefield use of firearms as developed in early modern European warfare: firepower was most effective when coordinated for delivery so that volume would com-pensate for the innate inaccuracy of weapons and (some of) their users. The net effect of this tension between everyday use of weapons and their use in formal combat was to render militias generally unpromising ma-terial for military purposes other than home defence. Consequently, the significance of training for effective military operations kept colonial set-tlements reliant on the mother country for specialist expeditionary forces in any effort to expand the frontiers through conquest that involved direct confrontation with other Europeans.

MORALE

Amongst Europeans confronting the indigenous societies of the littoral, morale, from early after first contact, was sustained by an inflated sense of their technical and technological superiority in military encounters. Their experience was that resistance by the Guanches was overcome in a relatively short period, and most of the peoples of the Caribbean islands put up little or no serious resistance to invasion; the empire of the Mexica collapsed when confronted by a tiny force of Europeans; the Pequots and later the Narragansett were wiped out. These victories influenced colonial attitudes more than did reverses at the hands of indigenous peoples. For some early modern minds, morale was never simply a matter of numbers but was more a reflection of innate courage and stomach for a fight. As expressed by Francis Bacon early in the seventeenth century, "number itself in armies importeth not much where the people is of weak courage,"[10] and commentators as diverse as Machiavelli and Montaigne remarked on the importance amongst the martial virtues of courage and commitment.[11] When in combat against societies around the littoral, Europeans could enjoy in some respects the kinds of advantages (although not to the same degree) possessed centuries before by Roman armies confronting "barbarians": tighter discipline, drill and body armour made formations robust in the face of superior numbers, helped to minimise European casualties, and delivered the available firepower to maximum effect. Like Roman armies, however, early modern European armies were vulnerable to sheer weight of numbers if their opponents were willing to press home their numerical advantage and sustain heavy casualties. The attitude to casualties was a measure, in effect, of morale amongst opposing forces around the littoral.

When discussing casualties, we should distinguish between those sustained in combat and those injuries and fatalities sustained as a consequence of more everyday activity whilst on campaign: the illnesses arising from poor sanitation, contaminated food and water, infectious diseases spread more easily amongst numbers of people in close proximity to each other or encountered in adverse environmental conditions; and the accidental injuries from animals—for Europeans, principally falling off horses[12]—in travel over any distance, in construction work for defence or assault. Noncombat casualties amongst European armies were always high during the early modern period, wherever they campaigned, and usually reduced fighting effectiveness far more quickly than losses arising in or from actual fighting. These could sap morale but might be sustained with greater fortitude if the campaign aims—and rewards—were regarded as achievable. To quote only two examples: the sweep through what is now Florida led by Pánfilo de Narváez (1528) suffered disastrous casualties, but this did not deter the launching of a further major incursion into the region, led by Hernando de Soto (1539–42). Soto's expedition ranged further afield and was more brutally successful in overcoming such local resistance as it encountered, but what deterred the colonial authorities from mounting follow-up expeditions was the absence of significant rewards, not the loss of manpower.

Injury in combat, even of the slightest kind from the point of view of the twenty-first century, was likely to be fatal because of post-traumatic infection. Individuals might survive extraordinary wounds but these were, statistically, the rare exceptions: Bernal Díaz described how he and his commander were seriously injured by arrows in their fighting escape from the people of Champotón, fighting that killed 50 of their companions.[13] The risks of infection were increased if the injuries were penetration wounds, from bullets or blades, although injuries from heavy blows would, of course, have their own complications. With the weapons most favoured by the Europeans, penetration wounds were the more likely to be inflicted, and their style of fighting sought to maximise these types of injuries. Stone clubs or arrowheads, bronze or copper alloy blades, however, were less likely to cause injury through even the ordinary European soldier's body and head protection, let alone his officer's armour and helmet. Even after their opponents acquired European weapons—iron and steel blades as well as firearms—the injuries that were inflicted on Europeans were less likely to incapacitate or kill because the wearing of such body protection and armour was commonplace amongst European soldiers until the latter part of the seventeenth century. The prospects for Europeans of survival in combat against the other peoples of the littoral were, therefore, usually better than for their opponents, notwithstanding the regard expressed by some of the conquistadores for the light-weight cotton armour of the Mexica, or the deadly effectiveness of the poisoned arrowheads used by the indigenous peoples of Guatemala. In any case, recurrent episodes of torture encouraged amongst Europeans a view that fighting to the last man was preferable to being captured, whether by the Mexica,[14] the Powhatans,[15] or the Hotinonshonni.[16]

For indigenous peoples, any attempts to perpetuate a view of war in which the principal objective was to drive the opponents away rather than to kill them[17] did not survive the initial encounters, whereas a willingness on their part to fight on despite sustaining large numbers of casualties would always have been decisive in combat with Europeans. What undermined that willingness in the Western Hemisphere was the impact of fatal disease. Certainly, indiscriminate killings were also carried out by European invaders and settlers of all kinds in all parts of the Western Hemisphere, and these methods were used in attempts to terrorise the indigenous peoples into submission: for example, in the Caribbean islands the first years of the sixteenth century, by Soto and Coronado c. 1540, amongst the Pequots in 1633, or amongst the Narragansetts in the 1670s. In comparison with the numbers killed by disease, these horrors might have been sustained and indeed might have stiffened resistance amongst indigenous peoples. Time and again, however, contacts with Europeans right across the Western Hemisphere were accompanied by epidemics that killed the strong as well as the weak, the great and the humble, without discrimination. Not only did disease significantly affect the numbers of men available for combat, it also affected the pool of female labour from which to sustain agriculture, so that disease would be followed by famine. Europeans also died from their contacts with new environments, not only in tropical jungle zones but also in the more temperate environments further to the north. Whilst the European casualties to disease could be, in relative terms, as devastating as those suffered by the indigenous peoples, in absolute terms the European deaths were never sufficient to halt colonial projects or to stem the flows of incomers.

In West Africa, by contrast, European penetration was long deterred by the hostility of the natural environment, and combat with Europeans could be avoided by temporary flight to the interior. That West African societies did not simply overwhelm the small European outposts reflected the symbiosis that developed between the societies. In the absence of a realistic threat of conquest and occupation by Europeans, West African societies suffered less damage from such diseases as were introduced from overseas and could devote their military resources to competition struggles with their immediate neighbours.

MOVEMENT

Movement and manoeuvre were the areas in which the European invaders throughout the early modern period exercised a clear advantage over all of their indigenous opponents. First and foremost, the ability to transport their forces across the ocean and to deploy them at will on any coast, and thereafter to sustain such deployments by sea, was never matched by any of the other societies of the littoral. In purely military terms, the inability of indigenous societies to interdict the replenishment of European manpower and weaponry by sea in the long term was decisive. The rewards of that effective monopoly, however, were by no means immediate, in the ways that they were for the Europeans' contemporaneous naval efforts in Asia. Amongst Asian societies, the importance to some of them of maritime trade left them vulnerable to coercion and expropriation by the earliest forms of gunboat diplomacy. In conflicts with the indigenous societies around the Atlantic, by contrast, naval power was only the means to deliver military force.

Having once secured bridgeheads for their operations, the Europeans' introduction of the horse to the Western Hemisphere thereafter gave them the ability to overcome the vast distances that might otherwise have protected the peoples of the interior of the New World. In West Africa, Europeans made fewer efforts to penetrate the interior so that questions of mobility and manoeuvre did not arise in the same way as they did in the Western Hemisphere. Furthermore, African societies were already familiar with the power of cavalry and, in those areas where horses could be bred and deployed, had their own mounted forces capable of resisting attempts at invasion. Certainly, not every European soldier in the New World was mounted, and the ratio of cavalry to infantry amongst European fighting forces around the littoral was seldom in accord with the textbook advice on contemporaneous best practice. In any case, over the early modern period, expert opinion tended to recommend a reduction in the proportion that cavalry should form in any army. For war, however, the horse, even in small numbers, gave advantages over the pedestrian for reconnaissance, raiding, and speed of deployment. On the battlefield, the advantages in mobility and fighting power (principally weight and height) enjoyed by the mediaeval knight were restored to the man on horseback in the New World, just at the time when these had been undermined in warfare in Europe.

Despite the animals' initial strangeness, it soon became apparent to the indigenous peoples of the New World that horses could be, like European men, vulnerable in combat and in need of substantial quantities of food and water. They were, of course, also useless against prepared defences or in jungle and forest. Nevertheless, when combined with the other military assets of the European invaders, horses further undermined the initial advantages of numbers that the indigenous peoples should have enjoyed. With time, of course, some of the indigenous peoples acquired horses for themselves to transform their lives and cultures in the Great Plains. In the early modern period, in the south-west of what is now the United States, the Dineh (Apache) developed into unrivalled light cavalry. They tended, however, to prey on the other indigenous societies that were settled in farming communities, as much as they did on colonists, and their numbers were not sufficient to prevent determined European occupation of key sites.[18]

FIREPOWER

With our muskets and crossbows and good sword-play we put up a stout fight, and once they came to feel the edge of our swords they gradually fell back, but only to shoot at us [with arrows] from greater safety. Our artilleryman Mesa killed many of them with his cannon. For since they came in great bands and did not open out, he could fire at them as he pleased.[19]

Describing this as the first battle of the Mexican expedition, Díaz captures for us the essential points about the Europeans' deployment of firepower in combat with the other societies of the littoral. Firearms could be very effective, particularly if the enemy deployed in close order, but guns were by no means the only projectile weapons employed, and their use did not prevent the enemy from closing in for hand-to-hand combat (the firearms' essential purpose being to injure the enemy at a distance), at which stage the sword was all-important. As Díaz goes on to explain, victory in this battle was secured by the timely arrival of Cortés and the cavalry, and when afterwards the enemy casualties were inspected, "most of [them] had been killed by sword-thrusts, and the rest by cannon, muskets, or crossbows. . . . For wherever the horsemen had passed there were great numbers of dead and wounded."[20] In this era before rapid-fire or magazine-fed firearms, it was at best unwise and probably dangerous to rely on gunfire alone to achieve victory on land.

Firearms were effective on the early modern battlefield in direct proportion to the numbers deployed. Whilst this might seem to be a truism, in the circumstances of early modern European styles of warfare, firearms could only be expected to affect the outcome if they were deployed in massed formations, because they were inherently unreliable in battlefield conditions. Regardless of calibre, their performance was adversely affected by inconsistencies in the quality of ammunition (both powder and shot), by the weather (spoiling powder, or the match used before the widespread adoption of the flintlock mechanism), giving rise to misfires and inconsistencies in effective range, even before consideration was given to the relative proficiency of the personnel using them. The crossbow, although by 1500 already an antique technology of war, remained a more reliable (and usually more accurate) projectile weapon for infantry use, although its performance could also be influenced by weather effects. Like firearms, however, its rate of reloading was slow. These deficiencies could be offset if sufficiently large numbers of firearms or crossbows were deployed, but firepower equated directly with manpower and not only in terms of the men to handle and fire the weapons. Across the period until the later seventeenth century, because troops equipped with portable projectile weapons—whether guns or crossbows—were capable only of relatively slow rates of fire, they had to be protected by others, usually pikemen and often in the ratio of one gunner to three or more pikemen,[21] to allow them the opportunity to reload. Yet as we have already observed, European manpower around the littoral was always in short supply.

These technological limitations to the effectiveness of firearms were only slowly overcome by refinements in design and manufacture of firearms and their munitions. The adoption of the firearm as the standard infantry weapon—rather than as that of a specialised corps—fully came about amongst armies in Europe only by around 1700. Even then, the limitations of the weapons and their users perpetuated the vital importance of massed formations fighting according to precise drills. These were moderately effective techniques when used against opponents employing the same approach amongst whom there was no wish to discriminate against individual targets, but virtually useless against irregular forces or guerrilla tactics. During most of our period, firearms were far more effective when used as artillery, from behind—or to bombard—fixed defences, or aboard ships. In such deployments, the users were less exposed to danger during the intervals for loading, and they could employ firearms in the artillery role for which they were ideally suited, as standoff weapons with which to hit (and keep) an opponent at arm's length.

Why, we should ask, did the European invaders of the littoral employ personal firearms at all for close combat on the battlefield? It is striking to note that a well-known alternative weapon for, in effect, close infantry support, was readily available: the longbow. Still carried for combat use aboard the English warship *Mary Rose* in the 1540s, the longbow had a faster rate of fire than either firearms or the crossbow; was relatively cheap to manufacture, maintain, and supply with projectiles; and, in the hands of a practised user, could be employed effectively over a number of ranges and with considerable accuracy against individually designated targets, such as officers. Whilst it did not always possess the armour-penetrating power of the firearm or crossbow, it did not require massed formations to be effective. These were performance standards that personal firearms did not attain until at least the later 1600s.

Nevertheless, from the late mediaeval period, the longbow was progressively abandoned for warfare in Europe as a consequence of a firearms race, in which field artillery and then personal firearms were adopted as much as symbols of conspicuous consumption and state power[22] as in the hope of any enhanced military effectiveness. Possession of firearms was itself a statement about wealth and power. In this regard, big could be beautiful, as illustrated by the (for the time) enormous gun Mons Meg, now in Edinburgh Castle,[23] or by the preference of successive Ottoman sultans for a few of the largest calibre artillery instead of greater numbers of more adaptable (and mobile) smaller calibre weapons.[24] To some extent, the adoption of personal firearms on the battlefield was encouraged by their fashionability, for they proved of limited effectiveness until at least the early seventeenth century, when tactics began to be adjusted seriously to take their use into account.[25] Personal firearms, however, did possess one advantage over the longbow: they could be used after only relatively limited training, and practice did not necessarily produce significant improvements in accuracy or rates of fire.

European soldiery became to some extent fascinated by the technology of firearms, despite the evidence for their limited effectiveness as battlefield personal weapons. Around the Atlantic and particularly in the Western Hemisphere, more important than their possible military effectiveness, firearms exemplified a technological superiority of Europeans over the indigenous peoples. Whilst it was true that it took relatively little time for a soldier—European or indigenous—to learn to use a personal firearm, only the Europeans could manufacture them. Even in West Africa, where the skills of the gunsmith were known before the arrival of the Portuguese, the trade in low-quality European-made personal firearms became quickly established as a major item in the commerce between Europeans and Africans. Around the Atlantic, personal firearms therefore were, to Europeans as much as to indigenous peoples, a highly visible (and noisy) expression of the superiority that Europeans wished to assert over the societies with which they came into contact. Whatever short-term psychological advantage may have accrued from the first occasions on which firearms were used on the battlefields of the New World, these weapons did not secure for the European incomers an immediate—or even eventual—mastery of the military situation. During the early modern period, the Atlantic was won by West Europeans at the point of a sword, not at the muzzle of a gun.

This contrasted greatly with the West Europeans' contemporaneous penetration of the Indian Ocean and south-east Asia. There, firearms, particularly naval artillery, were vital in securing for West European intruders a place in the regions' politics and economies. As in the Atlantic, West Europeans were always at a numerical disadvantage, and they likewise sought allies amongst the indigenous societies with whom to pursue their objectives, but the fundamental difference between the situations was the existence of thriving marine commerce in the Orient, which was vulnerable to West European naval firepower. In the Atlantic, naval artillery was important in the conflicts between Europeans but was not vital for the outcomes of their armed encounters with the other indigenous peoples.

Indigenous peoples were not slow to adopt European weapons, including personal firearms, when opportunities to do so presented themselves, whether by trade, theft, or capture, although they were generally less enthusiastic about artillery because of the difficulties of moving pieces and their munitions. They did not, however, develop the technology of firearms manufacture and thus remained dependent on the invaders for the weapons, even though they could improvise for the gunpowder and ammunition.[26] Not the least of the attractions for the indigenous peoples was that possession of firearms could also be for them symbolic: of their superiority over indigenous rivals, in much the same way as firearms symbolised Europeans' claims to superiority, or of their parity with European or colonial soldiers. Personal firearms were generally more effective than traditional weapons against men in armour, as well as against horses, thus offsetting some of the other tactical advantages of the Europeans. Firearms did not, however, transform the military capabilities of the indigenous societies; rather, they were integrated into those traditional tactics that already held out the best prospects for defeating the incomers, such as the ambush and the raid.

Significant progress in the technology of firearms, giving measurably improved accuracy and rates of fire, did not occur until towards the end of our period, when mechanisation and standardisation were introduced to the manufacture of firearms, with enhancements not only in quality and reliability but also availability. The real breakthroughs for firearms, technologically and tactically speaking (and sufficient to change the course of history), did not occur until the nineteenth-century development of inexpensive, rapid-fire, magazine-fed handguns, courtesy of Mr. Colt.

COMMAND AND CONTROL

The area of command and control might suggest itself as one in which the West Europeans enjoyed an advantage over the forces of the other societies around the littoral. The narratives of the conquistadores lend themselves to an interpretation in which the professionalism, tight-knit discipline, and mission focus of the tiny European forces, dominated by the personalities of key individuals, contrasted with both the voluntarist associations amongst so-called tribal peoples and the loose formations based on tribute and noble clientage that characterised the empires of Mesoamerica. On closer enquiry, by the standards of modern armies the level of command and control exercised, either in the field or strategically, was for much of our period strikingly poor amongst all the fighting forces in the early modern Atlantic. Amongst the European adventurers and settlers of all societies, mutiny or conspiracy were not infrequent, and stories of efforts to undermine the authority of one or another governor, *adelantado,* or proprietor, recur across the whole period, whether by relatively poor compliance with formal chains of command or by readiness to seek favour directly from royal governments in the mother country. Amongst the indigenous peoples, rather than be portrayed as passive victims of European invasion, the fact of defeat might seem to demonstrate an inability to exercise proper command and control in military situations, for how otherwise might we explain the failure of overwhelming numbers to be victorious?

The question is perhaps misconceived: across the whole of our period issues of command and control seem in practice to have made little difference to the degrees of success—or failure—that European and colonial forces enjoyed in conflict with other indigenous societies or between themselves. As we have seen, garrisons were not cost-effective, settler populations lacked the manpower to spare for permanent military establishments, and specialist military forces tended to be deployed from Europe for particular campaigns. These deployments grew in size over our period, and issues surrounding command and control only emerged when significant numbers of regular soldiers were deployed from the mother country in campaigns that sought to coordinate actions in a number of theatres. The high point of these deployments in our period were the campaigns of the French and Indian/Seven Years War.

For much of our period, the numbers of European or colonial soldiers available were too few to put into effect set-piece manoeuvres or to prosecute a major siege—with the notable exception, of course, of Cortés's investment of Tenochtitlán—and instead placed a premium on adaptability and improvisation. Yet these were the features of military activity that were contemporaneously being reduced by the spread of formal drill and attempts to create armies on the model of ancient Roman legions, in which the troops' loyalty would be secured for something other than cash payment as mercenaries. At the tactical level, combat around the littoral provided limited opportunities for innovations of the kind that would feature in contemporaneous textbooks, largely because the fact of effectively limitless space for manoeuvre was outside of the soldiering experience in most of western Europe. There is nothing to suggest that, for example, the Swedish king Gustav II Adolf or France's Marshal de Saxe were influential over or influenced by the experiences of warfare around the Atlantic.

Amongst indigenous societies of the New World, failures of command or of a proliferation of chiefdoms to unite in the face of the outsiders' threats were probably of less significance in the out-turn of events than were the effects of disease. We need not accept the suggestion that an absence of a cultural celebration of individualism predisposed the indigenous societies of the Western Hemisphere to poor leadership,[27] but whether expressed through the hierarchical structure of Mesoamerican societies, or through the collective and consensual models amongst the communities of the Iroquois Five Nations, the qualities of indigenous leaders were unequal to the challenges of catastrophic mortality and European relentlessness. That the indigenous societies were overcome by West Europeans was not a simple consequence of superior organisation or more effective articulation of command and control. It was, rather, that with some honourable but few exceptions, European incomers were distinguished by their collaboration in a consistent determination to assert control over the indigenous peoples, by conquest, by expropriation of their land and labour, by their marginalisation, and, in some cases, their extinction.

LOGISTICS

The logistics requirements of all armies included supplies of food and water, and all armies expected to some degree to expropriate these from the lands in which they campaigned. The needs of European and colonial forces, however, were substantially different to those of the indigenous forces around the Atlantic. In contrast with most of the indigenous forces they encountered, European and colonial forces possessed—and needed to maintain—specialised animals and equipment. Although the invaders usually brought with them the skills and means—principally, the blacksmith—to maintain their animals and repair their equipment, if killed or lost, these central items of inventory could not, for much of our period, be replenished or replaced on campaign. In the early years of occupation and settlement, these items could be replaced only from across the ocean. Even after the establishment of European colonies in the New World, the distances covered on campaign made replenishment from a home base impractical. One spectacular illustration of this was the two-pronged attempt in 1540 to replenish the Coronado expedition, overland by Melchior Diaz and up the Colorado River by Hernando de Alarcón, neither of which managed to make contact with the intended recipients.

In effect, the kind of thinking that already applied to the logistics of ocean travel continued to apply to military operations on land around the littoral: if you had not brought it with you, you were not going to find it along the way, even if the natives were friendly. For certain key items, particularly horses, firearms, and swords, there were no indigenous alternatives or substitutes with which to make do and mend. Consequently, decisions to slaughter horses for fresh meat or to abandon equipment could be justified in only the most dire of circumstances, such as the lengths to which were driven the members of the expedition in upper Amazonia (1540–42), led by Gonzalo Pizarro. Amongst other desperate measures, the expedition blacksmiths turned horseshoes into nails with which to build the riverboat in which Orellana was sent in search of food.

In addition to their specialised inventory for fighting, European forces introduced two significant logistical supports in their campaigns in the Western Hemisphere: beasts of burden (horses and mules) and meat on the hoof or trotter (cattle and pigs). In the absence of native species suitable for these roles, indigenous societies relied on human portering and foraging. The employment of animals in these ways to an extent reflected the same thinking as we have already discussed—that everything that might be needed had to be carried along. On one hand, the invaders were generally unwilling to travel light, over and above their fighting kit, and stores that were self-propelled reflected the Europeans' preference for a high-protein diet. Both these developments, however, reveal the limits to the Europeans' ability or willingness to come to terms with the indigenous ecology of the Atlantic littoral. Whether for transport or meat, such livestock themselves significantly magnified the logistics challenge for an expedition. These animals also had to be herded, cared for, fed, and watered, which in turn required additional personnel, possibly noncombatant, who in turn required supplies. The logistical tail of European forces could become enormous relative to the size of the combat spearhead.

From the perspective of the Europeans on campaign, the ability to transport their own supplies could ease their dependence on indigenous expertise. It was recurrently the experience of Europeans that they would face near-starvation in environments that yielded sustenance to the indigenous peoples, and that the incomers' initial survival depended on indigenous peoples to feed them, either directly from their surpluses or indirectly by teaching the incomers how to exploit the unfamiliar ecology for food. Such relationships required the Europeans to engage sympathetically with the indigenous societies, thereby revealing the Europeans' weaknesses and encouraging the indigenous peoples to tolerate, rather then fear, the incomers. More complex forms of this European dependence were expressed in the use made by the invaders of indigenous people as porters, either as allies (for example, in the case of Tlaxcalans) or as part of the process of the expropriation of labour, amongst other indigenous resources. Notwithstanding the military logic for Europeans of travelling light, living off the land, and maintaining the smallest practical number of noncombatant personnel to service the fighting force, it would eventually be the indigenous peoples of the Great Plains, exploiting the now-feral populations of horses, who most effectively overcame the logistical challenges of campaigning in the New World.

CONCLUSION

If we return to the questions with which we began our exploration of warfare around the littoral, it is difficult to argue that, notwithstanding their initial advantages of firearms and steel blades, West Europeans either already possessed at the start or developed during our period an intrinsic superiority in warfare, with which they overwhelmed the indigenous peoples of the Atlantic. As in the case of travel, there was comparatively limited technological advance for warfare in this period, in stark contrast with the period after the mid-1700s, since which period war has been a forcing house of new technologies, aided by the permeability of the boundaries between military and naval technologies and civilian life. This would be symbolised by the development of the Wilkinson cannon lathe (perfected 1774), a power tool capable of drilling out to unprecedented tolerances the metal tubes that were equally suitable for the barrels of naval artillery and the condensing chambers of Watts's steam engines. The early modern Atlantic was undoubtedly transformed by war, but the instrument of transformation was not itself transformed.

Rather, Europeans deployed in the Atlantic with the same proficiency as in their homelands, their existing technologies of war in ways that were skillful enough to secure them bridgeheads in the territories they sought to colonise. In the combat equation that we have discussed, disadvantages in manpower were overcome by successive asymmetrical alliances in which the indigenous allies always lost more than they gained; military training might encourage proficiency with arms but in general had no lessons of tactical value for war around the littoral; beasts of burden facilitated the movement of men and equipment but were rarely decisive; firepower was of questionable effectiveness until the latter part of our period; command and control were of limited significance in determining the outcome of warfare until late in our period; and the logistic needs of the invaders were met by the replenishment of men and equipment from Europe, because the command of the sea was never challenged by the indigenous peoples, and only intermittently by rival European societies.

On the part of the indigenous peoples, their overwhelming numerical superiority was undermined by disease; they learned to deploy the weapons and horses of the invaders, but not with sufficient strength to prevent the spread of European settlement; they became dependent on the Europeans' weapons and tools, without acquiring the metallurgical skills to make their own in quantity and of quality. The costs of defeat were exploitation, and it is to that topic that we turn in the next chapter.

A NOTE ON FORTIFICATIONS

In early modern practice almost as much as in early modern theorists' writings, a pre-eminent inspiration for West European military technical and technological developments in the period from the Renaissance through the mid–seventeenth century was the impact of gunpowder on fortifications. Around the North Atlantic, beyond the zones of most intensive artillery warfare, substantial resources were devoted by West Europeans to constructing the most modern style of defences against gunfire, for example, at Safi (from 1519) and Mazagão (from 1541) on the Atlantic coast of Morocco; Funchal in Madeira (from 1542) and Porto Delgado in the Açores (from 1551); around the Caribbean, at Havana, San Juan, Cartagena (from the 1560s); and at Natal in Brasil (from 1603).

Such complex fortifications, unlike those constructed contemporaneously by Europeans in Asia, were intended to deter other Europeans rather than to defend against indigenous peoples. Despite the importance of the so-called gunpowder effect on the designs for European fortifications, military experience of the New World taught that against indigenous forces, simple stockades were as likely to be effective as more elaborate fortifications, and New World warfare contributed little or nothing to the development of European military engineering.

FURTHER READING

For: classic statements of the terms of the debate on the military revolution, see for example those by M. Roberts, *The Military Revolution, 1560–1660* (Belfast, 1956), G. Parker, *The Military Revolution: Military Innovation and the Rise of the West, 1500–1800* (New York and Cambridge, 1988), and J. Black, ed., *European Warfare, 1453–1815* (New York and London, 1999), or a summary of these themes in C. J. Rogers, ed., *The Military Revolution Debate: Readings on the Military Transformation of Early Modern Europe* (Boulder, CO, and Oxford, 1995); a recent, concise introduction to the general themes of early modern warfare as practised by Europeans, with helpful illustrations, see T. Arnold, *The Renaissance at War* (New York and London, 2001); concise but thought-provoking introductory accounts for particular themes in context, see the series *Warfare and History*, J. Black, gen. ed., in particular, J. Glete, *Warfare at Sea, 1500–1650: Maritime Conflicts and the Transformation of Europe* (New York and London, 2000), J. Black, *European Warfare, 1494–1660* (New York, 2002), and J. Black, *European Warfare, 1660–1815* (London, 1994); analytical accounts of indigenous societies and their military practices, see R. Hassig, *Aztec Warfare: Imperial Expansion and Political Control* (Norman, Okla., and London, 1988), J. K. Thornton, *Warfare in Atlantic Africa, 1500–1800* (New York and London, 1999), and A. Starkey, *European and Native American Warfare, 1675–1815* (New York and London, 1998); a detailed scholarly account of the conquest of Mexico, see H. Thomas, *Conquest: Montezuma, Cortés, and the Fall of Old Mexico* (New York, 1995); a synoptic, concise account of fortifications in Europe and around the globe in this period, by way of context for the fortifications built by Europeans around the north Atlantic, see C. Duffy, *Siege Warfare: The Fortress in the Early Modern World* (1979; reprint, New York and London, 1997).

CHAPTER 4

Exploitation

Across the globe between c. 1450 and 1500, empires rested on technical capabilities, to mobilise and deploy money, manpower, and *matériel*. Yet even within Europe, the capability to assemble and deploy resources was neither confined to nor best exemplified in the societies that later became prominent in the occupation and settlement around the Atlantic. Manoel I's Portugal, relatively underpopulated and undercapitalised, not only carved out an empire of plunder east of Suez but also successfully laid claim to Brasil. By contrast, at the same time, Henry VII's England, also technically proficient for maritime enterprise and better resourced than Portugal, failed to exploit the early opportunity for Atlantic expansion provided by the Caboto expeditions. Later, the Habsburg Charles/Karl V/Carlos I's empire mobilised the resources to capture the king of France and even to sack the Roman Eternal City, yet its tiniest military forces seized vastly wealthier prizes in Central and South America. By contrast, the French monarchy achieved remarkably little in the North Atlantic before 1600, notwithstanding its considerable resources of manpower and marine expertise. There is to be explained, therefore, a contrast between prospects and outcomes.

We may propose that, in the pursuit and creation of imperial presence in the early modern North Atlantic, there was a relatively low threshold of technological capability and technical proficiency,[1] required as the price of entry to participate and to show a return. This threshold was, at best, a necessary but not sufficient condition for successful transoceanic enterprise, and notwithstanding the technical challenges, societies with very limited resources did very well. In this respect, we may consider whether there was any significant technology gap between West Europeans and West Africans that gave the former either an uncatchable lead or decisive advantage. Such technology deficits did exist with respect to the indigenous peoples of the Caribbean and American mainland, but the gap might have been bridged or overcome because West Europeans had no unchallengeable monopoly of the purportedly key skills and technologies of shipbuilding, navigation, and firearms. Despite the enormous numbers of people involved, however, African contact with the New World was essentially a one-way transaction. This contrasted dramatically with the experiences of the indigenous peoples of the Western Hemisphere, who were extensively exposed to European and African peoples, flora, and fauna and to the experiences of peoples remaining in Europe, where the products of the New World, extracted as often as not by African labour, were adopted extensively. Africa did not begin the cultivation of the plants of the New World, did not directly receive the bullion or trade goods of the Western Hemisphere in return for those enslaved, and did not adopt for use elsewhere a model of colonial exploitation developed in the Western Hemisphere.

In the history of what did not happen, the drives to exploit the wealth of the North Atlantic littoral did not provoke an early modern agricultural or industrial revolution, even though superficially similar conditions in the later eighteenth and early nineteenth centuries in north-eastern America—resource-rich and relatively people-poor, particularly a shortage of skilled people—prompted mechanisation, whilst in western Europe at the same time population pressures and rising incomes encouraged the enhancement of agricultural and industrial productivity. A dependence on technical and technological superiority was a development of a later period with different dynamics—the Industrial Revolution—not a consequence of the manner in which the North Atlantic became subjected to European domination.

Instead, the exploration and exploitation by West Europeans of the North Atlantic proceeded by deploying existing technologies and technical skills, which were enough for the immediate needs of their users. If the North Atlantic empires were not dependent on technological and technical capacity for their emergence and development, does this foreshadow in more recent historical experience the examples of low-tech societies achieving extraordinary outcomes, such as the Vietnamese victory over the United States, just as the opposite case may be illustrated in that technologically innovative U.S. missions to the moon have not been the start of lunar colonisation and exploitation? We might suggest that the crucial element in all these cases was not technology, but determination—the will to succeed. Is it therefore to motives and incentives as origins of determination and will that we might turn? Amongst authors and commentators within the early modern period, there was certainly a great interest in the role played by outstanding leaders, men (seldom women) who might stand as heroes, exemplifying the power of the will and comparable to those celebrated in Europe's classical literature and mediaeval culture.

Over the almost three hundred years of our period, we see the transformation of the North Atlantic region by war and slavery, and, for a post-Freudian, psychologically self-aware, twenty-first-century Western mind-set, perhaps the most interesting question to ask of this collective past is, why did people behave the way they did? To identify motives for the actions of ancestors is for modern Western readers a simple means by which to bring the ancient experiences closer to our own time, to identify literally and metaphorically with those motives, and indulge a modern sensibility in passing moral judgements on the rights and wrongs of choices made along the journey to the present. Yet the evidence at our disposal by which to establish their motives is obscure, difficult to evaluate, and, of necessity, directly representative of only a tiny fraction of the millions of individuals caught up in the drama. Inevitably, therefore, we are tempted to impute motives to the actions we observe, by drawing on our direct experience of human behaviours in our own times. If the past is another country, then we seek to identify features within its landscape that we believe we understand.

Greed, utopianism, religious conviction, political ideology, enterprise, desperation—we may find examples of each and all of these contributing in some part to the choice to travel the North Atlantic made individually by thousands of European men and women in the period between 1492 and 1763. It is difficult to imagine that anyone willingly embarked on such a voyage from East to West without some notion of a particular destination and what was to be found there. Even if in many cases expectations were disappointed, these travellers nonetheless *had* expectations, derived from a cocktail of speculation, promotional literature, and reportage, that developed across societies and across the period. Enough individuals, enough of the time, in enough European societies continued so much to believe in an "Atlantic dream" that the influx of people willing to stay, cumulatively exceeded mortality amongst West European settlers in the islands and the New World, if not along the African littoral.

Yet in this proposition we have already distorted the reality of the period: Europeans and those of European heritage were not the only actors free to choose in our drama of transformation, and motive had a different significance in the cultures of the other peoples around the littoral. Amongst the indigenous peoples of the littoral, their motives and incentives were of course as complex and intermingled as those of the Europeans. Need, perpetuation of one's own culture and heritage, faith in a religious explanation for why the world was the way it was, and simple profit may jointly or severally explain, for example, alliances between

Tlaxcalans and conquistadores, or the help given to early English settlers by some of the indigenous peoples of the Chesapeake, or the willingness with which some in West African societies consigned their neighbours to the slave trade. In their detailed workings, however, lay literally a world of difference between the motives of a European settler and a Native American, even whilst they cooperated in the works of transformation.

If we recall our original proposition that it was calculation, rather than blind desperation, that prompted West European excursion and then emigration, we may summarise the outcomes of calculation as decisions to pursue discernible opportunities for relative enrichment where the benefits were believed to outweigh risk by a significant margin. Were the elements of calculation the same or different for women as for men? How did early modern Europeans evaluate the prospects of religious (and social) self-determination, plunder, land, and status enhancement against the potential for disaster and untimely death? Were any of these calculations comparable to those made by the indigenous peoples of the littoral? In the reality of life around the littoral, amongst Europeans a further aspect of the appeal of emigration and settlement may have been the plurality of opportunities to achieve betterment in the economic, social, and spiritual spheres, simultaneously.[2] Perhaps more than anything else, the appeal of voluntary emigration lay in the dream of achieving betterment of whatever kind, in the lifetime of a single individual. Speed of change was thus the great prize of adventuring oneself around the Atlantic.

Cutting across the consideration of motives, however, is the fundamental distinction to be drawn across the whole period and region, between the free and the unfree. Not only were there millions of people who were unwilling victims of circumstance, both political and material, but also millions who were immanently coerced by their fellow humans: to work for the profit of their conquerors, to cross the ocean, to discard their inheritances of culture, belief, and language. Overwhelmingly but by no means exclusively, the distinction between free and unfree was made manifest through skin colour as a simple marker for cultural difference, but it should also be recalled that throughout the period, amongst peoples sharing common languages, cultures, and faiths there were those who were made unfree by their own cultural kindred, whether as criminals or as prisoners of war.

In this chapter we consider aspects of the questions of exploitation, noting the (literally) world of difference between the free and the unfree, by reference to the means employed for the exploitation of the North Atlantic and its peoples. These means were, for the most part, by plundering (of the peoples of the littoral and of the natural resources of the region), by slavery (and the creation of the plantation economy), and by trade (and its early modern European partner, mercantilism). To begin, however, we shall reflect a little further on the question of European will, expressed perhaps most clearly in leadership.

LEADERSHIP

If we choose in our histories to privilege accounts of European "great men," we need not look for long to find candidates for the North Atlantic, starting with explorers such as Columbus or Champlain, soldier-conquerors such as Cortés or Wolfe, or settler-exiles of conscience such as John Winthrop or William Penn. Were heroic individuals—that is, inspirational leaders of their fellows—necessarily central in the stories of the European empires in the North Atlantic? Could empires be created only by such heroes and their companions? If so, were they a cause or a product of these empires? Did the Europeans' discoveries, conquests, and empires rely on heroic individuals to create them: the vital spark of inspirational leadership? Was such a model of heroism a characteristic essential to success? Alternatively, were certain individuals elevated to heroic status by their contemporaries or near-contemporaries to draw out the parallels with ancient models, because within the early modern period writers on historical events preferred to seek explanations for events through significant individuals rather than impersonal forces?

The Idea of the Hero

Stories of heroic figures—in myth, literature, or history—were already established in West European culture c. 1500, whether as Mallory's *Morte d'Arthur*, Amadis of Gaul, or Rodrigo Díaz de Vivar (El Cid), respectively. These figures were to be admired as heroes because their behaviour was marked not only by physical courage and fortitude (characteristics also of mere adventurism), but also by a devotion to late mediaeval conventional notions of justice and honour, service, duty, and faithfulness.[3] Such a model of heroism need not be confined to military men. The founders of the Franciscan or Dominican religious orders, for example, were role models for the more peaceful conquest of people's hearts and minds, and the rich traditions of late mediaeval Roman Catholicism inspired spiritual heroes for the early modern age, such as St. Ignatius or Las Casas. Once the Christian Scriptures became more widely available from the mid–sixteenth century, through print and in the European vernacular languages, they could provide further illustrations of heroism, both spiritual and military, male and female, drawn from the Old as well as the New Testaments. In addition, knowledge of a European past—through classical Greek and Roman literature—revived idealised foundation myths in European culture. This tendency was represented, for example, by the perhaps mythical figures of Solon or Romulus, to whom could be added a mythologising of the achievements of Charlemagne, in which stories an heroic individual laid foundations for his society by establishing a code of law. A revival of interest in and knowledge of classical learning, combined with an expansion in educational opportunities and with the new technology of print, made literary models of the hero more widely available for comparison and imitation, just as our period of transatlantic endeavour was beginning.

The availability of literary models of heroism created, whether or not intentionally, a context within which accounts by Europeans of their adventures in the North Atlantic could be set. Certainly, early accounts by West Europeans noted parallels with events in ancient history (and myth):

The few have conquered the many before. They say Alexander the Great with thirty-three thousand Macedonians undertook to conquer the world. So with the Romans too. But no nation has with such resolution passed through such labours, . . . as the Spanish have done.[4]

[Chieftains] carried great presents of gold to Cortes, and even brought their small children to show them Mexico, pointing it out to them in much the same way that we would say: "Here stood Troy."[5]

Everything that has happened since the marvellous discovery of the Americas has been so extraordinary that the whole story remains quite incredible to anyone who has not experienced it at first hand. Indeed it seems to overshadow all the deeds of famous people of the past, no matter how heroic, and to silence all talk of other wonders of the world.[6]

The opportunity to emulate the deeds of classical heroes celebrated in Renaissance literature and imagination, to be a new Alexander or Caesar, for some at least matched if not exceeded the pursuit of riches for their own sake. Herein, however, lies the interpretative challenge: did the enormity of the transformations to which these authors were witnesses and chroniclers, demand by literary and cultural convention that they be achieved by heroes? Or, as in the case of less successful endeavours, did some chroniclers nevertheless seek to heroise the participants, as, for example, in Hakluyt's account[7] of the valiant (but failed) efforts of Elizabethan English explorers?

In early modern western Europe, there were already celebrated some contemporaneous heroic individuals who could be likened to the ancients, such as the generals Gonzalo Fernández de Córdoba (El Gran Capitán) or Gaston de Foix, whose eminence as exemplars of both military leadership and chivalrous behaviour could be envied even by kings. Such figures could as readily emerge from Protestant as from Roman Catholic societies, as the later celebration of Willem the Silent as the leader of the Dutch Revolt, or of the Swedish king Gustav II Adolf as saviour of the Protestant cause in the Thirty Years War, showed, although these latter were more often compared with biblical than classical models. Yet these men, like Alexander the Great or Julius Caesar, were born into all of the advantages of princely families, and their greatness might be said to have emerged as they fulfilled a natural duty to their existing high status.

Renaissance culture, however, may be said to have reorientated aspects of the hero concept during the politicomilitary turmoil of the fifteenth-century Italian peninsula. These Italian heroes were, above all, dynamic individuals who, from modest or even humble backgrounds, sought fortune and glory through the leadership of companies of military adventurers. Building on Burckhardt's classic formulation,[8] we may see these self-made men as seeking legitimation and social acceptance through celebration of their *virtù*, derived from classical exemplars and later notoriously described from observation by Machiavelli in *Il Principe*.[9] Some even sought to heroise their achievements by imitation of the Virgilian epic: in his *Sforziad*, Filelfo attempted to do so for the *milanese* duke Francesco Sforza;[10] more famously, Ariosto sought to elevate the origins of the Este clan in *Orlando furioso*, published from 1508 and in its final form in 1532. Certainly, the Italian Wars and subsequent European conflicts presented opportunities for rewards—personal wealth and social advancement—for politicomilitary entrepreneurs, but such careers needed significant initial capital investment to raise and equip forces of size sufficient to gain the attention of princes and kings. The era when the free captains, the *condottieri*, could carve out fortunes in the Italian peninsula was by and large ended with the French invasion in 1498. Restless young people seeking fortune and glory might continue to go to the European wars, but from c. 1500, numbers of them looked instead to the North Atlantic.

Secular heroes could be identified by reference to the extent of their achievements, relative to the perceived strengths of their opponents. These heroes might appear as the least calculating of men, because they took such huge risks without regard to rational assessment of likely outcome. Did Cortés, for example, seriously expect to overcome the political and military power of the indigenous Mexica empire, with a few hundred soldiers, or was he a gambler of iron resolve and ruthlessness, committed to do or die?

Self-Proclaimed Heroes: The Case of Cortés

Modern scholars have noted how Cortés, in particular amongst the conquistadores, noted in his correspondence that there was to be found in the New World fame and glory to rival those of the ancients.[11] To Cortés's Cyrus, Bernal Díaz played Xenophon to write his own *Anabasis*. Amongst his contemporaries in the Caribbean, however, Cortés was by no means the most obviously heroic, in the sense of daring to pursue challenges of nature and the unknown to find fame and riches. Of this kind of daring, perhaps Balboa in reaching the Pacific, or Narváez in Florida, showed more. By contrast, Cortés may be more representative of the motives of a majority of those who took up a challenge in the early modern Atlantic, as an adventurer.

In fifteenth- and sixteenth-century England, *adventurer* denoted one who would risk an investment in an enterprise that might reasonably be expected to make some profit, and the men who were recruited by prospective investors were likewise adventurers, rather than necessarily bandits or outlaws, or reckless gamblers. Cortés had already established himself as a figure of some wealth and significance[12] within the limits of Cuban settler society when in 1518 he ventured so much of his personal fortune on the costs of recruiting and equipping an expedition to explore the Yucatán.[13] We may surmise that the cash-equivalent of Cortés's investment, coupled with the resources lent him by friends and associates, exposed him to bankruptcy.[14] Such sizeable investment was ill advised if purely speculative, and for some commentators, Cortés was a man noted for his caution.[15] Thus, his decision to join the expedition suggests some prior and credible intelligence about what he should expect to find. This intelligence had been gathered in the reconnaissances in which Bernal Díaz describes himself participating, first with Francisco Hernández and later with Grijalva.[16]

According to Díaz,[17] Cortés's appointment to head the expedition was the fruit of a conspiracy between Cortés and two leading officials, to share the expedition's expected profits between them. In his modern scholarly account, Thomas[18] says that Cortés's appointment arose out of Cuba's governor Velázquez's anxiety to have one of his dependants, *un criado* rather than a potential rival, in charge of the expedition. Then there was a further personal motive: a potential dispute between Cortés and his wife's family, which included Velázquez, might have encouraged Velázquez further to believe that Cortés was dependent on him, but as the expedition put to sea the governor tried in vain to revoke the commission.

With European manpower at a premium in the still-infant Cuban settler society, quite apart from the commitment of *matériel*—ships, arms, and food supplies—authorised by governor Velázquez, the decision to mount a major expedition to the west of Cuba surely could only make sense in terms of projected profit at acceptable risk. In terms of profit, Velázquez's main concern was to beat possible rivals in order to claim new lands by possession, whilst waiting to receive confirmation from the crown of his appointment as *adelantado* of Yucatán, rather than to find himself confirmed as regional governing deputy to Columbus's son, Diego Colón. In terms of risk, Velázquez himself had direct experience of ineffectual resistance amongst indigenous peoples, when he perpetrated the massacre of the "queen" Anacaona and her followers, an event that may have been witnessed by Cortés. Of Cortés's possible credentials as expedition leader, military prowess was not noted and should not have been necessary, given the limited resistance thought to be expected. Instead, Cortés possessed a number of singularly unheroic attributes. Of first importance was his skill as a politician, shown in his success in cultivating support for himself as a popular and dynamic leader, symbolised in his wining and dining before the expedition's departure. Secondly, Cortés possessed a working knowledge of the law (and hence an ability to safeguard the hoped-for profits of the expedition from rivals) gained as a sometime student at the university in Salamanca and as a judge in the colonies. Finally, he was an investor, in which role he was also active in recruiting men and in his attention to the details of equipping the expedition: expedition members were promised shares in wealth, and not all of them joined with their own arms or horses. Rather than a self-consciously heroic expedition intent on furthering the achievements of the *Reconquista*, Cortés made his preparations in the manner of a merchant.

In his exploitation of the opportunities presented to him in the Mexican adventure, Cortés undoubtedly displayed to a high degree at least some of the characteristics identified as heroic in his own time and since, such as leadership, and certainly courage in the face of physical, mortal danger. He was neither the first amongst the conquistadores to display these attributes nor the only one to secure a materially rewarding outcome. As he became more aware of the extent of his conquests on the mainland, however, Cortés sought to heroise the undertaking to inflate his own reputation as a defence against the criticisms of those he offended—not only amongst his fellow colonists but also at the court of the new monarch, Carlos I. Not only did his letters to the crown address his monarch as Caesar, he also claimed to be acting to promote Christianity amongst the "heathens" as a major aim of his expedition,[19] and he coined the title New Spain[20] for the Mesoamerican territories, when there was not yet (and would not be for nearly two hundred years more) a united state or society in Old Spain. In this deliberate drawing of a self-portrait as hero, Cortés distinguished himself from others of this period: his rewards included the grant of aristocratic status, as marquis; their reputations, in their own lifetimes as well as subsequently, were more commonly true-to-life characterisations as murderous risk-takers, to be brought to heel as soon as practicable by "real" aristocrats sent out to the empire as the agents of the crown. The achievements of the Pizarro brothers in South America, for example, were (from the point of view of colonisers and the crown) if anything more amazing and certainly more profitable than those of Cortés, yet the Pizarros' fates included death in battle, assassination, and execution as invaders, conspirators, and rebels.

The identification of further heroes depended, in part, on the circumstances of their mother country. Within Hispanic culture, already by the early seventeenth century the idea of the heroic individual had become tarnished to the point of pathos, as in the portrayal of Don Quixote de La Mancha. For the English, on the other hand, heroes could be sought from conflict with the Iberian empire, rather than from exploration or encounters with the indigenous peoples of the littoral. Francis Drake and later, Henry Morgan, won knighthoods in part for portraying their piratical expeditions as promoting their nation's cause in the wider world, in contrast with the limited official recognition accorded John Smith's efforts in the earliest colonial days in Virginia, or the scant acknowledgement of William Dampier for his hydrographical attainments (as opposed to his mixed success as pirate or privateer), notwithstanding Smith's and Dampier's respective efforts at self-advertisement.[21] Indeed, a heroic mythology was deemed necessary amongst the later seventeenth-century English population of Jamaica, for example, who portrayed the early period of their settlement in exaggerated terms of struggle for supremacy with their Hispanic predecessors.[22] Such stories answered a contemporary social and political need to amplify and elaborate the achievements and to reassure their compatriots at home that something more than material profit was at stake in their Atlantic endeavours.

VOLUNTARY MIGRATION

For much of our period, the commodity in shortest supply within European settlements around the North Atlantic was European people. There was a vital need for human labour—skilled and unskilled—in all aspects of colonial exploitation and development, because, from the perspective of European incomers, the indigenous societies were not all sufficiently advanced in their exploitation of the natural environment. From the clearing of land for agriculture and settlement, the recurrent work in farming of crops and livestock, the provision and maintenance of clothing and equipment, the maintenance of contact and trade with the mother country and other colonies, to the administration of settlers' affairs in law and government, European labour—or at least, supervision—was deemed essential. In contrast, however, with some imperial-colonial projects of earlier periods, for example the Roman Empire, the extent to which any European colonial project in the Atlantic would prosper was a direct function of the numbers of European emigrants it could attract, because no early modern West European society was content—or able—to create an imperial outpost staffed solely by indigenous peoples newly acculturated to the Europeans' values and aims. Europeanised indigenous or mestizo communities emerged, in effect, only as side effects of colonial projects, not as their rulers' primary objective.[23]

In the West European homelands, economic and social pressures arising from renewed population growth across the early modern period, continually prompted both internal and external migration.[24] The voluntary movement of individuals and families—in search of casual or seasonal employment; entering service as domestic, business, or estate servants; seeking to be bound in apprenticeships in any number of trades—rendered migration a comparatively familiar experience. Indeed, we should also note that numbers of migrants of European heritage also moved from the New World to the Old, reflecting shifting perceptions of advantage and opportunity, and amongst them are some individuals who played significant parts in developments in Europe.[25] Recruitment of migrants was also familiar; encouraging migration to particular destinations was the challenge, and there were significant differences in the degrees of success in recruitment of emigrants to different extra-European destinations. Perhaps the most difficult destinations for which to recruit were those in the Indian Ocean and Asia, but the reluctance of men to serve in those regions (and the rate of desertions amongst those who did go) derived not simply from the horrifying risk of premature death by disease, but perhaps more importantly from recruits' concerns that the rewards of service and effort, if paid at all, would not be as great as individuals believed that they deserved or that they saw rivals achieve through underhanded means.[26]

We might expect that mortality rates in colonial enterprise deterred recruits, particularly when we consider the numbers who died amongst West Europeans recruited to service in West Africa[27] and in the Caribbean.[28] In practice, death rates in the colonies could be comparable to those in many European cities, and certainly with those of London, for example. Life expectancy remained generally low across early modern Europe, and in periods of epidemic disease, life expectancy was no better for those with wealth. The risk of death from natural causes anywhere in Europe was unremitting, whereas the risks associated with colonial emigration might be no greater than those at home, and might possibly be well worth taking if migration brought better prospects for improved lifestyles, particularly for those from humble backgrounds with limited life chances at home. Nevertheless, European emigration across the North Atlantic in the early modern period was never more than modest in numbers: over the sixteenth century, perhaps an average of 1,000 emigrants left Iberia each year to settle in the Hispanic New World, whereas over the same period the population of Sevilla grew from perhaps 50,000 people in the 1480s to perhaps 122,000 in 1588.[29] English migrants to New England in the 1630s probably averaged about 2,000 per year; this compared with late Stuart London, where perhaps "8,000 or so net immigrants . . . [were] absorbed every year."[30] For both Sevilla and London—as with most other European cities—population increased only by reason of inward migration, because urban death rates always far outran urban birth rates.

The practical challenges for any emigrants who were the first to establish a settlement were of course substantial, as the desperate struggle for survival of the first settlers at Jamestown proved, as much as did the early experiences of the so-called Pilgrim Fathers. Once a settlement had begun, however, prospects could quickly improve if the numbers of new arrivals could be sustained, and for emigrants to long-established settlements, even small-scale settlements, prospects could be promising. Unlike migrants to the European cities, who might simply exchange rural poverty for urban poverty, those who crossed the Atlantic could expect opportunities for employment for all those who were willing to work. The chronic shortage of European labour of all kinds was in effect a guarantee of work that was likely to be rewarded in direct proportion to the amount of work undertaken. This was particularly so for those with any kind of craft skills, even those skills associated with luxury lifestyles. Each successive wave of emigrants who survived the crossing and the first seasons in the colonies was an encouraging example for others to follow. Advertising for initial recruits to found a settlement might make extravagant claims for the prosperity to be enjoyed, but migration would continue only because of real improvements in lifestyle and life chances—and the European settlements that failed were those in which settlers experienced little or no improvements in life. For those with relatives in the mother country, settlers' letters describing the material benefits were the most effective means for sustaining recruitment, whether to the Hispanic empire or to the Anglophone colonies of the islands and mainland in the West.

If material prosperity was a substantial reward for emigrating, early modern opinion also commonly attached great significance to formal recognition of social status. In England, for example, the grant of a coat of arms (along with a family tree to prove the entitlement was by birth) was the vital symbol of social standing, for which large cash sums would be paid. In Iberia and France, membership by birth of the ranks of the aristocracy was thought to need both protection and assertion of its formal privileges, however miserable the material circumstances of the possessors. New grants of aristocratic status were the greatest of rewards for service to a crown, and for most of our period in most European societies such grants were closely guarded, by jealous aristocrats if not always by kings themselves. Wealth was an important attribute but was not the sole qualification for entry to the ranks of publicly acknowledged social élites.

Formal social hierarchies—differentiation expressed through legal and taxation privileges or rights to participate in public life—existed in the indigenous societies of the littoral and were early established in European colonies. Most commonly, these were differentiated by perceived ethnicity and were expressed in the ways with which we are familiar into the modern age—through the different legal status accorded to individuals on the basis of parentage, and the place to which their ancestry and appearance were thought to put them on the spectrum from new immigrants from Europe, through all the varieties of parentage that were regarded as mixed, to the latest African slave immigrants. These ethnic identities and social distinctions were generally much more complex in reality than the formal legal categories might comprehend, and they might, but need not, correspond to the economic status of the individuals concerned. Although the gradient of social differentiation on ethnic grounds was generally steeper and more punishing amongst Anglophone than Iberian colonial societies, it remained, of course, an important part of a white colonial identity myth for the poorest white to assert that he was innately superior to the richest person of any other ancestry. For women of non-European or mixed origin, the social boundaries might prove more porous.

In one important respect, however, we see a limit to the potential rewards of migration, from the narrow perspective of the European immigrant. Ennoblement—the awarding in perpetuity of aristocratic titles and status, predominantly to men, because of service to the crown or in recognition of wealth—was not common amongst the conqueror-settlers in the Western Hemisphere, even though it was an important reward for service and wealth in the mother countries. No sizeable, formal Creole aristocracy, endowed with titles reflecting their colonial origins, was allowed to emerge in any of the European projects around the Atlantic. In some cases, service to the crown was rewarded by entry to the most junior ranks of the formal social élites, with knighthoods and their equivalent titles from European court societies, but entry to the higher levels of aristocracy was accorded to only a very few individuals. Columbus, for example, although initially promised various offices of state that included extraordinary powers of government and trade,[31] did not become a grandee with a territorial title. Only later, as part of the settlement of the family's claims against the crown, was his grandson ennobled as duke of Veragua (in Panama) and marquis of La Vega. Cortés was created marquis of the valley of Oaxaca, a title that reflected his enormous personal holdings in that region of Mexico. Cortés, however, was born an hidalgo and behaved in that manner, so that his ennoblement—though resented—need not have affronted Castilian sensitivities about social status as much as such a grant might have if made to men of lower social origins, regardless of their achievements or worth. Francisco Pizarro—as vicious and cunning as Cortés, not only lacking the polish of a university but illiterate and thought vulgar in his preferred pastimes—was awarded a knighthood and later a marquisate, but even he was an hidalgo by birth, although illegitimate. Aristocrats by birth might travel to empires to seek the financial backing for their social status, but there were few cases of men who, having acquired the wealth, also secured formal status recognition with a noble title rooted in their colonial experience. This is not to say that the wealthy and capable of the colonies were denied status recognition, but it did mean that, perhaps more so than in the mother countries, wealth was early the immediate measure of social worth in colonial societies. For those seeking formal acknowledgement of improvement in their social status, the colonies might be a means to an end, through the acquisition of wealth, but securing a title generally required presence nearer the fount of honours, the court of a king.

This reluctance to award titles of nobility to the leaders of settler societies contrasted sharply with, for example, English practice in their colonisation of Ireland, another part of the Atlantic littoral subjected to invasion and colonisation. Admittedly, native Irish princes and chiefs were granted recognition of noble status by the English crown as part of intermittent attempts to reconcile them to colonisation, but from Tudor adventurers onwards, amongst the rewards for incomers were grants of aristocratic titles. Richard Boyle, for example, arrived penniless in Ireland in 1588 and formally marked the success of his career as government servant, sometime embezzler, and ruthless opportunist when he became the earl of Cork in 1620. He founded a dynasty whose members included titled nobles who served each of the regimes of seventeenth-century England, exemplifying the permeability of the early modern English aristocracy to admit those of Welsh, Scot, and Irish birth,[32] provided that they would serve. Yet there was no grant of aristocracy bestowed on the Boyles' equivalents across the Atlantic, no earl of Massachusetts or marquis of New York.[33]

In these respects, the experiences of European women emigrants to the Atlantic colonies were, for the most part, not fundamentally different from those of the men. Unmarried women crossed the Atlantic to the Iberian settlements from the first quarter of the sixteenth century, seeking opportunities through service, marriage, or both. Although always fewer in number than the European men, they might enjoy wider choice of partners only in those societies that attached particular importance to European birth. In Hispanic laws, notwithstanding social prejudice, formal marriage between immigrant men and indigenous women was as valid as that between any persons. Amongst Anglophone settlers, however, European women enjoyed much more of a premium.

From the present-day perspective, perhaps the most attractive feature of early modern colonial migration was what might seem to be the prospect of enlarged personal freedom, arising not simply from material prosperity, but also from the supposed lighter burden of government on the settler in the New World, in comparison with his peers in the mother country. Clearly, personal choice could be extensive for those who were either rich enough to secure good relations with their colonial governments, or who chose to live out of easy reach of the colonial officials. For the most part, however, European colonial settlements largely emulated the social conventions and fashions of Europe, with some practical adjustments for local conditions. In the Iberian Empire, urban life with forms of representative town government and participation in broadly orthodox religious observances, combined with conventional works of charity, largely resembled practice in the mother country: the marked variations arose in the extent to which syncretism amongst the practices of the indigenous peoples were encouraged or permitted. In the French settlements, although the most energetic early explorers and settlers were often willing to adopt the lifestyles of indigenous peoples, government policy sought to encourage settlement by (in every sense) orthodox, farming families and to exclude undesired elements, such as Huguenots, even whilst difficulties in recruitment to some regions led to the forced migration of criminals and other outcasts. Dutch settlements followed the practice of parts of their homeland: considerable latitude in personal beliefs and practice were tolerated, provided that good order and commercial advantage were maintained. During the early modern period, no separate communities were envisaged for Jewish would-be migrants, although their presence was tolerated in some places, and no provision was made for Islamic communities, not even those expelled from Iberia.

Only in the case of the English were there significant attempts to create in the New World, havens for those who would otherwise be subjected to intolerance or persecution at home, which also provided for these emigrants to enjoy civic and political rights: Protestant separatists in New England, Roman Catholics in Maryland, Quakers and other Nonconformists in Pennsylvania, Scots-Irish Presbyterians in New Jersey, for example. Religious conviction, as the prevailing ideological frame of reference throughout the period, potentially provided for Europeans a powerful justification for migration to the New World, in the work of making God's Kingdom on earth in a virgin land. In this respect, however, the Pilgrim Fathers were atypical, even in the English experience, because the majority of emigrants from the British Isles were orthodox in their formal adherence to the Church of England. Nonconformity at both ends of the (Christian) spectrum produced Puritan New England *and* Roman Catholic Maryland, although this tolerance did not readily extend to Brownists, antinomians, or Quakers. This limited toleration of religious diversity, perhaps, reflected the relative difficulty encountered in recruiting enough people willing to make the journey to the New World in the early seventeenth century. By the later seventeenth century, the prominence of sectaries in the government and commerce of certain English colonies caused dispute and tension both within the settler communities and between these colonial élites and London. At no time did the sectaries number a simple majority amongst all settlers, or as the dominant voice in a majority of colonies.

In the Caribbean and later along the Carolina and African coasts, however, there emerged amongst European settlers a few genuine free zones— the havens of buccaneers and pirates. Only in these communities do we see develop any real alternative versions of European settler societies, with social customs that departed from those of the communities from which these groups had withdrawn. This was not mere criminality, although joining a pirate crew was invariably preceded by a criminal act; plenty of those of European origins or culture around the Atlantic engaged in raiding against the settlements and commerce of their mother country, as well as those of other European societies, moving back and forth across the line between legitimate commerce raiding as licensed privateers and outlawry. Nor were buccaneers necessarily more habituated than their contemporaries to violence; as already noted, early modern Europeans were both armed and argumentative. Amongst pirates, however, there were expressions of counterculture, at odds with those that prevailed amongst most European colonial settlements.

First and foremost, pirates were volunteers, when some serving at sea were impressed or oppressed by circumstances into service. As companies of volunteers, they "placed authority in the collective hands of the crew," an arrangement that was often formalised in articles of agreement for service.[34] Egalitarianism extended to common messing shipboard with no distinctions or privileges for captains, a powerful symbolic rejection of the hierarchies of all other European societies. In the making of decisions, in the settlement of interpersonal disputes and grievances, in the division of spoils, and in rewards for ability, pirate crews practised a value system based on participation and majority vote that flatly contradicted prevailing European conventions. In perhaps the ultimate rejection of convention, pirate crews tolerated greater ethnic and cultural diversity than other Atlantic communities and, in a few celebrated cases, acknowledged women as their leaders. Fundamentally, of course, these groups were judged deviant and were persecuted as such: "Beyond the church, beyond the family, beyond disciplinary labor, and using the sea to distance themselves from the powers of the state, they carried out a strange experiment."[35]

PLUNDERING

Although various types of trading were established from early in the West Europeans' contacts with West African societies, in the Atlantic islands and Western Hemisphere, plundering—expropriation of goods or labour by force or threat of force—was the first and foremost means of exploitation of the new lands. We might speculate that this situation would have been different, had the European incomers possessed any commodities for trade that the indigenous peoples in the West particularly valued, but there was little in European material culture from the time of first contact that attracted immediate or sustained interest amongst indigenous societies, other than metal blades and implements. From the point of view of the Europeans, however, plundering's great attraction was that, by comparison with almost any form of trade, the returns on the effort and resources invested could be for individual participants both relatively swift and disproportionately large.

Plundering, manifestly and recurrently, worked: not only did it succeed in giving returns to the earliest European explorers and conquerors, it continued to show significant returns to almost any group willing to pursue it vigorously. Thus, the fruits of exploitation from the Iberian Empire in the West were in turn plundered by French, English, and Dutch raiders, just as the profits of their later colonial enterprises were likewise plundered by stateless raiders, buccaneers and pirates, until well into the 1700s. Although some religious and other intellectual figures in European societies might debate the morality of plundering or condemn the activity as a manifestation of the innate sinfulness of humanity, plundering was attractive for as long as indigenous peoples of the littoral were unable or unwilling to defend themselves from West European incomers, and for as long as European societies were unable or unwilling to enforce significant moral or legal restraints on the use of violence by their own people.

In many ways, the phrase "no peace beyond the line" may seem to exemplify the circumstances within which plundering began and was continued. For one modern scholar,[36] the physical distance from the mother country, living in almost exclusively male and martial groups, combined with the experience of being outnumbered by peoples very different in culture and beliefs, gave a kind of psychological licence to some European incomers to abandon restraint when dealing with the indigenous peoples of the Atlantic. In reality, lack of restraint was never confined to the margins of European experience; whilst clearly not on the same scale as some events in the New World, we may cite as examples of extreme cruelty and inhumanity, events at the heart of civilised Europe such as the massacres of Huguenots across France that began on St. Bartholomew's Day, 1572; or the Spanish Fury of 1576, when elements of Felipe II's army in the Low Countries went on the rampage against civilians in Antwerpen; or the massacres of defenders and civilians at Drogheda and Wexford in Ireland, by Cromwell's English army in 1649. These events were, by the standards of the European continent, on a relatively large scale, but they were matched by countless numbers of small-scale, everyday cases of cruelty and torture; criminal proceedings commonly involved physical mutilation, short of death; execution, including burning at the stake, was regarded as public entertainment, as much as ritualised expressions of the power of the state; corporal punishment of children, servants, and any woman was commonplace.

The establishment by conquest of European settlement in the Americas was rarely, if ever, built on a deliberate placing of or by the immigrants beyond the legal framework of the society of origin, except in the cases of buccaneers and pirates, as already noted. There were no sustained attempts to create a lawless frontier of brigandage and outlawry as a regular mechanism by which to extend West European domination over indigenous peoples. However much in practice lawless behaviour might go unpunished, from relatively early in the development of their colonial empires, Iberian and later English home governments, in particular, sought to give legal protection to indigenous peoples and to restrain the behaviour of their European settlers.

What distinguished the early modern Atlantic littoral was the extent to which plundering was carried on, in terms both of its geographical distribution and its practice over time. Europeans discovered around the Atlantic what were, by the standards of their previous experience, unprecedented opportunities for plunder, encouraged initially by the generally ineffective resistance of the indigenous peoples and thereafter by the apparently limitless natural resources of the land. Unrestrained exploitation first became a practical possibility around the early modern Atlantic, because the consequences of despoilation—of peoples, ecologies, and landscapes—were always experienced away from the European mother countries by peoples who were not Europeans. The age of plunder passed, we may suggest, only when there became established in the Atlantic world sufficiently large communities of settlers of European culture enjoying lifestyles and material culture recognisably comparable to those of their mother countries, that their governments sought to impose their normal rules of civil and international order. In effect, state enterprise replaced private enterprise in the business of plunder.

PLUNDERING THE NATURAL ENVIRONMENT: THE CASE OF MINING

Notwithstanding the enormous mineral wealth of the New World and West Africa in all of the commodities of value to early modern European consumers—tin, copper, iron, for example—around the littoral, this period saw an overwhelming preoccupation with the extraction of gold and silver bullion from the region. This was an extractive activity of the most primitive kind: destructive of the natural environment with no mitigating side effects, such as, for example, improving the area or quality of agricultural land. Instead, bullion had no greater intrinsic value or utility than the exotic birds' plumage so besought by the indigenous peoples of Mesoamerica, or the seashells used as the medium of exchange amongst peoples of the North American interior. Bullion was already, however, vital to the functioning of the international economy, such as it was, amongst European societies and particularly between Europe and Asia, in which role it remains the subject of considerable scholarly attention.[37] It was also vital in the development of an Hispanic imperialism.

The lure of gold may first have drawn Spain and Spaniards to America; but it was the reality of silver that kept them there.

By the end of the sixteenth century, silver mining was clearly the most heavily capitalized productive activity in Spanish America, the one showing most pronounced specialization and division of labor, and the one in which imported technology played the largest part.

Thus has one modern historian characterised the mining and refining of bullion in the New World.[38] With the incentives of the discovery of rich ore deposits[39]—of gold in the streams of the main Caribbean islands from the first contact and thereafter in the highlands of Nueva Granada (in modern-day Colombia) in the late 1530s; and silver, particularly at Zacatecas in northern Mexico, from 1546—and almost limitless demand for the product, here we see how, with sufficient motivation, more productive technologies were identified and deployed, at least in the refining of silver ores, if not in the technologies of mining.

From the late 1550s, shortly after the discovery of new silver mining deposits in Mexico, there was the speedy adoption of the elaborate and capital-intensive mercury amalgam method of refining silver. In addition to the industrial chemistry of the amalgamation method, water- and animal-powered milling machinery was employed to crush the ore, and industrial-scale washing and processing facilities for recovering the refined metal afterwards. The mining of ore remained dependent on human muscle, for the most part that of indigenous labourers drafted in by the government, and it was not until later in the eighteenth century that improvements in drainage techniques had an impact on mining itself.

The mines presented not only technological challenges, in the search for improved productivity, they also presented significant logistical challenges, in terms of the supply of foodstuffs and materials to the workforces. The most extreme case was, of course, that of the mines at Potosí (in modern-day Bolivia), which were at altitudes approaching 4,000 metres and the "extreme limit of habitability."[40] Elsewhere, however, the mines of northern Mexico were in wild country, occupied by peoples hostile to the incomers, to which substantial quantities of supplies had to be transported on the hoof and by mule trains, and all at significant cost. Yet these challenges were confronted and effectively overcome for the century and more of peak production.

We shall give further consideration in a later chapter to the consequences for the development of the Hispanic empire of the availability of such riches, but for now we should note the extent to which the exploitation of the natural resources of the North Atlantic was exemplified by the flow of bullion out of the New World mines. By the reign of Felipe IV (1621–65), it would be said by one leading figure that the remedy to the empire's ills would be that "God will send us another Potosí," a statement symbolic at once of the empire's dependence on bullion and of a presumption that there should be no limit to the plundering of the earth. It is no doubt anachronistic to ask why the statement was not, "God will send us an improved technology for deep-cast mining or improved returns on long-range maritime trade," but it was perhaps in its progressive loss of influence and participation on its own account in European trade that the Iberian Empire was in the long-term undermined.

The mining of gold and particularly silver sustained the Iberian Empire not only in the Atlantic but around the globe, and envy of these riches in some way motivated all other West European participants in colonial activity around the littoral. The story of *El Dorado* might provide a convenient focus for the dream of unparalleled wealth, but the reality of substantial riches torn from the environment without the need to make restitution either in nature or to indigenous communities affected by the processes established behaviours and attitudes that could become habitual and unquestioned.

PLUNDERING THE HUMAN ENVIRONMENT: SLAVERY

Beginning after the initial phase of plunder, the early modern North Atlantic was transformed from the physical barrier for trading intercourse amongst the autarkic societies of the littoral, to the busy highway for exchange of people and commodities in an increasingly complex transoceanic economy. This transformation seems to have derived from a widely felt urge to profit, pre-eminent amongst though not exclusive to those of European origin but shared, for example, by African slave traders as much as by truck farmers and sharecroppers on the central Mexican plateau. A North Atlantic economy was created that serviced lifestyles beyond simple subsistence, for which lifestyles the accumulation of surpluses—of foodstuffs, materials, and labour—was deemed by its beneficiaries, principally those of European origin, to be essential. The process of accumulation was characterised by three elements: a desire for fast profits, on minimum investment, with the maximum rates of return.

For the development of an Atlantic economy, the significance of these three elements was that, if they could be secured, there was a compelling case for pursuing economic opportunities around the littoral, rather than opportunities closer to home. Within European societies, attitudes to profit were tempered by, for example, concerns such as academic and theological debates about fair prices and lending at interest, and government policies to keep subsistence prices low for the benefit of the poor—and for the maintenance of public order. Trade with other societies around the Atlantic could for a time bring Europeans substantial returns for modest investment, as demonstrated in the fifteenth-century trade in West African spices (of inferior quality to those from Asia) and the seventeenth-century trade in North American furs (to the point of exhaustion of the supplies), in both cases in exchange for what (by European standards) were inferior manufactures (principally firearms and blades). These transactions, however, only temporarily offset the circumstance prevailing through most of our period, that there were only limited commodities produced by Europeans for which there was any significant demand amongst the other peoples of the littoral. If trade with indigenous peoples was inconsistently profitable, plundering and piracy could satisfy all of the three characteristics—speed, minimal investment, maximum return—and as such remained attractive for some peoples into the 1700s. These methods, however, increasingly relied on the seizure of products and profits arising from the establishment of successful forms of longer-term exploitation, usually by other Europeans, derived from the two simplest ingredients in economic activity, land and labour.

In more complex economies, surpluses could be generated from trade in manufactures or services, with value added, as well as from primary production, and indeed this value-added trade was to become a growth area across the Atlantic from the mid–eighteenth century. For much of our period, however, the principal traded outputs of the littoral were (apart from the substantial trade in labour) primary products and semiprocessed raw materials, derived from the direct exploitation of the natural environment. This was because these were commodities that could be exploited with minimal numbers of skilled personnel. The backbone of surplus accumulation for Europeans in the early modern Atlantic was relatively low-skilled agricultural productivity and the mining of precious metals, traded on into West European processing and consumption.

From an economist's perspective, the challenge of rapid wealth creation over successive generations around the North Atlantic might be characterised as follows. West Africa remained an innately hostile physical environment for West Europeans, although its indigenous peoples might find incentives to exploit the region's natural resources and participate in the emergent Atlantic economy. On the islands of the Atlantic and Caribbean, as well as on much of the American mainland, vigorous exploitation of indigenous labour, plants and animals led rapidly to the despoiling of all three. With rapidly declining indigenous populations from whom resources could be expropriated and in the absence (until the eighteenth century) of any sizeable class of colonial consumers much above the level of subsistence, the profits needed to support luxurious lifestyles in the New World could be sustained only from trade with European markets. Transatlantic journey times rendered trade in services uncompetitive with European providers, and with finite shipping resources, low bulk–high value commodities represented the most profitable items for export. Bullion was the pre-eminent commodity of this type, but notwithstanding its enormous importance for the wider economic history of the Atlantic and of Europe, its greatest profits were directly returned to only a fraction of the American colonial population, even if by trickle-down those profits were disseminated. Within a labour theory of value, low bulk–high value goods for export might have been created by the skills and craftsmanship of workers in the Americas; this would have been equivalent to the early modern trade in luxury hardware from Asia, such as silk cloth, porcelain tableware, or lacquerwork. The New World's indigenous art- and craft-work, however, were generally at a discount for settlers and had only limited appeal amongst European consumers, whilst New World imitations of European objects and styles were at once too expensive (after transport) and of inferior quality to compete effectively in European markets. In the context of early modern European consumption, however, the archetype of the low bulk–high value commodity was spice: a consumable with a limited shelf life (thus requiring constant replenishment), having wide appeal across European markets sufficient to command premium prices, derived from scarce agricultural resources but by essentially low-skilled farming. From the first, Europeans sought to find American equivalents of familiar spices[41] or to cultivate them by transplantation from Asia, but with little success in either endeavour. Thus, the challenge for West Europeans was to identify a commodity for trading into European markets, that was of high value relative to its bulk (to offset shipping costs), perishable (to ensure rapid stock turnover), consumable (to ensure sustained demand), requiring limited skill to produce (because of the shortage of skilled personnel in the New World), and agricultural in origin (because of the ready availability and hence low capital cost of land for farming).

The engine of profitability in this mode of production was the dramatic expansion in the appetite—literally—amongst the peoples still resident in western Europe for the exotic products which could be grown in the tropics of the Western Hemisphere, pre-eminently sugar and tobacco. These, however, were by no means the only agricultural products traded to West European consumers, so that there were in effect two, contrasting models of agricultural exploitation of the landscape and peoples of the Atlantic. These two models were powerfully transforming of the environments in which they were set down by their European beneficiaries, but these models were themselves imitative, rather than innovative. Both were cash-crop activities, derived from Iberian models: on one hand, extensive pastoralism broadly of the kind practised in Castilian sheep-farming and its attendant wool trade, epitomised by the *mesta;* on the other, the exploitation of dependent workers in labour-intensive cultivation of fruit and sugar, as exemplified in the agriculture of *morisco* Valencia.

For the first century or so of the European settlement of the littoral, particularly in the Caribbean islands and Mesoamerica, farming was essentially about sustaining a new exploitative caste of conquistadores to a high level of ordinary subsistence, through the *encomienda* system. Notwithstanding the introduction of European food crops and tastes, preconquest agricultural practices largely continued and their products were predominantly those traditional to the farming economies of each region, because not all European varieties of food plants prospered in these conditions of soil, climate, and pest infestation.[42] The transformation of agriculture, however, was effected by the early introduction of large-scale pastoralism, of sheep and cattle, to regions previously ungrazed and unmanured by significant numbers of livestock. As indigenous populations declined, so the opportunities increased to adopt extensive livestock farming plus modest truck farming: hacienda ranching. Land—of which there was, in effect, limitless area—could be exploited with the minimum of inputs, to produce for cash returns chiefly hides and tallow. This was essentially a traditional, *castellano* style of exploitation of natural resources, but transplanted to contexts in which the needs of indigenous peoples could be ignored with impunity, and scales of operation vastly greater than those contemplated in Iberia could better assure the desired levels of return. This mode of production allowed small numbers of herders to manage large numbers of animals at low densities (and therefore low return) per unit area. High nominal returns were achieved through the combination of modest start-up and running costs, with extravagant wastage of the by-products—meat and manure—which were not passed into the subsistence resources of the bulk of the population, despite their great potential benefit as human foodstuffs or soil nutrients.[43] No technological or technical innovations were required to render this form of agriculture either profitable or sustainable; all that was required was an indifference to the suffering of the indigenous peoples and a disregard for the damage to the environment. For settlers from Europe, this style of agriculture generated moderate returns from very low inputs of capital and labour, but it produced for export commodities of which there was no particular shortage in Europe, and so could command no special premium at the point of sale. Substantial volumes had to be shipped to produce modest returns, so that the accumulation of great wealth from ranching was a relatively slow process.

To satisfy the formula for optimum wealth creation—high value, perishable, consumable, low skill, agricultural products for export to Europe—some form of agriculture other than ranching was needed. Labour could be made to generate surpluses by means of its ruthless expropriation through slavery, particularly in agriculture and in mining. Whilst slavery existed on the margins of West European societies,[44] it was employed on a substantially greater scale around the Atlantic, even before Columbus's first voyage. More capital intensive than livestock farming—because slaves had either to be captured or purchased—this mode of production nevertheless generated substantial returns because of the higher value per unit volume of the products, chiefly luxury consumables and, later, bullion. Again, the commodities produced did not contribute to subsistence, and there was considerable wastage—in human life. Replacement costs for labour inputs throughout the period, however, remained low, relative to the output per worker, thereby removing an economic incentive to technological or technical innovation. Slavery could from this perspective make good economic sense—until its moral repugnance became overpowering—and slavery in agriculture enabled the principal innovation in the economic history of the early modern North Atlantic: the adoption of the plantation system of primary agricultural production, chiefly of sugar and tobacco.

Cane sugar and tobacco became the commodities of choice in the early modern period, to be joined later by cotton (and later still by marijuana and the coca leaf). Sugar from cane was already an established consumer item in mediaeval western Europe and was cultivated around the Mediterranean, particularly in the eastern lands but also in Sicilian, Calabrian, Valencian, and Mallorcan farming, which by 1504 were all territories within the empire of Fernando of Aragón. Cultivation expanded into the Atlantic islands of the Canarias, Madeira, and São Tomé,[45] before being introduced to the New World, where the first sugar mill in Hispaniola dated from 1503. Tobacco, on the other hand, although native to the Americas and first encountered there by Columbus,[46] was being cultivated in Europe for its claimed medicinal properties from the 1550s and the plant was found to be readily adaptable to a wide range of climate and soil conditions. Its plantation cultivation as a commodity for European markets was, in effect, like that of sugar, a European introduction to the New World. Substantial cultivation of both these plants, however, did not begin until the seventeenth century, and in the hands of rivals to the Castilian Empire's settlers—the Portuguese, Dutch, and English. Sugar and tobacco were grown in preference to subsistence crops, but in the Caribbean, the wealth of plantation owners allowed them to import the meagre rations on which their slaves survived.

Outputs of agricultural products (or minerals) could be increased by enlarging the area to be worked—generating the same unit of output per unit of land but confronting technical challenges of organisation—or by increasing the unit of output per unit of land through improved methods or technologies. The Europeans' twin emphases on speed and size of accumulation might be thought to have been sufficient incentives to inspire technology and technical improvement, particularly in some resource-rich and people-poor regions of the Western Hemisphere, to aid accumulation of surpluses. Such surpluses might perhaps have been generated through technological advances in primary production—through irrigation projects for agriculture or drainage projects for mines, for example. In fact, around the early modern Atlantic, West Europeans failed to meet these technological and technical challenges, and this period saw no significant innovations of these kinds applied to colonial agriculture, even though there were in this period considerable developments in agricultural practice amongst, for example, Dutch farmers.[47] Instead, the desired surpluses were derived from the exploitation of the simplest ingredients, land and labour, for the production of commodities that were far from necessary for subsistence. In effect, low-tech approaches were adopted to facilitate the production of cash crops, for the swiftest return on a minimum of capital investment.

Europeans' demands for size and speed of accumulation led them in certain contexts to reproduce, whether wittingly or not, a mode of production—and thence the lifestyles—characteristic of the ancient Mediterranean world. Instead of technological or technical innovation, West Europeans turned to models of surplus accumulation and exploitation derived from their own history, in the expropriation of labour through slavery. Slavery had provided the economic underpinning of classical Mediterranean societies, of ancient Greek and Roman life, enabling the exploiters to sustain complex military-bureaucratic states, with rich literary, philosophical, artistic and architectural cultures, over several centuries. Roman experience, in particular, had demonstrated the productivity of plantation agriculture—*latifundia*—the surpluses of which could sustain not only relatively sizeable commercial and political élites but also extensive urban settlement and monumental architecture, the physical remnants of which were still apparent in much of western Europe. Forms of slavery were also long known in West Africa and in the Western Hemisphere, so to a degree perhaps apparent only in retrospect, the concept of empire was intertwined with that of slavery.

By this account, it is important to recognise that slavery would not have been predestined to be an important element in the exploitation of the natural environment, but was selected from amongst a number of alternative solutions to labour shortages. Indeed, the availability of slave labour to some extent encouraged the adoption of types of exploitation that could rely on large amounts of unskilled labour, even though alternative activities with lower demand for labour were also available to be practised. In agriculture, sugar cane was not the only route to wealth; as we have seen, modest fortunes could also be made from ranching, which had much lower labour inputs. If plantation agriculture were the method of choice, then indentured labour from Europe could be brought to the New World to work on the islands and the mainland colonies. Across the period, significant numbers of West Europeans remained willing voluntarily to trade their labour for the costs of passage and subsequent board and lodging for an agreed term of years' service on plantations, as the price of new opportunity. Alternatively, as was to occur in North America from the later 1700s, when demands for commodities outstripped the capacity of limited numbers of skilled craftsmen to meet them, entrepreneurs turned to forms of mechanisation and technical innovation to improve output. Certainly, an economic argument might be made that slavery represented the most cost-effective—short-term—solution to the Europeans' problems of exploitation, but the choice of slavery as the principal mode of labour exploitation derived from several powerful elements other than relative economic advantage. Instead, we might argue that in their exploitation of the natural resources of the Atlantic, West Europeans ignored the incentives and opportunities for technological developments that labour shortages presented, in favour of an altogether cruder, more cruel, and, in the longer-term, less effective remedy.

By choosing to pursue labour-intensive forms of agriculture and thence to meet their labour requirements with slaves, European settlers—first Castilians but later also French, English, and Dutch—inhibited the development within their own communities of independent and small-scale producers of commodities that might otherwise have been in demand amongst wage labourers. The subsistence requirements of slaves did sustain the incomes of those who supplied the slaves' very restricted consumption, but there would be no economic take-off of demand for a whole host of consumer items for as long as slaves were the main workforce. The small volumes of demand for luxury commodities amongst the owners or overseers were often met by imports from Europe or small-scale local craftwork, and in the absence of significant demand in slave-owning societies for cheaper consumer goods, there were limited incentives to develop broader-based craft or service activities in these economies. By contrast, in the absence of significant slave and plantation agriculture, in New England settlements there emerged relatively sizeable numbers of modest consumers for a wide variety of manufactured domestic commodities, beyond the bare minimum of subsistence, which in time produced surpluses of hardware and foodstuffs for the islands and their plantation agriculture. Notwithstanding the commercial importance of fishing to the emergent New England economies and the significant demand for labour that fishing represented, slavery was not adopted as the major source of manpower for this other, essentially low-tech, form of exploitation of the natural environment.

Why was slavery the preferred route to increased output? Or, to pose the question in another way, why did those of European origin choose not to explore further technological or technical innovation in pursuit of increased productivity? Our answer here is to suggest that slavery presented the quickest, least technically challenging remedy to the short-term but intensive demands for labour in the cultivation and processing of sugar cane. The catastrophic decline in the numbers of indigenous inhabitants in the Caribbean islands, Mesoamerica, and North America provided an excuse but not an explanation. Once identified with the plantation cultivation of one tropical agricultural product, its adoption for others arose from the convenience of an existing system of supply: the slave trade. Did slavery remove incentives for technological and technical innovation in the pursuit of quick riches? As we have already seen,[48] the transatlantic slave traffic would never have begun if there had not been well-founded expectations of shipping people in large numbers with calculable prospect of successful survival for onward sale. The need to keep the cargo alive was the business imperative that could prompt limited innovation in ship- ping techniques. Once the slaves were delivered to their destinations, their unwillingness or inability to reproduce themselves in the time or the num- bers sufficient to meet the labour needs of their owners, sustained the inhuman trade.

Beyond any economic calculus to justify slavery, however, there was also a social incentive amongst European settlers to perpetuate the prac- tice. Slave ownership was attractive because it could bring immediate status recognition in societies in which the number of his followers or servants was a measure of the power of the master, and, as we have al- ready noted, formal recognition of status through ennoblement was rare in the Europeans' Western Hemisphere. Like apartheid in South Africa, to have numbers of people of another culture at one's beck and call made the small men feel grander, and exemplified a community of interest amongst the slave-owning whites that transcended any other political, commercial, or social rivalries. Anglophone settlers, for example, were constantly concerned about the possibility of slave revolts, even though these were relatively rare occurrences on any scale sufficient seriously to challenge white supremacy.

Once commitments had been made to the exploitation of the natural environment with slave labour, inevitably there became established com- mercial vested interests in its continuation, if not commercial arguments for its extension. Slave labour ensured that technological and technical innovation in agricultural practice would emerge in areas other than the plantations of the Western Hemisphere, where the issues of changing con- sumer taste and more intensive price competition would be drivers for innovation. Only by cutting off the supply of replacement slaves, did the moralist opponents of the institution of slavery effect the undermining of the "economic case" for slavery.

TRADE

In his monumental study, *Capitalism and Material Life*, Fernand Braudel proposed that, at its simplest, Europeans needed the rest of the world for its resources and not vice versa, so this is why European societies were the first to venture forth across the globe in pursuit of trade, plunder, and settlement.[49] In a similar vein, Immanuel Wallerstein explored a model in which European societies at the core of a global economy, exploited the raw materials and natural resources of a (shifting) periphery.[50] In a sense, both models propose that need, rather than greed, provided the motive for exploration, preparatory to exploitation. Whilst this general proposition may broadly hold true of European engagement with the wider world over the whole of the period from c. 1500 to c. 1950, it is less useful as an explanation for the details of the several endeavours of societies around the North Atlantic during the early modern period.

First and foremost, for the purposes of this study, any explanation is deficient that takes no account of the needs or desires of extra-European societies indigenous to the littoral. As we have already remarked, the earliest contacts between West Europeans and the other peoples of the littoral, beginning with the Portuguese in West Africa, suggested that relations could be established on some form of exchange. In particular, cheap trade goods from Europe were acceptable to some West African peoples in exchange for commodities that they either had in abundance or to which they attached less value than the items offered in trade. Terms of trade became established that were regarded as profitable to both sides. In contacts with Asian societies, in contrast, West Europeans had little or nothing by way of material goods to offer for which there was a demand or need amongst the indigenous peoples, with whom bullion and force, by turns, were the currency.

Around the Atlantic, as we have already remarked,[51] a vital characteristic of the era was the development and maintenance of alliances or coalitions between West Europeans and the peoples they encountered—asymmetrical coalitions, certainly, but nevertheless coalitions in which the indigenous societies engaged because of the prospect of rewards to themselves. In Mesoamerica, societies exploited by the empire of the Mexica allied with the conquistadores to reduce their burden of tribute. In West Africa, indigenous societies acquired arms and sometimes allies against their neighbours and sold them—and sometimes their own people—into slavery to Europeans who transported this surplus population across the ocean. In the North American interior, Algonquin and the so-called Cherokee tribes allied with French and English governments in return for weapons and manufactured goods. Indigenous peoples could engage with Europeans and expect to derive benefits from the transactions.

Second, in a model of need as the driver for European engagement with the Atlantic, we might expect that the goods for which there was most enthusiastic trade or competition were those in which within the competing societies there was unmet demand and short supply. Across early modern Europe there were, for example, recurrent local shortages of foodstuffs, pig-iron, salt, small denomination coins, and timber for naval and building construction. Yet apart from timber, the materials brought in to Europe from the North Atlantic littoral were luxury foodstuffs, such as sugar; items for which a demand had to be created, such as tobacco; and gold and silver bullion, which arrived in sufficiently large quantities that it added to inflation and currency problems, such as the shortage of small denomination coins. Amongst the other indigenous societies around the littoral, the greatest demands were for cheap but effective metalwares, and they were encouraged to seek supplies of firearms, whereas the commodity preferred for profitable export amongst many West European traders were textiles, usually woollens.

In the development of transatlantic economies over our period, the commodities that eventually figured the largest in trading balances were not those either that were initially in great surplus on either side of the transactions or that responded to pre-existing unmet demands. Having "discovered" the Atlantic, West Europeans searched for ways in which to make their discoveries show a profit, because only clear profits would sustain interest and investment of their homelands' people and money. Dumping was not an option, despite the Europeans' surpluses of woollen textiles and their willingness to coerce others to participate in exchange, and European commercial interests were unable to identify a cheap commodity to which the indigenous peoples could be encouraged to become addicted, as opium became in nineteenth-century Asia. To profit from the Atlantic, therefore, Europeans transformed it into sources of commodities for which they created otherwise nonexistent demand. Plantation agriculture filled a gap in the market that was not there, in the mass consumption of narcotics for which a public taste had to be generated: for sucrose, for nicotine, and for caffeine. In modern times, perhaps only Beanie Babies went one better in creating a demand not previously imagined and then ensuring a shortage of supply to sustain the market value of the commodity.

We may therefore speak of need as a driver of European exploitation of the North Atlantic only in the sense of the need amongst some to identify ways of generating profit from the enterprise. For individual settlers on the (by European standards) vast and (soon after first contact) relatively empty lands of the New World, comfortable and sustainable subsistence could be realised within a relatively short period of agricultural improvement, using at the minimum a combination of European livestock and indigenous food crops. For communities of settlers, however, surplus was a prerequisite for the adornments of civic life—for instance, public buildings, the arts, consumption of luxuries—and surplus was another word for profit. The acme of the transformation through and for trade was the famous/notorious Triangular route around the North Atlantic: low cost–low value manufactures, surplus to European consumption, were shipped to West African communities that drained people from the interior of the continent; who provided the labour for underdeveloped, artificially sustained, cash-crop monocultural societies; that compromised their own subsistence to supply inessential commodities to growing numbers of European consumers with small disposal incomes. The spinoffs from the trade were substantial: the development of large merchant fleets to ship the commodities; the encouragement of surplus agricultural production in other parts of the North Atlantic to sustain the concentrations of population in the plantation zones; the opportunities for raiding and piracy, and so the incentives for the development of naval forces to protect colonies and their trades; the growth of governments' interests in all of these activities.

By the early seventeenth century, European thinkers were pursuing the proposition that profit through trade should benefit society as a whole, and that one role for the state could and should be the encouragement and protection of profitable external trade. This proposition, combined with a view that all commerce was essentially a zero-sum game in which one person's (or nation's) profit could only be at the expense of another's, has become known in retrospect as mercantilism, about which we shall have more to say in a later chapter.[52] For the purposes of the present discussion of exploitation, however, we should note that if such a phenomenon as mercantilism does have interpretative value in our understanding of the early modern period, it emerged only after the exploitation of the Atlantic had been underway for over a century and was in that sense a product rather than a primary cause of transformation.

Transoceanic trade became the defining characteristic of the early modern North Atlantic, even though alternative models of development would have allowed for some European and (a much smaller) African migration, to offset population pressures in the homelands and reoccupy the territories in the West that were depopulated by disease. Certain groups would have been willing to migrate, irrespective of the prospects for profitable trade: persecuted religious minorities were sufficiently numerous in West European states to encourage them to seek to leave, so that the Pilgrim Fathers and English Roman Catholics could have been joined in the New World by Iberian Jews or *moriscos*, or by German Anabaptists, or French Huguenots, or Savoyard Waldensians, in ways similar to those by which the United States later gave haven to such groups in the nineteenth-century migrations. Instead, the early modern pursuit of trade encouraged attempts to replicate societies from the homelands, with their hierarchies of property and status enshrined in legal frameworks, largely supported by the oppressive expropriation of labour.

CONCLUSION

Through the scale of their efforts and their capacity to cross the ocean, but wildly out of proportion with their actual numbers, West Europeans took the lead in the exploitation of the early modern North Atlantic. Their collective determination to secure rewards quickly, to achieve personal prosperity and higher standards of material existence within the lifetime of an individual, was potentially undermining of the established social structures of the West European homelands, in which ability frequently ceded precedence to status. The greatest improvements in personal fortune could, however, be rendered harmless to prevailing social structures by being described as the work of extraordinary individuals—heroes—or by being condemned as monstrous criminality in the cases of some of those who profited from the Atlantic world as pirates.

The North Atlantic world presented early modern West Europeans with extraordinary opportunities to accommodate through emigration a growing diversity of religious and social practice within their homelands, and to negotiate conditions of economic exchange with indigenous peoples on the basis of collaborative development and mutual benefit. In reality, neither of these opportunities was grasped. The urge for quick rewards made Europeans impatient of the rights and interests of other groups around the region. The readiness of some indigenous societies to collaborate in these endeavours encouraged European incomers to be forceful with those peoples who were more recalcitrant. From the perspective of the European incomers, the geographical extent and apparently limitless resources of the littoral were invitations to exploitation without regard to the consequences for the environments: profligacy with nature's resources became habitual.

Slavery was neither essential nor efficient as the route to profit in the European exploitation of the North Atlantic region. That it became, however, a defining characteristic of the region and its commerce for three hundred years was not accidental, and its adoption so widely in the Caribbean and southern colonies of North America contrasts sharply with the economic prosperity that could be secured without significant recourse to it, for example, in the more northerly colonies and in the exploitation of nature's wealth through fisheries. Short-run advantage became long-term vested economic, and hence political, interest, in the promotion to consumers in Europe of foodstuffs that were as addictive as they were inessential.

FURTHER READING

For: aspects of the hero concept, see R. Starn, "Reinventing Heroes in Renaissance Italy," in *Art and History: Images and Their Meaning,* ed. R. I. Rotberg and T. K. Rabb, 67–84 (Cambridge, 1988), and I. Leonard, *Books of the Brave* (Cambridge, Mass., 1949); a readable, one-volume survey of early modern European societies, see H. Kamen, *European Society, 1500–1700* (London, 1984), and more recently, for a concise and scholarly introduction to social and economic contexts in early modern European states, see S. R. Epstein, ed., *Town and Country in Europe, 1300–1800* (New York and Cambridge, 2001); population history in the New World, see M. R. Haines and R. H. Steckel, eds., *A Population History of North America* (New York and Cambridge, 2000); illustrations and examinations of the Atlantic migrant experiences, see, for example, I. Altman, *Transatlantic Ties in the Spanish Empire* (Stanford, Calif., 2000), especially for its analytical account of early modern migration from Brihuega in Castilla to Puebla de los Angeles in Mexico; J. Lockhart and E. Otte, *Letters and People of the Spanish Indies* (Cambridge, 1976), especially for illustrations of the sentiments expressed by migrants regarding their motives and experiences of migration; A. Games, "Migration" in *The British Atlantic World, 1500–1800*, ed. D. Armitage and M. J. Braddick, pp. 31–51 (Basingstoke and New York, 2002), especially for a concise introduction to the Anglophone experience; and D. Cressy, *Coming Over: Migration and Communication Between England and New England in the Seventeenth Century* (New York and Cambridge, 1987), especially for an exploration and illustration of migrant experiences; a concise, recent account of issues of identity in the Anglophone experience, see J. E. Chaplin, "Race" in *The British Atlantic World, 1500–1800*, ed. D. Armitage and M. J. Braddick, pp. 154–72 (Basingstoke and New York, 2002); a useful collection of essays on various detailed aspects of the subject over the period c.1500–c.1800, see I. Altman and J. Horn, eds., *"To Make America." European Emigration in the Early Modern Period* (Berkeley and Los Angeles, Calif., 1991); an accessible general introduction to the phenomenon of piracy over the whole of our period, see P. Pringle, *Jolly Roger. The Story of the Great Age of Piracy* (1953; reprint, Minneola, N.Y., 2001), and for a more thoughtful consideration of its context and significance, see M. Rediker, *Between the Devil and the Deep Blue Sea: Merchant Seamen, Pirates, and the Anglo-American Maritime World, 1700–1750* (New York and Cambridge, 1987), esp. chapter 6 (pp. 254–87); an account of the importance of bullion in the early modern economy and its impact on monetisation and inflation, see J. J. McCusker, *Money and Exchange in Europe and America, 1600–1775* (Chapel Hill, N.C., and London, 1978); discussion of mining, see the general account by M. Lynch, *Mining in World History* (London, 2002) and the more focused P. J. Bakewell, *Silver Mining and Society in Colonial Mexico, Zacatecas 1546–1700* (Cambridge, 1971); a careful and judicious analysis of the workings of English Caribbean sugar plantation agriculture, see R. S. Dunn, *Sugar and Slaves: The Rise of the Planter Class in the English West Indies, 1624–1713* (New York, 1973); an account of tobacco and its role in the economic development of British trade, see J. M. Price, *Tobacco in Atlantic Trade: The Chesapeake, London and Glasgow, 1675–1775* (Aldershot, 1995); a concise introduction to the issues and some of the extensive bibliography, see M. L. Bush, *Servitude in Modern Times* (Malden, Mass., and Oxford, 2000); and in more detail, R. Blackburn, *The Making of New World Slavery from the Baroque to the Modern, 1492–1800* (London, 1997), J. Thornton, *Africa and Africans in the Making of the Atlantic World, 1400–1800,* 2nd ed. (Cambridge, 1998), D. Eltis and S. D. Behrendt, eds., *The Transatlantic Slave Trade: A Database on CD-ROM* (Cambridge, 1999), and D. Eltis, *The Rise of African Slavery in the Americas* (Cambridge, 2000); a sweeping, accessible account of the economic and social development of the early modern world, the classic text remains F. Braudel, *Civilisation and Capitalism, 15th–18th Century,* trans. S. Reynolds, 3 vols. (New York and London, 1981–1984), although there are other editions in English; this account may be contrasted with that of I. Wallerstein, *The Origins of the Modern World System,* 3 vols. (New York and London, 1974–1980), as well as with the more recent A. G. Hopkins, ed., *Globalization in World History* (London, 2002); a specific account of the economic interests of those culturally European around the Atlantic in the eighteenth century (despite the promise of the title), see J. J. McCusker and K. Morgan, eds., *The Early Modern Atlantic Economy* (New York and Cambridge, 2000).

CHAPTER 5

The Availability or Absence of Alternatives to North Atlantic Expansion

Put simplistically, if the pursuit of empire by European societies was motivated by a lust for material gain, then the cost in blood and treasure of acquiring an empire in the Western Hemisphere was demonstrably lower than that needed to assert imperial supremacy in Europe, and in some key respects likely to be more profitable in terms of the ratio of investment to return, than pursuing alternatives in other parts of the world. In this chapter, we consider some alternatives and reflect on their relative attractiveness. From the European perspective, these alternative forms of imperial endeavour were, in order of geographical proximity, first, within the European continent; second, at the margins of the European continent; third, in North and West Africa; fourth, at the margins of the Atlantic littoral; and fifth, in the south Atlantic and Asia. In addition, we give consideration to alternative models of expansion which might have characterised the experience of the peoples of the North Atlantic. In particular, we consider the significance of monopoly, and its antithesis, economic communities based on free trade.

EMPIRES WITHIN EUROPE

Between 1492 and 1763, first Habsburgs then Bourbons were liable to be characterised by their opponents as bent on pursuit of hegemony in western Europe, employing as their means shifting combinations of dynasticism and war. Denominational controversy within western Christianity recurrently lent some ideological colour to dynastic rivalry, but in essence, these may reasonably be characterised as struggles for mastery. We may describe these endeavours as imperial because of their essential multicultural and collaborative nature: as was reported of the Habsburg emperor Charles/Karl V/Carlos I, in private he spoke a different European language to each of his confessor, his wife, his secretary, and his horse, quite apart from the vernacular languages in which he spoke to his diverse subjects. More telling an illustration, perhaps, is that Felipe II's 1588 Spanish Armada against England, was made up of men and ships from all over the Iberian and Italian peninsulas, with guns and armour from Italian and German craftsmen, all of which participated in a combined operation intended to link up with land forces including Flemish-, German-, and Italian-speaking soldiers and officers, in what is now the Flemish-Walloon Belgian state. When Armada contemporaries spoke of the Empire, they meant the territories of central Europe that were bound together under the antique slogan of Holy Roman. "Real" empires, congeries of states and peoples directed by the will of a common sovereign, existed for Habsburgs and Bourbons, as well as for Stuarts and Vasas, in the lands in which they were hereditary rulers or which were governed by their dependants.

That West European monarchs entertained ambitions for the conquest of their neighbours was already evident at the beginning of the early modern period. Notwithstanding the public invocation of religious differences or historical precedents as justification, the shifting policies of the contending states invariably revealed the self-serving quality of these public reasons, and in reality naked aggression in pursuit of narrow advantage was as much the explanation in this period as it was in any other. If we consider only a few illustrations from the beginning of this period, we may see how little regard was actually paid to considerations of common cultural or economic interest, or of collective security in the face of external threats. In Iberia, for instance, the conquest of Granada completed in 1492 might be characterised as the reunification of the peninsula under Christian monarchy, which also neutralised a potential bridgehead for Ottoman expansion. In reality, this was the overthrow of a legitimate (i.e., popularly supported) regime by military might, followed by the enforced integration or migration of the conquered peoples. Instead of conciliation, in the longer-term, coercion, and persecution of the *granadino* population provoked the revolt of the Alpujarras (1568–70). In the Italian peninsula, French attempts from the 1490s to seize some of the economically most prosperous territory in Europe triggered a cycle of wars with Fernando the Catholic of Aragón and subsequently with his Habsburg heir. These struggles comprehended the extraordinary spectacle of Habsburg imperial forces sacking the Papacy's Roman centre of western Christianity (1527), before eventually reaching a peace in 1559, that only in retrospect proved lasting. In central Europe, the Habsburg dynasty took the opportunity of the defeat of the Mágyars by the Ottomans at Mohács (1526), themselves to seize Hungarian lands. The rivalries between dynastic states led to a bewildering succession of shifting alliances and leagues, and even led to alliances with the power most often characterised as the greatest threat to all of western Europe, the Ottomans: thus far could rulers in the period subscribe to the notion that "my enemy's enemy is my friend."[1]

Unlike in the Europe of Napoléon or Hitler, however, no state in western Europe in the early modern period was able to achieve, let alone maintain, a lasting military superiority over its neighbours or rivals. The military triumphs of Pavia (1525) and Mühlberg (1547) brought no permanent resolution of struggles for hegemony, any more than did the great land battles of Breitenfeld (1631), Blenheim (1704), or Dettingen (1743). During this period, size of population or access to resources did not always ensure victory, as the aphorism of Francis Bacon noted[2] and the successes of "imperial" adventures by seventeenth-century Swedish kings illustrated. Within the period there was, nevertheless, dramatic inflation in the size of European armies and of the *matériel* for their support. The need to pay for these armies, some have argued,[3] contributed to the development of states that were bureaucratised to exploit the financial resources of their populations through enlarged taxation. It is, therefore, striking that, relative to the resources employed, so little of lasting significance was achieved by such prolonged periods of warfare, and that most of the so-called successes in the struggles were attained largely by dynastic means. Over these roughly three centuries, experience should have taught that warfare on the European continent was an expensive and unreliable means by which to secure policy objectives.

In effect, early modern empires that were constructed by marriage and inheritance generally proved more robust than those created by warfare, provided that one took a sufficiently long view. Once brought together under one sovereign, the constituent parts of empires in Europe were likely to be subjected to growing demands by their sovereign for money, men, and materials to defend the imperial projects, in a primitive form of arms race with their neighbours. The burdens that these states placed on their subjects provoked a succession of crises that in many respects proved far more challenging to their regimes than did the attempts by their rivals to dismember their empires. In contrast with their ambitions for imperial expansion within early modern Europe, the experiences of the leading monarchs of the continent were that their efforts to marshal the resources to pursue these ambitions were likely to provoke crises of allegiance amongst their existing subject peoples in uprisings against crown authority, which could meld into wider conflicts as neighbours sought to exploit domestic unrest.

This trajectory of state development was demonstrated in each of the largest imperial states in western Europe, and to some extent amongst the lesser powers also. Illustrations of this may be drawn from across the whole period and the whole continent. The Danish crown provoked rebellion amongst its Swedish subjects that fractured the Union of Kalmar and led to the election of the first Vasa king of a newly independent Swedish state (1523). The pursuit of the German imperial title by the new Habsburg king of Castilla, Carlos I, provoked the revolt of the *comuneros*, Castilian and Valencian townsmen (1520–22). Successive attempts to resist the imposition of fiscal and labour dues culminated in the *Bauernkrieg* (1524–25), the "peasants' war" of the southern and central German lands. To defend their seizures of Church property and authority as sanctioned by Protestantism, German princes subscribed to the Schmalkaldic League (1531) to coordinate their resistance to the authority of the Habsburg emperor, until the political and denominational truce formalised by the Peace of Augsburg (1555). Although the French monarchy persisted in its attempts in the first half of the sixteenth century to absorb more or less of the Italian peninsula and significantly extended the size and authority of its domestic bureaucracy to increase tax revenues, from the 1560s until the end of the century, the French state was recurrently disabled by civil war, religious persecution, and political assassination. A Huguenot "state within a state" was created across the south and west and the privileges of its inhabitants guaranteed by the Edict of Nantes (1598). Attempts by the government of Felipe II to exact larger contributions towards the costs of his imperial policies provoked the revolt of the Netherlands (1567–1609, 1621–48), which became wars for Dutch independence and which, like the French experience, were given further colour by confessional differences. Austrian Habsburg attempts to reassert political authority across the German states provoked the Thirty Years War (1618–48), whilst the efforts of Felipe IV's government to take this opportunity to reassert Madrid's wider imperial authority provoked popular secessionist revolts within the Iberian peninsula, in Catalunya (1640–52) and Portugal (1640–68). French successes internationally did not save the state from the risings known as the *Frondes* (1648–53). In the first years of the eighteenth century, the grand imperial struggle of the War of the Spanish Succession/Queen Anne's War also comprehended civil war in Iberia, between the partisans of Felipe V in Castilla and those of the Archduke Karl/Charles "Carlos III" in Catalunya and Valencia (1705–14).[4] Notwithstanding the experience of insecure short-term gains and the dangers of domestic resistance to the costs, across this period substantial efforts and resources were deployed in European warfare for no lasting benefit.

War in the North Atlantic, on the other hand, taught the opposite: tiny forces of West Europeans could challenge and defeat not only "primitive" hunter-gatherer societies, but whole empires of peoples living in complex, urbanised cultures and governed by politicomilitary hierarchies. For a very modest investment of men and *matériel*, lasting changes could be effected within a single lifetime. For Europeans, however, it was crucially significant that these victories were achieved against indigenous opponents, and not in war with other Europeans. Even on those occasions when the indigenous peoples managed effectively to deploy European weapons, as, for example, in the later stages of the overthrow of the Inca Empire, the supposedly innate superiority—in weapons technology, armour, ruthlessness, and morale—of the conquistadores overcame indigenous resistance. The losers in these wars could thereafter be characterised by their conquerors as weak, uncivilised and immoral, and a tradition of West European military superiority could be cultivated (even while contemporaneous experience in Asia often suggested the opposite) because, more often than not, the European forces were simply good enough against their indigenous opponents.

War between Europeans in the Western Hemisphere, however, was for much of our period almost as unrewarding as the wars they fought in Europe, although for different reasons. From a military perspective, the chief characteristic of the Western Hemisphere was its almost limitless space. Whether by sea or on land, any position could be outflanked, if not tactically than strategically. As we have already explored in chapter 3, the costs of effective garrisoning were prohibitive, so that against other Europeans, the relatively small numbers of European military personnel could not defend every natural harbour, mountain pass, or river crossing, and local allies could be problematic. To meet the objectives of particular campaigns, specialist forces were sent from homelands, but the cost of maintaining them in idleness in the inevitable interludes in campaigns were not easily offset by trying to exploit indigenous peoples for supplies. Thus, the most effective forms of warfare between Europeans were those of manoeuvre and of the raid, rather than of occupation.

That there was so much space which, from a European perspective, was unoccupied should perhaps have encouraged a form of peaceful coexistence, for wherein lay the merit of direct confrontation where there was already more territory than could be effectively occupied and defended? This notion was in part reflected in the efforts made particularly by French, English, and Dutch expeditions to establish outposts on the North American mainland in areas remote from the Iberian presence. More immediately profitable in purely cash terms, however, were raids on the shipping and settlements of the expanding Iberian Empire, so that already from the 1520s (symbolised by the loss of Mexican treasure intended by Cortés for Carlos I, to French privateers licensed in the war between Habsburg and Valois), West Europeans seem to have begun to calculate the possible balance of strategic advantage between warfare in Europe and warfare in the Western Hemisphere. Whilst a general policy of "No peace beyond the line" was embraced in England only from the 1590s,[5] the proposition was being acted on for the previous 70 years by French as well as

English interlopers in the self-proclaimed Iberian monopoly. In turn, the government of Felipe II, when advised that it would be impossible cost-effectively to protect its American possessions from European marauders, pursued a strategic resolution of the question of its colonial security through prosecution of war in Europe, exemplified by the Armada campaign of 1588.

Central to this perception and to its perpetuation across the whole of our period was again the experience of the relative weakness of indigenous armed forces around the Atlantic. In the absence of serious military resistance to colonial incursions, Europeans could pursue their rivalries and enmities between each other, without having to give priority at all times to matters of defence against the natives. In the calculations of policy amongst Europeans contending for riches and territory around the Atlantic, the belief became established that European incursions of whatever kind were unlikely to be flung back into the sea by indigenous peoples: they were at risk of expulsion only from other Europeans. The pursuit of empire in Europe could therefore have a meaningful connection with the pursuit of empire overseas—around the North Atlantic. In contrast, contemporaneous experience of imperial endeavour in Asia showed that whereas profits might be immense, these derived not from the direct occupation of extensive territory, but through engagement with the complex systems of trade and rivalry that already existed amongst politically and militarily powerful indigenous states. Until the mid–eighteenth century and the progressive collapse of indigenous centres of power, Europeans in Asia held only enclaves and sought influence; empires came later.

The practice of pursuing wars amongst Europeans for essentially European aims around the North Atlantic owed much of its inspiration to the character of Iberian imperialism in the first century or so after Columbus's first voyage, and in particular as a consequence of the Habsburg accession to the Castilian crown. Established Aragonese interests in the south of the Italian peninsula and in the trade of the western Mediterranean had been to some extent promoted under the Catholic monarchs, whilst the Atlantic projects were largely Castilian interests, but under Carlos I/Karl V these endeavours became only some of the several vital interests contending for imperial attention. We might surmise that imperial expansion around the North Atlantic became in some way a compensation for the rebuffs to Habsburg imperial projects in Europe and that Iberian missionary work in the Western Hemisphere provided a form of comfort for the losses to the Roman Catholic communion of the lands of northern Europe to Protestantism. These views would not, however, be borne out by closer inspection of the relative sizes of forces and cash committed to the pursuit of war (or missionary work) in Europe, in comparison with the resources devoted to the pursuit of projects around the North Atlantic. Rather, the Western Hemisphere extension of the Habsburg Empire was expected by its sovereign to be a resource to be exploited for the needs of the European imperial heartland, rather than to be another liability requiring a substantial additional defence commitment. Had the western territories been more marginal in their contribution to the imperial treasury, particularly from the mid–sixteenth century, they might have been abandoned to whatever measures of self-defence their settlers could muster. Yet precisely because the Atlantic territories did contribute materially to the European empire's needs, these territories and their lines of communication inevitably themselves became targets for the empire's opponents and thus needed to be defended.

As we have already observed, practical considerations of defence in the vast open spaces in the West meant that the best way to defend the overseas empire from European enemies was by war in Europe. Such a perspective was intensified by the decision made by Carlos I/Karl V to divide his inheritance between east and west, with the ancestral Habsburg lands of central and eastern Europe passing to his brother Ferdinand, and his West European and oceanic territories bestowed upon his son, Felipe. Despite having in common the broadest of multicultural populations and recurrent concern with the Ottoman threat from the east, from this time until the end of the seventeenth century, within Europe these different portions of the Habsburg Empire were confronted by essentially different kinds of challenge, symbolised in the east by the Peace of Augsburg (1555) and in the West by the Treaty of Cateau-Cambrésis (1559). We may speculate that, if the Habsburg Empire had remained whole, including central and eastern Europe, would a successor of Carlos I/Karl V have been willing to concede territory in the Western Hemisphere as a price for secure frontiers in Europe, or to buy allies against the Ottomans?

In the east, with the Peace of 1555, Habsburg power had to decide on a response to confessional division (only partly recognised at Augsburg), amongst Protestant, Roman Catholic, Unitarian, and Orthodox Christianity, within the Holy Roman Empire and its adjacent territories. Successive Habsburg emperors had to judge the extent to which they would accommodate diversity or impose Roman Catholicism within their political and territorial programme. Significant Roman Catholic missionary endeavour proceeded with the connivance of the Habsburg crown. Allies and enemies were to be identified by their confessional labels. Any political or commercial interests around the wider world were the most minor of considerations on an agenda dominated by relations with immediate neighbours.

In the West, the Treaty of 1559 reiterated that the central challenge to the Habsburg monarchy was France. Although for most of our period at least formally Roman Catholic and so a coreligionist of the Habsburg Empires, France would ally with any state or group, regardless of denomination, that would confront Habsburg power. The obverse of this was that,

notwithstanding the public commitment to forms of orthodox Roman Catholicism, the crown in Madrid was not inhibited from prosecuting war
against the other leading Roman Catholic state in western Europe. Over
the whole of our period, French territorial expansion would progressively
seek to encompass all of the Francophone lands, including those of the
ancestral Habsburg Burgundy and within the Low Countries, up to the
Rhein River. Possessed of an extensive Atlantic coastline and maritime
resources sufficient to mount transatlantic expeditions, it was perhaps inevitable that the French crown would seek to pursue its wars with the
Habsburgs at whatever points amongst its global possessions where the
Habsburgs were found to be vulnerable. Whenever civil war within
France inhibited these maritime assaults, their English or Dutch allies (until the mid–seventeenth century) were willing to take up the challenge.
Until the War of the Spanish Succession/Queen Anne's War and the international recognition of the Bourbon succession to a united Spanish
crown at the Peace of Utrecht (1713), governments in Madrid had to confront the challenge of how to contain France.

For more than a century, the European enemies of the Habsburg Empire
sought to weaken her continental power by diversionary raids on her
Atlantic possessions. The benefits to the attackers were twofold: successful
assaults brought substantial plunder to the intruders, and even unsuccessful assaults caused the Iberian state to devote more of its military and
naval resources to defensive postures far from the main theatres of war
in Europe. Not until the seventeenth century, however, was a serious attempt made permanently to wrest control of a colony from the Iberian
monarchy. In 1630, as part of the long-term Dutch war effort against the
Iberian Empire worldwide, a Dutch expedition successfully seized Recife
and the province of Pernambuco in north-east Brasil, settled by Portugal
but at that time part of the empire of Felipe IV.[6] Although the Dutch
eventually abandoned the enterprise in 1654, allowing the territory to be
reoccupied by the newly independent Portuguese crown, the precedent
was established for the seizure of territory already occupied (and not simply that claimed but uninhabited by Europeans[7]) by another European
state.

Dutch efforts, however, were driven primarily by their estimates of the
size of immediate profit. In the Western Hemisphere, their seizure of Nya
Sverige in the Delaware valley (1655) was not comparable. The original
settlement had been sponsored by Dutch enterprise and was only refounded by Swedish and Finnish families in the 1640s, the settlement's
trading profits were extremely modest, and its real value lay in denying
opportunities to other European rivals. Around the African littoral and in
Asia, however, Dutch forces aimed to seize strategic bases founded by the
Portuguese and thereby secured control of the most profitable trades, in
commodities and people.

In the event, it was to be highly significant for the long-term transformation of the early modern North Atlantic that the state that proved most proficient at capturing other peoples' colonies was English. In 1654–55, the English republic launched a major expedition to the Caribbean with the explicit purpose of seizing an existing Hispanic colony. Although this Western Design (as it was called in the English popular press) failed against its prime objective, Hispaniola—the longest-established European colonial settlement in the Western Hemisphere—the expedition tried to make the best of its misfortunes to seize the relatively lightly defended (and sparsely inhabited) island of Jamaica (1655). The strategic and economic significance of the island was not apparent to the government of Oliver Cromwell in England, but the decision was taken in principle to retain the island (made easier by the absence of a serious attempt by the Iberian Empire to dislodge the English), even after the peace with Madrid and the restoration of the Stuart monarchy in London (1660). From the 1660s, however, the island became a haven for raiders preying on the commerce of the Caribbean and Central American colonies, a bridgehead for future wartime operations, and eventually a substantial addition to the sugar plantation economies of the English Western Hemisphere.

These benefits were only imperfectly appreciated when the next opportunity for colonial seizure was taken, this time against the Dutch, in the 1664 occupation of Neiuw Nederland, renamed New York. Unlike in Jamaica, a serious attempt was made by the founding colonial power to retrieve the territory, which was briefly re-conquered in 1673 but was surrendered again to the English in the peace treaty of 1674. In retrospect, the acquisition of the colonial territory between the Anglophone settlers of New England and of the Chesapeake seemed to be a logical step in a grand colonial project for the North American mainland, providing further opportunities for emigration from Britain. In the short-term, however, the reality was that the conquest provided an important propaganda gesture by the still-new Restoration monarchy that military and naval effectiveness were not the exclusive preserve of English republican regimes. In contrast with this colonial expansion, there had to be considered the humiliation of the English state in the destructive raid on its fleet at anchor in the Medway by the Dutch in 1667. It took almost a further century for the English, now British, state to embrace thoroughly the concept of territorial acquisition around the North Atlantic at the expense of an already-occupying European power, in Canada (conquered 1758–60), in West Africa (1758), amongst the islands of the Caribbean (1759, 1762), and Havana (seized in 1762 and returned at the peace), rounded out by the ceding to Britain of Florida in the Peace of Paris (1763).

For most of the early modern period, wars in the colonies were not necessarily wars *about* colonies. The North Atlantic and the lands around it, provided a vastly larger geographical canvas on which to pursue essentially domestic European rivalries. Colonial presence therefore had a twofold significance: the rewards of empire could be substantial in plunder and in agricultural exploitation, but colonies could also be additional venues for what were essentially European wars. Only in the Seven Years War did European states prosecute campaigns around the globe in pursuit of colonies for their intrinsic worth and rewards, and only in the Seven Years War did military victory in colonial campaigns have a determinative effect on European outcomes.

In contrast with the experiences of later periods, particularly in the twentieth century, European empires around the Atlantic did not contribute manpower or *matériel* in significant quantities to the mother countries' wars in Europe. Despite the common practice of recruiting significant numbers of soldiers from other nations, even if as mercenaries—Italians and Germans in the service of Madrid; Irishmen in the service of the English, French, and Castilian crowns; Scotsmen in the armies of France and of the northern European states; Finns in Swedish armies—and notwithstanding their military prowess, our period saw no serious effort to deploy in European theatres of operations, the indigenous forces of the Atlantic littoral. We might be tempted to speculate about a generalised reluctance to "arm the natives," were it not for the fact that in North America, in particular, the rival European colonial powers operated under no such constraint. More likely, whilst the shortage of fighting manpower justified recruitment of allies and equipping them with firearms around the littoral, there were no such chronic shortages of recruits for the armies on the European continent. Amongst the settler populations of European origin, individuals might serve in armies and navies in Europe, but there were no battalions or frigates of colonials deployed in the European struggles.

EUROPEAN MARGINS

In addition to the aggressive pursuit of territorial expansion amongst the states of the European continent, there were opportunities for "colonialism on the doorstep." The margins of the continent were defined as much by topography as by lineal distance from the metropolitan core, and by mentality as well as geography. Given also the limitations of land transport in this period, there were parts of Europe to which in practice it was more difficult to travel, than it was to cross the Atlantic.

The topographical margins were the islands, mountains, marshlands, forests, and desert in which the challenges of climate and cultivation made them less attractive prospects, unless there were other inducements. Within most European states there were territories that in previous centuries had supported larger populations. In some cases, these lands had been abandoned in the aftermath of the Black Death (from the 1340s) and had remained unattractive because changes in climate[8] as well as the collapse in populations had made more readily available, more easily productive agricultural land. With the renewed growth of Europe's population in the early modern period, however, the arithmetic of viability once again began to alter, and new settlements were founded—or refounded—which, as in the late thirteenth century, began again to push arable cultivation to the margins of altitude and fertility. Over the early modern period, however, a broad decline in grain yield ratios has been observed in much of eastern Europe,[9] so that the incentives to extend the total area of cultivation also increased.

Across the continent, recurrent increases in population notwithstanding the Malthusian checks of disease and famine, provoked different responses from those who held land and needed labour. In the west of Europe, a growth in population could undermine the premium that free, waged labour had been able to command in the century after the devastating mortality of the Black Death: more hands seeking work brought real wages down. In addition, there emerged a temptation for some who owned and worked the land to reduce their labour needs by converting to pastoralism or to seek economies of scale through enclosure: either of these developments could decrease the opportunities for work amongst the landless and encouraged migration to the places of employment opportunity and maximum mortality, the towns. In eastern Europe, by contrast, landowners sought to reduce their exposure to direct labour costs by reinforcing or re-imposing traditional dues of service, seeking to tie the rural workforce to the land as serfs.

Migration within continental Europe could take several forms. Most commonly, there was short-range relocation from rural hinterland to local urban centre, but for some migrants, distance was no obstacle, as, for example, in the recurrent recruitment of western Europeans to serve as technical experts and advisors in the Russian Empire, as well as settlers in the Volga region, particularly from the reign of tsar Pytor I the Great. Voluntary migration crossed political and cultural frontiers, such as in the numbers of humble French artisans who migrated to the Madrid region in the eighteenth century. Involuntary migration necessarily ignored linguistic or economic barriers, as in the numbers of Huguenot refugees who left France after 1685 for religious toleration in England, or the Portuguese Jews who fled to the Dutch states. For all these migrants, relocation within the continent could become attractive, without the need to confront the physical challenge and initial expense of transatlantic travel.

Economic and fiscal factors could render some naturally well-favoured locations unattractive, such as in the progressive de-population of central Castilla over the course of the later 1500s. On the other hand, mining was the spur to settlement in some otherwise unpromising regions, such as for lead in the English Lake District, for silver in the German Tirol, for copper at Swedish Falun, for mercury at Idrija,[10] because the demand for these valuable minerals could encourage the enterprising (or desperate) to confront the natural obstacles of climate and topography. In some instances, deliberate economic development opened up new areas for profitable cultivation, such as made the draining of the eastern English Fenland attractive from the 1620s, using technologies newly improved by Dutch engineers from the late 1500s.

On a map, the distant corners of Europe appear to be Ireland, the Swedish/Finnish northlands, and the western edges of the steppes. These areas were indeed targets for colonial settlement, that is, explicitly identified as preferred destinations for migrants with the deliberate encouragement by governments for their subjects permanently to transplant from the metropolitan centres to these distant territories. The Ulster Plantation (from 1608), for example, was the preferred project of the new British king, James VI of Scotland/James I of England, for the settlement overseas of enterprising Scots and English, with the dual aims of displacing the indigenous inhabitants and promoting economic opportunities for the settlers. Encouraged by Dutch entrepreneurs, the mineral- and timber-rich lands traversed by the nomadic Suomi people of Lapland were targeted by the Swedish crown for settlement across the seventeenth century, with government recruiting agents at work in the German-speaking lands, the Low Countries and Scotland, whilst from 1673, several thousand Finns were brought to Umeå Lappmark to settle the territory against the rival claims of the Danish crown. Ivan IV the Terrible and his successors promoted the settlement of Muscovites on the lands to the south and east of the central Asian peoples of the Tatar khanates and across Siberia. These efforts were as much to create security buffers as they were intended to enlarge the area of settlement and exploitation, and at the same time some of the tsars' domestic policies encouraged peasants to flee to the margins of settlement to escape the burdens of service and state terror.

The greatest challenge for the would-be colonialist was perhaps to confront the cultural margins of the continent. If the variety of European languages was the principal measure of cultural diversity, then this diversity was beginning to be compromised by the development from c. 1500 of the first true revolution in the continent's communications that was brought by the printing press. The potential for mass production of reading matter encouraged greater standardisation of the written languages, in favour of the dialects of metropolitan centres of production and government. In extreme cases, this could provoke rebellion, as for example played a part in the Western Rising (1549) of Cornish opponents to a prayer book that was not only novel in doctrine but English (not Cornish) in language. Other linguistically "marginal" societies were confronted by educational and civilising programmes designed to achieve rapid integration with the governing culture: Bretons, *moriscos*, the Gaels of the Scottish highlands and islands, the *Gwerin* (Welsh)—all were subjected to programmes of linguistic colonialism, often accompanied by missions to promote particular forms of religious observance. In contrast, whilst often motivated by a similar desire to promote Christian beliefs, in their engagements with the indigenous peoples of the Atlantic—who still greatly outnumbered them—at least some amongst West European settlers showed a willingness to render indigenous oral cultures into printed, literary versions of the native languages.

Perhaps not surprisingly, endeavours to colonise the margins of Europe met with varying degrees of success. The outcomes were not simply a direct function of the levels of investment—human and material—but instead reflected very different relative rates of return on that investment. Perhaps the most financially profitable of these colonisations was the draining of the English Fens, which quickly became the richest arable land in the kingdom, with high yields per acre and substantial growth in rental incomes for their landlords, including the crown. The cost, in strictly cash terms, was modest and the human cost as measured in lives lost was, by the standards of the period, trivial, although there was some popular resistance to the destruction of traditional lifestyles.[11] Such opposition, however, was overcome with vigorous police action, rather than requiring armed invasion and pacification.

This contrasted with the experience in the Irish projects of successive English governments—Tudor, early Stuart, but particularly republican and Orange[12]—that eventually by the mid–eighteenth century made Ireland a well-populated and productive component in the economy of the West European archipelago. The cumulative cost in blood and treasure to invade and "pacify" the island in the face of recurrent armed indigenous resistance, however, far exceeded the income returned by these projects, which were perhaps more important as means of strategic defence against, successively, Felipe II, Roman Catholicism, Cavaliers, Jacobites, and Louis XIV. In the seventeenth and eighteenth centuries, however, neither drained fens nor Irish returns per unit of land could approach the scale of profits to be enjoyed by all those participating willingly in the English Caribbean sugar islands trade, for example.

Colonial projects in the Western Hemisphere absorbed relatively small numbers of people, modest amounts of capital and, until the mid–eighteenth century, limited resources from the homelands, so that, when unsuccessful, the failures of these enterprises did not lead to the collapse of the homeland's political or economic position.[13] When they succeeded, however, the Atlantic enterprises could show enormous percentage returns which were sustained over many years. This was an ideal environment for what in the modern age we would describe as venture capitalism. The evidence for profit was real and not only imagined, for those formally excluded from it, in France, the Italian peninsula, the Low Countries, and

England. Of these, only the English possessed immediately to hand a colonial alternative potentially to rival those of the Americas: Ireland. Measured in cash and manpower, early modern England was materially more engaged with its neighbouring isle than it was with transatlantic enterprise. Nevertheless, investors pursued projects in both spheres, sometimes in tandem, to the extent that mid–seventeenth-century governments could deport Scots and Irish prisoners of war to populate Caribbean settlements. For English colonial pretensions, was Ireland like Iberia's Atlantic islands, a place to practise and perfect colonial exploitation? Or was it like North Africa, a land of beleaguered outposts where settlement was for long too great a challenge in the face of indigenous resistance?

AFRICA

With the fall of Granada and without Isabel's fateful audience to Columbus, the natural next step in the Iberian *Reconquista* might have seemed to be to North Africa. The apparent advantages of such a development were considerable and may be summarised as proximity, familiarity, and continuity. Proximity—on a clear day one might see across the Straits of Gibraltar—meant short lines of communication and supply, flexibility in the choice of sites to occupy on the coast with attendant advantages of maritime resupply (or evacuation) in the face of counterattack, and relatively simple integration into existing patterns of Mediterranean and eastern Atlantic trade. Familiarity meant an understanding of the social and political cultures with which the struggle would be pursued, awareness of the opponents' military and naval capacities and of potential allies and preparedness for the challenges of governing conquered Muslim peoples. Continuity, perhaps most important of all, meant the perpetuation of the centuries-old crusader mentality and all that implied for promoting what, in retrospect, could be portrayed as Fernando and Isabel's great project of Iberian political and religiocultural unity: the diverse societies of early modern Iberia could sink the considerable differences within and between themselves in a common cause against the Moors.

That part of the justification for exploration to Europe's south and west was to outflank Islam was acknowledged in da Gama's supposed riposte that he came to India in search of "Christians and spices." Yet Habsburg Iberia maintained what was for periods only a cold war with the Ottomans, and there was no sustained crusade, for example, to Catholicise the Maghreb. From the 1530s to 1560s, Carlos I and Felipe II despatched expeditions to the Maghreb to seize military footholds—Tunis (1535), Algiers (1541), Djerba (1560), Oran (1563)—but these attempts were never wholly successful, always expensive, and, on occasion, disastrous. Nevertheless, more than 80 years after Columbus's first voyage, King Sebastião of Portugal was sufficiently concerned with the North African dimension to launch the invasion of Morocco that led to his death at Al-Kasr al-Kebr (1578).

Iberian policy toward the Maghreb was, of course, bound up with the wider question of how West European societies were to deal with the Ottoman Empire. There was no simple or consistent position. Notwithstanding the evidence suggesting that the Ottomans sought territorial expansion in central and eastern Europe and the Mediterranean, as much in the 1680s as in the 1520s, and despite moments of particular crisis when desperate pleas from the Papacy coincided with mutual advantage to allow for cooperation, West European societies were generally at odds amongst themselves about what a later century would call the Eastern Question. Although Ottoman conquest of the Balkans brought Islam's land frontier to the heart of Europe and recurrent clashes between the invaders and Mágyar, Polish, and Lithuanian forces, yet the subjugation to Islamic rulers of Orthodox Christians did not sufficiently interest the rest of Christian Europe to inspire a new round of Crusades. Italian societies usually sought some modus vivendi to minimise interference in trade in the eastern Mediterranean and beyond, overland to Asia. French rivalry with the Habsburgs encouraged recurrent alliance with the Ottomans. German-speaking Protestants in central Europe were willing to exploit the Ottoman threat to extract concessions from their Habsburg Holy Roman Emperors. Despite the excitement across Christian Europe at the victory over Ottoman power at the battle of Lepanto (1571), there was no consequent redefinition of the balance of power between, broadly speaking, an Iberian western Mediterranean and an Ottoman eastern Mediterranean.

Although Iberia was throughout the early modern period amongst the frontline states, Ottoman power did not provoke a consistent European commitment to assist Iberia to stem or reverse an Islamic tide. On the other hand, Ottoman commitment to the extension of their conquests in the Mediterranean and Europe was not uniform across the period, which inconsistency reflected the significance for policy of the changing personalities and interests of successive Sultans and their courts. In addition, although from a simplistic, European Christian perspective, Islam represented a geographically broad and militarily powerful menace, the reality was that the Islamic societies along the eastern and southern Mediterranean littoral were generally far from united in political purposes and structures: North African city-states were at odds with the tribal kinship groups of the interior, and recognition of Ottoman suzerainty was, at the best of times, loose and contingent on clear benefits being derived by the client states.

In effect, despite opportunities during the period for the Iberian Catholic monarchy to pursue territorial expansion in the Maghreb—rather than containment—these opportunities were passed up in favour of a policy of limited engagement. At the heart of this policy, we may suggest, lay a calculation that, distance notwithstanding, conquest and settlement were perceived as easier in the Atlantic and America than in Africa. The experience of the century following Columbus's first voyage was that for very modest investment of resources—cash, military, and human—a disproportionately large return was made by the Iberian crowns, in pepper, sugar, bullion, and slaves. Although the Maghreb harboured challengers to the security of maritime trade in the Mediterranean and was feared as a possible springboard for Islamic invasion of Iberia, occupation of territory there was not only militarily challenging but could not be expected to show returns comparable to those already being received from the Atlantic islands and the New World. In the view of Andrew Hess, "the cost of absorbing the Muslim sultanates was too high relative to the cost of imperial activities elsewhere,"[14] and the measurable profits in cash continued to grow.[15]

To the south, along the West African littoral, the indigenous societies gave little indication across the period of ambitions to extend their political or economic control beyond the continent, although they were ready to pursue trade and politicomilitary alliances with West Europeans. The rewards of engagement were mutual, and the prospective and real returns encouraged all sides to compete for the best terms of trade and alliance. In contrast with their dealings with the societies of North Africa, West Europeans perceived no hint of threats to the security of their homelands, and the indigenous African societies always retained the advantage of overwhelming numbers if there were recourse to force of arms. Unlike in other parts of the North Atlantic, the potential profits of settlement were insufficiently clear to encourage significant numbers of European migrants to confront the hostility of the diverse climates and terrains of the West African littoral. For leaders in politics and commerce amongst West African societies, the profits and benefits of direct engagement in the wider Atlantic world—selling their slaves directly to Western Hemisphere plantations, or setting up their own plantations—were likewise insufficiently greater than the benefits and profits already enjoyed through the West European intermediaries: the Western Hemisphere did not possess anything that West African societies did not already have or could not already more easily obtain.

MARGINS OF THE ATLANTIC

The Faroe islands, Iceland, Greenland, Labrador, Acadia/Nova Scotia, and Newfoundland, trace a great arc of territories accessible—at least in the summer months—by the waters of the North Atlantic ocean, rich in the primary, renewable products of nature: from fish, whales, seals, and, in places, forestry. Demand for these commodities in Europe remained buoyant across our period,[16] access to these territories was in effect open, and there were few if any indigenous peoples to resist incomers. The climates were challenging, but no more extreme than those of some parts of Europe; subsistence agriculture could sustain modest lifestyles; and regular contacts with West European homelands were practicable. For West European societies seeking outlets for surplus populations; places of exile for criminals, paupers, political or religious dissidents; or largely virgin lands to occupy and populate, this northern arc surely provided opportunities.

West European societies did compete for the resources of the arc: rival fishing fleets were by turns guarded and raided by naval units of the homelands, such as those of the English and the Dutch; colonists were planted to substantiate claims to possession, such as in the Avalon peninsula of Newfoundland; military expeditions were despatched to destroy or seize strategic points, such as Port Royal (twice) or Louisbourg. These were territories judged worth claiming, settling and fighting for, but never consistently or on the same scale as pursued in the lands further south. Plantation agriculture was not attempted, slaves were not imported to exploit the natural resources, colonies of settlement for migrants were not consistently attractive, yet there were no environmental or commercial obstacles that would have rendered such efforts inevitably doomed to failure. The Caribbean islands might offer conditions favourable to sugar plantations, but life expectancy amongst settlers remained short. Tobacco plantations in the Middle Colonies became profitable, but expansion risked conflict with indigenous peoples and European rivals. New England became prosperous, and its settlers were often enthusiastic participants in expeditions to seize the more northern territories. The northern arc did not necessarily present greater challenges to West European settlement and exploitation than did other territories around the North Atlantic, so that the prospects for successful colonial endeavour were reasonable.

Yet the early, obvious, and abundant commodities to be exploited from the northern arc were superseded by the higher margins offered by another natural resource: fur. The profits of the fur trades so exceeded those of fishing and forestry—offering low bulk with high value—that exploitation of the northern interior of the western continent leapfrogged development of its shorelines. For a European adventurer, metalwares, firearms, trinkets could purchase from indigenous hunters substantial quantities of fur, for much less effort than that required to achieve enrichment from the fisheries and forestry resources, let alone farming.

If we may, for a moment, imagine a world in which the North American landmass does not extend farther south than the 49th parallel, would the story of the early modern North Atlantic be told in cod wars and rival fur plantations? If we accept that European interest in western settlement was sustained by the development of consumer tastes, beyond subsistence, then colonies around the Atlantic needed to identify commodities that would command long-term homeland interest and consumption. If we imagine the absence of the sugar and tobacco plantations of the Caribbean and North American mainland, Atlantic fish products might have provided a staple of consumption, whilst furs might have continued to command premium prices through fashion. We may then surmise that the exhaustion of the wild fur resources of the northern interior might have prompted the development of commercial fur farming, possibly sustained by fishmeal by-products of the commercial fleets on the Grand Banks. Basque and *gallego* fishing fleets were as capable of and interested in the exploitation of the north and West Atlantic waters, as were French, English, and Dutch mariners. Thus, rivalries may be presumed to be as likely to lead to raiding and armed conflict, interloper trading with settlements on the mainland, and the pursuit of European war aims in colonial Atlantic settings, as we actually see occurring in and around the Caribbean, for example. What, perhaps, might have been absent was African slavery, because there would not have been the same demands for unskilled physical labour.

In the event, the northern arc became drawn into the conflicts and rivalries of West European colonial powers only to the extent that they sought to control the major access route to the continental interior, the St. Lawrence. No attempts were made to interdict rival fishing fleets by seizing bases for privateering in either the Faroes or Iceland, the Atlantic coastal margins remained thinly populated by indigenous peoples and incomers alike, and the quality of life enjoyed by those who did settle these lands remained poor. If the spur to many adventurers in the North Atlantic was the prospect of large profits in a short period, then the south—its precious metals, its plantation products—was a more certain source than the struggle with nature in the north might promise.

THE SOUTH ATLANTIC AND ASIA

As is well known, over the course of the early modern period, Iberian colonialism profited hugely from the settlement and exploitation of territories and peoples in the Western Hemisphere south of the mouth of the Amazonas, and established bases on the African continent from the mouth of the Kongo, around the southern tip and into the Indian ocean and Asia. The maritime routes from Europe to each of these regions were also established from the early 1500s, yet the stories of European engagement with them are significantly different from each other, as well as distinct from the story of the North Atlantic.

A preliminary reading of the European engagement with south America might suggest that it was a continuation of the North Atlantic story. With more detailed scrutiny, however, we may observe significant differences over our period: competition between West European states for territory was substantially less pronounced to the south of the Amazonas than in the regions to the north, and the colonial societies established by the Iberian incomers from the 1530s, remained linguistically and culturally more numerous and politically pre-eminent into the modern age. It is striking to observe that our period saw no equivalent transformation of the south Atlantic from Iberian to Anglophone, nor the establishment of any substantial alternative European colonial presence, for example, by the French or the Dutch, even though they were contemporaneously all fiercely competitive with each other in Asia. Yet the profits of empire in South America—actual and potential—were surely as considerable as those to be enjoyed around the North Atlantic: precious metals from the interior, rich plantation agriculture on the coasts, slave trading across the ocean from Africa, diverse climates and terrains to be settled, and ecologies to be altered, in the aftermath of the devastation of indigenous populations by European pestilence. Apart, however, from a Dutch interlude around Recife, Hispanic and Portuguese colonial dominance remained largely unshaken until the era of independence movements in the nineteenth century. Only in Brasil do we see in our period the development of colonial societies and economies, comparable in wealth and demography to those of the North Atlantic.

In the Eastern Hemisphere, we see in the early modern period some limited success in colonial settlement: in Angola, around the Cape, at strategic points around the Indian Ocean, in trading stations amongst the so-called Spice Islands, and at specified locations on the fringes of the Chinese and Japanese Empires. Competition amongst Europeans for the most advantageous sites and relationships remained intense, at least amongst those small numbers of Europeans present in these regions. From the perspective of the incomers, the same incentive of enormous profits existed in contacts with the Eastern Hemisphere as could motivate engagement in the West: European consumers continued over the period to pay premiums for exotic products—not only perishable foodstuffs but also handicrafts. The Europeans' presence, however, was never in the early modern period equivalent to the numbers or power of their contemporaries in the western side of the Atlantic, north or south. Whereas the European presence—in governance, language, religion, agriculture, architecture—displaced or subordinated the indigenous forms in the Americas, in the Eastern Hemisphere, European forms were adopted where useful, adjusted when convenient, or ignored. These experiences, however, did not deter or deflect European efforts in the Eastern Hemisphere as much as they attenuated them, at least until the onset of the decline of the indigenous empires in India.

We may suggest that what particularly distinguished European engagement in the south and the Orient, from that in the North Atlantic was distance and time, which in the early modern period were effectively the same. Average journey times to and from South America and by sea to and from Asia were not so very much greater than those for the North Atlantic crossings that they became unthinkable or unendurable, but there was a distinct difference in the duration of the undertakings, which had an impact on the ways in which they were organised. For example, at Madrid's insistence the maritime link with the New World was for much of our period characterised by regular convoys across the North Atlantic, and these convoys drew cargoes and personnel to and from the viceroyalty of Peru, as well as to and from the Caribbean and Mexico. Convoys, of course, reflected concerns about exposure to possible attack by raiders or pirates, but the system was made viable by recurrent demand for volumes of traffic in goods and people that justified the assignment of such numbers of ships, just as the regular availability of capacity within the convoys itself encouraged use of the space.

On the other hand, single ships of quite modest size might reasonably undertake the North Atlantic crossing, notwithstanding some risks from weather or raiders, but such vessels were not readily deployed in the South Atlantic. Later in our period, some shipping made more routine the journey from Iberia to the Rio de la Plata and profited from an illicit trade with Peru, but voyages from Sevilla or Cádiz across the South Atlantic to the Pacific were far from frequent; more likely it was that vessels rounding Cape Horn were sent by various kinds of interlopers, rather than by authorised traders. The portage of goods across the isthmus of Panamá as the way to and from Peru remained not only customary but also attractive: it was quicker, safer, and more comfortable than the seaborne alternatives.

Sea journeys to Asia presented logistical challenges, not in kind but in extent, beyond those of the North Atlantic crossing. Transit times were significantly longer—some six months from England to Calcutta was not unusual—although there were of course opportunities for replenishment en route. Capital investment in expeditions was necessarily higher, for equipment, stores, personnel, and the bullion that was so often the only commodity in which Asian trading partners were interested. For preference, larger vessels with substantially bigger crews (to allow for ordinary shipboard mortality as well as self-defence) undertook the voyages to the East. Convoys were also employed, by Portuguese, English, Dutch, and French operators, but these were by no means as consistent in the numbers of vessels employed or in their frequency, as were operated on the North Atlantic run. Expeditions to Asia could be characterised by extended duration because delays were encountered in securing cargoes of appropriate value, volume, and perishability, even if there were only limited interruptions arising from political or military conflicts. The longer an expedition lasted, the more likely it was that the crews would be reduced by disease or desertion, with limited prospects for finding replacement hands willing to serve all the way back to Europe, without in turn reducing the crews of other vessels. We should note, however, that neither the experience nor the fear of disease prevented Europeans from pursuing adventures around Africa or Asia any more than they inhibited adventurers in the North Atlantic.[17]

For the potential colonial settler, particularly if accompanied by or intending to bring out a family, the Southern or Eastern Hemispheres presented opportunities and challenges over and above those of North Atlantic emigration. West European cultural identities were more likely to become hybridised in the colonial settlements of southern Africa, the Indian Ocean, and further Asia, because their indigenous cultures were at once more assertive in the face of European claims and more attractive to the incomers than were commonly those of the indigenous peoples of the New World. For the same reason, a proportion of those for whom a successful tour of duty in the Asian trades brought wealth were more inclined to return with their rewards to Europe, than was commonly the case amongst emigrants to the West, for whom a recognisable variant on their homeland cultural identity could more easily be created and sustained in the New World. Neither Africa nor Asia could ever be made to be—at least in the early modern period—a form of home from home, although some parts of the Portuguese Empire came closest to achieving something of this sort, for example, in Goa. The transformation of parts of Africa and of Asia into imitations of France, Holland, or England, would not occur until the nineteenth century, with its telegraphs and steamships that truly conquered distance.

MONOPOLY VERSUS COMPETITIVE FREE TRADE

The treaty of Tordesillas (1494) at the behest of a Spanish pope[18] conveniently divided the world in two for Iberia. Regardless of its pretensions to assigning sovereignty, the treaty reflects attitudes of mind to global imperialism and spheres of influence which prefigure those of Europeans in the nineteenth century: that any indigenous societies encountered need not be respected in their prior occupation of territory or integrity of beliefs; that continents could be owned, plundered, and partitioned; and that exploitation might comprehend ownership and extermination of peoples. Equally significantly, the treaty asserted a principle of noncompetition by the designation of regions of exclusive rights, thus making monopoly a further defining characteristic in the early modern model for the exploitation of the Atlantic. Within early modern European monarchies, however, monopolies were awarded in the expectation of investment at higher than usual risk: an enhanced return on some part of a venture would offset losses expected on others. Competition became confused intellectually with seizure; formal condominium, if not impossible, was extremely rare: St. Kitts in the 1620s provided a workable, if strained, example. Yet for Iberian America, exclusivity was in practice abandoned from the mid–sixteenth century, and the eventual formal transfer of the *asiento de negros*, first to France (1701) and subsequently to Great Britain (1713), merely symbolised the end of more than two hundred years of the pretension to monopoly. The reality was cooperation and trade between the subjects of different *imperia*, driven by the inability of any single part of European economies to meet the needs of the settler-exploiters and to service the purchasing market.

From the perspective of West European governments, progressively articulated over the early modern period to become what historians have labelled for convenience as mercantilism, formal monopoly remained the most attractive model of economic exploitation because uncertainty and misfortune—storms, poor harvests, shipwrecks, epidemics, wars—always posed greater risks to commercial prosperity than could purely market forces, such as changes in taste, improvements in productivity, or favourable exchange rate movements. Profits might be more likely if the risks of commercial enterprise were distributed across as many activities as possible; profits were only certain if the conditions of the market could be dictated by a monopoly provider of goods or services for which there was an inexhaustible demand. Lacking expertise and capital for development, European governments were willing to share profits with nominated, favoured individuals or consortia, who would generally further redistribute the risk and the returns through forms of subcontracting or licensing. Such forms of enterprise could only be attractive to franchisees, however, if they were offered some sort of guarantees that whatever returns were achieved would be exclusively theirs. Competition, particularly between rival providers from different societies, further undermined what were already uncertain prospects for returns on investments.

Italian and, later, Dutch societies exhibited, in the forms perhaps most easily recognised by the modern observer, the characteristics of competitive capitalism in our period. Notwithstanding the relative sophistication of their economic activities, in banking, insurance, international commodity trades, and exchange, it is striking to note how limited were Italians as direct participants in the development of the Atlantic economies. Some merchant groups within the Italian peninsula had long, mediaeval, experience of commercial and political dealings with non-European cultures, substantial technical and technological resources for maritime trade and settlement of outposts overseas, and the networks to connect extra-European commodity providers with consumer demands across Europe. All these characteristics made them important participants in Iberian exploitation of the Atlantic, as bankers to Portuguese and Castilian monarchs, and intermediaries for the onward trades across Europe in the North Atlantic's commodities, agricultural as well as mineral.

Merchants from the Italian peninsula, by and large, shared the prevailing ethos of commerce in this period, and so sought to secure and protect monopolies for themselves, as enthusiastically as did any other group. They did not, however, conceive of monopoly as only expressible through their direct participation in and control of the imperial territories, plantations, mines, and slaves, as franchisees of other monarchies. Some Italian commercial interests were served by providing the capital and credit systems to facilitate the expeditions of the Iberian societies. By these means they were no less exposed to disaster—recurrent bankruptcies and cancellation of debts by Habsburg monarchs in the 1500s had devastating consequences for Italian finance houses and their commercial dependents—and because these Italian groups did not themselves occupy colonial outposts around the Atlantic and physically control flows of commodities, they lacked means to compensate themselves immediately against such breaches of contract. Whereas we may in retrospect wonder how the history of the early modern Atlantic might have unfolded had groups from the Italian peninsula taken earlier, more prominent roles in the explorations and settlements to which their expertise and capital might have entitled them—would modern Italian now be the language of global exchange?—within the period itself, judgements that risks might best be offset by confining them to credit and cash exposure, seemed only prudent. This view may be justified by reference to the long-term prosperity of some Italian material culture and standards of living, compared with the rest of early modern Europe; this prosperity was in part built on commercial contacts, through intermediaries of various kinds, with the wider world, to both east and west.

Dutch enterprise, in contrast, did participate directly in the explorations, settlements, and exploitation of the North Atlantic, backed by technical and financial resources comparable to those of parts of the early modern Italian peninsula. That starting relatively late—a century or so after Columbus's first expedition—did not, in practice, damage prospects for Dutch success says much about the relative sophistication and determination of Dutch enterprise. Its mistake—if we may characterise it as such—was in failing to make emigration to the infant Dutch colonial outposts sufficiently attractive to encourage settler populations (perhaps recruited from the German-speaking lands) large enough to defend themselves from other, West European predators.

Neither Italian nor Dutch enterprises were fatally undermined by war. Ibero-French rivalries for hegemony on the Italian peninsula were recurrently damaging in the early modern period, but not catastrophically so, in the ways that, for example, the German lands were affected by the Thirty Years War. The Dutch wars of liberation took 80 years, a period that coincided with the societies' most spectacular economic and cultural growth. We may perhaps imagine that vigorous commercial competition around the Atlantic, between Italian and Dutch interests, might have provided more powerful spurs to the development of complex Atlantic economies, than the spurs actually experienced by Iberian or Anglophone colonialists. Instead of Iberian or Anglophone hegemony of the North Atlantic, built on numbers of settlers and military-naval presence, Italo-Dutch competitive capitalism might perhaps have encouraged forms of consumerism amongst indigenous peoples around the littoral, broader participation in emigration from societies across Europe, and an earlier onset of the kinds of exploitation and settlement that characterised the early United States, possibly also drawing on Italian and Dutch experiences of civic republicanism and religious toleration. Instead, Italian and Dutch interests chose the routes of *rentier* capitalism, allowing the economically more primitive societies of Iberia, France, and Britain to pursue their military-colonial rivalries to secure simple monopoly and direct exploitation.

CONCLUSION

Early modern West European empires in the North Atlantic, as elsewhere around the globe to which Europeans reached out, relied for their development and continuation on the participation of the willing. Notwithstanding the enormous numbers of unwilling migrants, mostly African, these victims of empire were drawn in to sustain projects that were already showing promise of profit for their willing participants. Enforced settlement by penal colonists, although experimented with by most West European governments, were not generally successful for the long-term development of colonial presence, and they often indicated the paucity of opportunity for personal advancement or profit.

Imperial projects were sustained by prospects and opportunities in the empires being more attractive than those which the adventurers or migrants expected in the homelands. Decisions by individual merchants, migrants, or soldiers to pursue opportunities overseas might derive from experiences—perhaps disappointments—closer to home: some early English settlers, for example, had tried Ireland before America.[19] The availability of alternative colonial destinations, therefore, provided constant reference points, standards of comparison by which to judge the attractiveness, relative difficulty, and likely return on the investment of human and material capital. Over our period, measured by the numbers of migrants and the growth of colonial populations of European culture, the North Atlantic and particularly its western littoral became and remained more attractive than the alternatives. Chief amongst the alternatives, of course, was to stay in the homeland, so we may attach considerable weight to the generally limited interest in direct participation in Atlantic colonial projects by the peoples of (by modern standards) the most economically sophisticated societies in early modern western Europe: the Italian and Dutch. Lacking effective centralising, authoritarian, aristocratic, monarchical, political, and social forms, these Italian and Dutch societies derived their profits of participation at one remove from the colonies of settlement pursued by Iberian, French, and Anglophone Europe. Although from the imperial perspective of 1763, their choices may seem to have been unwise, in terms of the life experiences of successive generations of early modern Italians and Dutch, the calculation seemed very sound.

FURTHER READING

For: a discussion of the development of the concept of empire as a composite or federal structure, see J. Muldoon, *Empire and Order: The Concept of Empire, 800–1800* (London, 1999), esp. chapters 1–4; a comparison of visions of overseas empire amongst major European powers, see A. Pagden, *Lords of All the World: Ideologies of Empire in Spain, Britain and France, c.1500–c.1800* (New Haven, Conn., and London, 1995); recent general introductions to early modern Europe, see R. J. Bonney, *The European Dynastic States, 1494–1660* (New York and Oxford, 1991), and D. J. Sturdy, *Fractured Europe, 1600–1721* (Oxford, 2002); a convenient, wide-ranging account of western European unrest, see P. Zagorin, *Rebels and Rulers, 1500–1660* 2 vols. (New York and Cambridge, 1982); a stimulating account of the interplay between indigenous peoples and incomers in near Asia, see R. J. Barendse, *The Arabian Seas: The Indian Ocean World of the Seventeenth Century* (Armonk, N.Y., 2002); a wide-ranging, ground-breaking account of the cultural "colonisation" of Europe in the wake of the printing revolution, see E. L. Eisenstein, *The Printing Press as an Agent of Change* 2 vols. (New York and Cambridge, 1979); a recent account that emphasises the suffering for the indigenous peoples, see N. Canny, *Making Ireland British, 1580–1650* (Oxford, 2001), but see also the review by Prof. Brendan Bradshaw in *English Historical Review* cxvii, 473 (September 2002): pp. 910–13, for a contrasting interpretation of Irish experience; a one-volume account of the Iberian interaction with north Africa, see A. C. Hess, *The Forgotten Frontier. A History of the Sixteenth-Century Ibero-African Frontier* (Chicago, Ill., and London, 1978), for the Ottoman empire in this period, see S. J. Shaw, *Empire of the Gazis: The Rise and Decline of the Ottoman Empire, 1280–1808*, vol. 1, *History of the Ottoman Empire and Modern Turkey* (1976; reprint, New York and Cambridge, 1985), and for West Africa, see J. Thornton, *Africa and Africans in the Making of the Atlantic World, 1400–1800*, 2nd ed. (Cambridge, 1998); a history of an important fishery in the north Atlantic, see the readable M. Kurlansky, *Cod* (New York, 1998); wider discussion of the Hispanic empire around the globe, see H. Kamen, *Spain's Road to Empire: The Making of a World Power, 1492–1763* (London, 2002), and for an authoritative and accessible Anglophone account of Portuguese maritime empire, see C. R. Boxer, *The Portuguese Seaborne Empire, 1415–1825* (London, 1969); a recent general account of Italian developments, see J. A. Marino, ed., *Early Modern Italy, 1550–1796* (New York and Oxford, 2002), and for the Dutch, see the monumental study by J. Israel, *The Dutch Republic: Its Rise, Greatness and Fall, 1477–1806* (New York and Oxford, 1998).

CHAPTER 6

The Push and Pull of Environmental Factors

Without wishing to invoke a narrow form of environmental determinism[1] to explain the transformation of the North Atlantic, we may nevertheless legitimately explore the possible interplay between, on one hand, the transformations in social, economic, and political relations we observe in this period and, on the other, the environmental contexts within which these transformations occurred. Were there significant or uniquely favourable environmental factors or circumstances which prompted or facilitated European settlement of the North Atlantic? Were there such or other environmental circumstances that help to explain the relative weakness of resistance amongst indigenous peoples to European settlement? Did such or other environmental circumstances constrain the contribution of African peoples, or facilitate the eventual Anglophone domination of the North Atlantic? For our present discussion, whilst acknowledging the interdependence of these environmental factors, we may explore them under the broad headings of climate, population, and natural resources. In addition, we can reflect on how the different societies around the North Atlantic responded to the environmental circumstances they confronted. To conclude, we should hope to offer some answers to our opening questions.

That beginning in 1492, there were substantial interactions between the ecologies of the eastern and western sides of the North Atlantic is beyond doubt, and there is much to debate about the relative enormity of the impacts of the transplantation, intentional and unintentional, of varieties of plants and animals, microbes, and viruses, between the Old and New

Worlds. The simplest observation we may make, however, is that human beings from Europe and West Africa were able to survive in the very different environments of the Western Hemisphere. This discovery, that the natural environments across the North Atlantic were not unmanageably hostile to them, gave experiential substance to the Judeo-Christian proposition that God had indeed bestowed command of the natural world upon Europeans, and that as a "species," Europeans were not confined to their own continent. Even if only at a subconscious level, this revelation was immensely empowering of European societies—not only in this period but also into the modern age. Overcoming the challenges of the natural world subsequently became a habit of mind amongst European and colonial societies. For the indigenous peoples of the littoral, in contrast, the experiences were of environmental transformations beyond their agency or control.

CLIMATE CHANGE

Perhaps *the* critical variable in the environment, climate had immediate impact on two vital aspects of early modern human life around the North Atlantic, as it continues to have on most of humanity in the present. Climate directly affected communications—not only for the establishment and maintenance of contact across the ocean but also for contact across the land, manifested, for example, in the limited capacity of early modern land travel for bulk goods, which in turn put a premium on waterborne—coastal and riverine—transport. Climate also directly affected (and affects) the suitability and output of land used for food production, not only in the cycles of cultivation and harvest but also with respect to determining, for example, by rises or falls in sea levels or water tables, the amount of land available and suitable for agriculture.

Even in our present age, climate variation has had substantial consequences for human development and prosperity. We see, for example, the consequences of below-average rainfall coupled with overcultivation in the midwest states of the United States in the 1930s that produced the Dustbowl. Still beyond the power of modern technologies, El Niño reminds us that even in respect of those climate events that we can regard as reasonably predictable, the scale and timing of those events can vary significantly, with dramatic consequences.

There is evidence worldwide for dramatic variations in climate but with the trend towards progressive cooling of mean seasonal temperatures and changes in precipitation patterns, from the high Middle Ages until perhaps the middle of the nineteenth century, which some experts have described as a Little Ice Age. Lower temperatures directly affected the length of the growing season, and the altitudes and latitudes at which cereal farming, in particular, could be practised effectively: "A fall of one degree

centigrade in overall summer temperature restricts the growing season
for plants by three or four weeks and reduces the maximum altitude at
which crops will ripen by about 500 feet."[2] Perhaps more significantly,
changes in the amounts, type, and timing of precipitation, reflected most
dramatically in such changes as the pattern of the monsoon or the extent
of glaciers, likewise had consequences for farming, as was recognised by
commentators within the early modern period as much as by farmers at
all times. Given that poor land communications largely determined the
maximum effective distance between urban centres and their sources of
food supply,[3] these changes in turn could influence patterns of settlement,
tending either to concentrate populations in those remaining areas of reasonable arable productivity or disperse them more widely over areas
where pastoralism had become more effective. The consequences of these
long-term changes could be extreme. In the case of European settlement
in Greenland, first established by Vikings in the more moderate climate
of the later tenth century, failure to adapt food production to progressively
harsher climatic conditions probably explains the extinction of these communities (dependent on forms of arable farming) by the early fifteenth
century, in contrast with the survival of Greenland's Inuit communities
(which depended on hunting and gathering).[4]

There is evidence that the early modern period experienced some
particularly severe climate effects, summarised in a recent account, as
follows:

... [the periods] 1570 to 1600, the 1690s, and the 1810s [were] probably the coldest
decades of the Little Ice Age.[5]

During the seventeenth century, an unusual frequency of volcanic events contributed to the volatility of climate change.[6]

Between 1680 and 1730, the coldest cycle of the Little Ice Age, temperatures plum-
meted, the growing season in England was about five weeks shorter than it was
during the twentieth century's warmest decades.[7]

That there is evidence of generally unfavourable weather coinciding
with periods of widespread political and social unrest has been added
to the ingredients of a general crisis of the seventeenth century.[8] Modern
understanding of complex weather systems at least implies that these
European experiences had correlates in the Western Hemisphere, possibly in better than average climatic conditions.[9] We may therefore en-
quire whether this connection extended to the early modern European
engagement with the Atlantic. What did the seventeenth-century freez-
ing of the Thames indicate about Atlantic currents within our period?

Although in modern times, richer northern Europeans have increasingly sought holidays and also homes in the sunnier, apparently more agreeable climates of the southern parts of the continent, it is not here suggested that climate effects, either alone or largely, prompted early modern European exploration of and emigration around the North Atlantic. Within the perspective of any individual's life experience, it is unlikely that effects of profound climate change were recognised by early modern Europeans: instead, observers in the period noted what they regarded as the significant short-term variations in climate—weather—and their immediate impact on agriculture, in particular. Awareness of these weather effects may have influenced the relative weightings of the ingredients within any individual's calculations of the attractions of emigration: greater short-term variations in weather conditions—colder winters, wetter summers, or the opposite—experienced in parts of the European homelands may have encouraged migrants to be more willing to persevere in the naturally more extreme climatic ranges they encountered in parts of the western lands. There is no doubt that in parts of the Western Hemisphere, the normal variations in weather—ranges of temperature and precipitation, incidence of storms—were and remain greater than the normal variations in parts of western Europe, even allowing for the differences of latitude. If, however, the perception of migrants was that the differences between weather extremes in the homeland and normal weather in the colony were relatively modest, then the challenges in making a success of settlement and particularly of farming may have seemed less daunting to them than the objective climate data might suggest.

At a superficial level, it might appear that the geographical distribution of West European colonial endeavours in the western lands reflected a search for environments comparable or equivalent to those experienced in the respective homelands: Iberian settlers in the southern heat, and the French, Dutch, and English in more northerly latitudes and temperate climes. Indeed, outside of the tropics, the natural variety of climate in each of their homelands (other than for the Dutch) meant that Iberian, French, and to an extent English settlers could potentially draw on their societies' existing experiences of life in climatic conditions that could be broadly comparable to those in some areas of the New World.

The major climatic challenge for settlers from western Europe was to establish themselves in the tropics. Normal ranges of temperature, humidity, and precipitation in the islands of the Caribbean, for example, were beyond the homeland experiences of Iberians, French, Dutch, English, or Scottish emigrants. Although the climates experienced on the North American mainland, particularly above 32°N, were generally of greater range than those in western Europe, they were at least clearly differentiated by season and so regularly enjoyed at least some periods of relief from extremes of any kind. Within the tropics, however, the climatic challenge for West Europeans was most pronounced. By representing these conditions as beyond the tolerance of West Europeans, a climatic justification could be proposed for the importation of West African labour, even though the prevailing climates of the principal places of origin of African slaves were not all consistent with Caribbean conditions, and certainly not consistent with mainland American climates.

If West Africans were brought to the Caribbean because they were judged to be accustomed to the climatic conditions in which they were forced to work, such could not be said of the climates to which they were brought further to the north. That in some respects there were, in retrospect, more limited numbers of West African slaves in northern colonies was not because these climates were easier or more comfortable for Europeans; rather, this reflected differences in form and extent of exploitation and profitability. In the Caribbean, the profits of sugar could readily withstand the costs of importing labour and foodstuffs. In the Middle Colonies, a balance could be struck between cash crops (principally tobacco) and subsistence farming for the workforce. In the more northerly colonies, a reluctance to employ slave labour on the same large scale reflected the more modest returns on the commerce arising from the exploitation of those regions' natural resources. If, for the sake of argument, we imagine that some activity as labour intensive as mining, for example, had become a major and profitable activity in seventeenth-century New England, then perhaps West African slaves would have been deployed there on a much larger scale.

Before the arrival of Europeans, it may be that climate effects had consequences for the development of indigenous American societies. Changes in levels of agricultural productivity, presumably arising partly as consequences of climate change and partly as forms of Malthusian check on growing numbers of mouths to feed, have been suggested as factors contributing to the decline of urbanised, agricultural societies in the lowlands of Central America—the Maya of Tikal, c. 800 C.E., for whom there is evidence of malnourishment;[10] in the Mississippi Valley around modern St. Louis—the Cahokia people, c. 1300 C.E., for whom perhaps crises of subsistence undermined the sustainability of urban living;[11] and in what is now New Mexico—amongst the predecessors of the peoples the conquistadores called Pueblos, c. 1200 C.E., amongst whom perhaps as a result of adverse weather conditions that reduced agricultural productivity, there was intensified warfare to capture the limited returns of farming.[12] In the absence of fuller indigenous accounts of the circumstances surrounding the abandonment of urban centres, environmental and particularly climatic change remain attractive explanations.

Weather effects outside the norms in the New World could be equally damaging for European settlement.[13] For example, uncharacteristically moderate weather encouraging good cereal yields could create false expectations amongst incomers about the productivity of land. Also, land clearance and cultivation in uncharacteristically wetter or drier periods could expose disafforested areas to rapid erosion when rainfall returned to normal levels. The climatic forces we still fear played their part in the early modern period; for example, the annual silver fleets were timed to avoid the hurricane season in the Caribbean and Gulf Stream, the course of the Río Grande altered as the rains came and went, and explorers to the interior of North America encountered rivers where months before were dry beds. Recognition of these challenges has led one recent commentator to conclude that uncharacteristic periods of drought contributed to the failure of the Hispanic settlement of what is now South Carolina in the 1560s and to the failure of the English settlement at Roanoke in the 1580s, which "may help explain why most people in the south-eastern United States speak English rather than Spanish."[14] He goes on to note the impact on the Jamestown settlement of drought, without drawing out the point that these challenges were generally not on a sufficiently large or prolonged scale to provoke European settlers to abandon their colonial efforts. Natural disasters linked to climate such as drought or floods or storms, when they did occur, were within the range of tolerance of the settlers of European origin so that whilst they might prompt individuals to pack up and return to the homeland, the immediate benefits or potential opportunities of colonial settlement seemingly were consistently judged to outweigh problems of climate.

CLIMATE AND COMMUNICATION

The realisation of the consistency with which the Trade Winds can take a sailing vessel west across the Atlantic by the southerly route, and the Gulf Stream return it by the northerly, injected a vital confidence into the exploration and exploitation of the Atlantic littoral that remained unchallenged until the advent of reliable long-range steam navigation. Because mean speeds of winds and currents varied seasonally, and to avoid the added dangers of the hurricane season, the transatlantic convoy route had, by the 1560s, become conventionalised as departing from Sevilla in April or May, with last landfall in the Canarias before the Greater Antilles, wintering in the Gulf of Mexico before assembling at Havana in March, for the return journey through the Florida Strait, before arcing north-eastwards back to the homeland.[15]

Notwithstanding its vital strategic importance, within only a few years of Columbus's voyages knowledge of this route became known amongst European Atlantic seafarers. There is evidence for documentary descriptions of the route circulating in the 1520s.[16] Detailed information about the most important landfalls became widely disseminated and, after all, although voyagers might wish to reach a specific destination, even with the indifferent navigation skills of captain Jones, the Pilgrim Fathers found

America was a difficult target to miss. Even in the more northerly latitudes, transatlantic crossings were regularly completed from the late fifteenth century, to exploit the riches of the Grand Banks. Fisherman from St. Malo and Bristol probably put ashore on the Newfoundland coast to smoke, cure, or salt their catches, so that at least in the summer months Europeans were likely to be found on the mid-ocean passage. A triangular trade from northern Europe to West Africa to the Caribbean and back to Europe was pioneered by Hawkins in the 1560s and, by the early seventeenth century, numbered amongst its regular users the French and Dutch as well as English seafarers, and occasionally some Swedes, Danes, and Brandenburgers. This traffic also developed a calendar, which experience taught should govern sailing dates from West European ports to the gulf of Guinea to allow an optimum crossing of the Middle Passage and a reliable passage home from American waters.

Fagan comments that throughout Europe, the period 1560–1600 was "cooler and stormier" than the twentieth century and that

storm activity increased by 85 percent in the second half of the sixteenth century, mostly during cooler winters. The incidence of severe storms rose by 400 percent.[17]

The volatility of weather, as much as its extremes, may have contributed to the adjustment of the optimum track and calendar dates for transatlantic crossings. Numbers of storm days or incidence of difficult weather, the varying southern limits of pack ice as measured at Iceland, the force and reliability of the westerly winds that brought European seafarers home from the New World—all these factors influenced journey times and the endurance of crews and cargoes. Average crossing times of around two months rendered transatlantic voyages, for the most part, reliably within the endurance of early modern Europeans, their food and water storage systems, and their naval architecture.[18] Columbus's crews had probably feared that they would not have stores enough for the return to European waters more than they had feared falling off a flat earth. Although the knowledge that the ocean vastness was bounded to both east and west did not diminish the inherent dangers of maritime travel, it could render acceptable the calculated risk involved. Journey times across the Atlantic could bear favourable comparison with some of those in the Mediterranean and were significantly better than the time needed to reach the Cape of Good Hope and far shorter than the usual time taken to reach Goa or Molucca.

Optimum journey times were achieved by exploitation of, just as successful agriculture obeyed, the rhythm of the seasons. Practical meteorology was perhaps a greater part of navigation than an ability to define one's location on the globe. Although during the early modern period patterns in the climate of the Northern Hemisphere shifted weather patterns north and south of the trend lines, communications across the ocean were never completely sundered by natural elements.

CLIMATE AND FOOD

As we have already observed, overlying long-term climatic change, of course, there remain significant short-term variations in weather that into the present age have economic and social consequences and that, in the early modern period, we may see reflected most significantly in the relative availability of agricultural staples—in general, higher food prices were a function of poorer harvests, resulting from bad weather. If we may use grain prices as a rough proxy for climate data,[19] we may see that within only the English experience, higher than average prices (and suffering for the poor) occurred in the late 1520s, the late 1540s–early 1550s, the 1590s, the late 1640s, the late 1650s–early 1660s, the late 1690s, the early 1700s, and 1739–42.[20] Across western Europe, and more immediately a function of weather, "the study of the tree-rings . . . reveals several bouts of prolonged bad weather and poor growing seasons: the 1590s, the 1620s, the 1640s and 1650s, and the 1690s."[21]

Climate factors not only influence plant and animal growth, they also affect the virulence of their pests: insects, vermin, plant or animal diseases. During the early modern period in Europe, the interplay of these factors was even more significant because, in addition, they affected provision for storage between harvests and the quality of seed available for the following year's planting. Decisions about whether to store supplies in grain pits or in granaries and barns, for example, depended on judgements about the commitment of resources needed to create and maintain these different modes of storage, relative to the risks of storage failure: pits may preserve grain more securely against vermin and are more likely to maintain low temperatures but may leave seed vulnerable to damp; granaries, although costly to build, can be accessed and monitored more easily, but supplies may be adversely affected by extremes of weather or by infestation.

There are, it should be noted, no easy correlations between periods of poor harvests (and by implication poor weather) in western Europe and flows of emigrants to the North Atlantic. To consider again only the English case, although periods of poor harvests could coincide with political unrest, for example, in the late 1540s and early 1550s, it is notable that despite the appalling harvests of the 1590s and the contemporaneous stories of deaths from starvation, there were no serious domestic rebellions against the Elizabethan regime at this time. By contrast, although the 1630s saw significant growth in English emigration to the New World, the harvests in these years were within the range regarded in retrospect as normal. In other words, weather and its correlate, agricultural productivity, provided only part of a background to decisions to emigrate. Famine in early modern Europe did not on its own spur transatlantic travel, but it set a different context in which to measure the environmental challenge posed by life in the Caribbean or mid-Atlantic seaboard, compared with life in La Mancha or Lincolnshire.

Famine in early modern Europe could arise in very local circum-stances,[22] not necessarily related to weather but simply as a function of poor distribution, and governments of towns as much as of states were sensitive to famine's effects, if not motivated only by charity then out of fear that famine might provoke disorder. The security of food supplies was therefore an established concern of government at every level in west-ern Europe[23] which in some societies—notably, France—lasted until be-yond our period. It has been argued that in places, European agricultural practices improved and diversified during the early modern period, and with them so did food security, particularly for Dutch and, later, English societies.[24] Yet the easing of subsistence pressures in England was not accompanied by declining interest in New World emigration. On the other hand, French peasants continued to suffer from dearth, causing falls in population in some areas,[25] and (it is argued)[26] long-term food insecurity contributed significantly to the outbreak of the French Revolution. Yet French migration to the New World remained modest throughout the period.

Over the course of our period, in some of western Europe the incidence and degree of subsistence crises eased, notwithstanding rises in popula-tion, not least because of the development of and expansion in the move-ment of grain supplies from the large-scale production areas of eastern Europe, encouraged by the growing wealth of West European economies as a consequence of their trade and empires. We should recall that the economics of international food supply were not favourable to the trans-atlantic shipment of food staples until the nineteenth century, but whilst there was not yet enough of an incentive to pursue colonisation as a source of food for the homeland, colonies at least potentially could become rem-edies for food shortages by becoming destinations for the motherland's surplus hungry mouths.

Certainly, in the long-term the food security of West European societies was significantly enhanced by the introduction of new crops to augment the staples, particularly cereals. Perhaps the greatest trophy of the Euro-pean conquest of the New World was the potato, not least because of its adaptability to a wider range of climate and soil conditions, its tolerance of lower temperatures and higher precipitation, and its higher yields per unit area of cultivation, than the traditional European cereal staples. But this must be numbered amongst the unintended consequences of the Eu-ropean settlement of the West, and in any case was a product of the Iberian conquest of the Americas farther south than we are considering in this study. We may not argue, then, that the needs of European food security either prompted or were satisfied by the colonial efforts in the North Atlantic.

In the New World, the search by European colonists for food security may be described as having two successive phases. In the first, incoming Europeans and, to some extent, their slaves were reliant on indigenous agriculture (not least because of the expense of regular supplies from the homeland), obtained either by expropriation of the native peoples' foodstuffs or by exploiting surpluses that continued to be generated in the aftermath of conquest. The dramatic fall in the numbers of indigenous populations then overlapped with the transformation of agricultural practice in favour of European farming techniques and products. These in combination allowed extensive agriculture to supersede intensive agriculture, whilst falling populations eased demand. Towards the end of the 1500s, food prices rose for the colonists in Mexico, but these were consequent on declining numbers of indigenous labourers and overgrazing, rather than strictly the result of climate effects.[27] Famine was, notoriously, experienced by English settlers in their earliest years in the Chesapeake and in New England, and in the short-term this was mitigated, by turns, through native charity and settlers' theft. For the majority of European settlers over the whole period, however, food security was not a long-term challenge because subsistence was achieved either by regular trade with indigenous neighbours or by successful adaptation to local agricultural conditions through the adoption of some indigenous food staples and the introduction of livestock. In the second phase, and particularly for the benefit of the mines of northern Mexico and for the island plantations, there developed significant commerce in agricultural foodstuffs between the Europeans' western settlements. Carts and mule trains moved large volumes of supplies to the northern mines over the flat lands of the Mexican *altoplano*. Sea- and river-borne transportation of foodstuffs in bulk, between colonies rather than between a colony and its motherland, allowed for the amelioration of local shortages arising from adverse weather or poor agricultural practice.

Between West Africa and the western colonies, transfers of food plants brought significant opportunities in agriculture. It has been argued that the introduction of native American crops enhanced food security in West Africa sufficiently to allow for sustained growth in population, notwithstanding the depredations of the slave trade. On the other hand, famines in West Africa and the interior could act as incentives to export people to avoid exposure to subsistence crises. We have already observed that, notwithstanding the availability of land and labour, West Africa did not in this period develop plantation agriculture in the products that became so much demand in Europe; a similar missed opportunity was that West Africa did not participate in volume trading in foodstuffs, either to export any surplus to the slave islands of the Caribbean or to offset the effects of poor harvests at home.

Agriculture is, of course, not the only form of food production. Fishing in fresh- and seawater was a significant component of diets across early modern Europe, and not only in coastal or riverine areas, nor only in Roman Catholic societies. Climate effects did influence long-term changes in the size and location of fish stocks in the seas near Europe and thus encouraged the pursuit of new fishing grounds across the North Atlantic, with consequent lessons in long-range maritime travel for the participating societies. Fishing and whaling later became important commercial activities for the northern colonies in the New World, with the attendant encouragement to local shipbuilding, outfitting, and supply, as well as navigation. Climate factors were relevant to the movement of shoals and hence of their fishermen, and fishing could provide another remedy for food scarcity, but fishing's productivity varied significantly and unpredictably in the short-term, not necessarily in step with climate effects on agriculture. There is little to suggest that fishing activity was able to expand significantly in periods of poor harvest, and fishing would not (because of its inconsistency of returns) have provided a sufficient spur to create colonies around the North Atlantic unless its profits could have been significantly raised. Rather, deep-sea fishing encouraged practice in the techniques that facilitated empires motivated by other rewards.

Around the littoral, the impact of climate change on food production was to a considerable extent masked by other substantial changes. Epidemic disease removed mouths to be fed but also the labour to produce the food. European crops and livestock—and pests—radically affected the landscapes and diets of indigenous peoples, for example, in the introduction of meat, dairy, and wheat products. Horses and firearms altered the patterns and intensity of hunting. The impact of these changes were immediate and lasting, beyond the subtler and slow-burning consequences of climate effects.

POPULATION

Contemporaneous with the discovery and first exploitation of the North Atlantic, Europe experienced renewed population pressure as it progressively emerged from the long-term consequences of the Black Death of the fourteenth century. That these might be independent variables is not incompatible with the observation that although population pressures may have provoked inflation and famine in Europe, this seems at odds with the Atlantic's potential to provide in effect a limitless resource for early modern Europeans. How far did real or imagined demographic growth rates spur efforts to exploit the Atlantic? What potential lay, realised and unrealised, in exporting surplus population from Europe? What were the consequences for (voluntary and involuntary) European and (enforced) African migration, of the catastrophic demographic experiences of the indigenous peoples of the New World? How are we to understand the epidemiology of disease, on either side of the Atlantic? In our consideration of these issues, we should note the recurrence of anomalies.

At a simplistic level, we may regard the classical motors of population movements as taking effect as population increase exceeds the resources available to sustain it, or as catastrophic events—pestilence, war—undermine an existing balance between numbers and resources. In the early modern West European context, overall numbers grew substantially in relative terms, provoking social and economic dislocation and reconfigurations, but in absolute terms broadly only to recover numbers lost in the demographic catastrophes of the fourteenth century.[28] The early modern period also experienced catastrophe, of which perhaps the Thirty Years War had the most prolonged destructive social and economic impact over the widest geographical area. Yet we do not see substantial numbers of central European refugees seeking to flee to new lives in the Atlantic, notwithstanding opportunities to do so. In retrospect, the substantial demographic changes of the nineteenth century were more closely interconnected with colonial migration than were the changes in the early modern period. Within our period, population movements, yes; but movement overseas was not the only nor necessarily the preferred option.

Amongst West African societies, there can surely be little argument that slavery constituted a substantial haemorrhaging of the demographic resources of the region, over an unprecedentedly long period. Despite the horrors of the millions of individual tragedies, populations in West Africa did not, as a whole, collapse, through any or all of flight, family limitation, infanticide, or abstinence, all of which we see amongst the indigenous peoples of North America in reaction to the West European incursions. We have some important quantitative information about life expectancy and mortality amongst the millions of these enforced migrants, but we lack comparable detail about the demographic fortunes of the peoples who, whether enslaved or not, remained in West Africa. Stripped of the vital sparks of emotion and compassion, and expressed in narrowly statistical terms, were the environmentally determined life chances of staying in West Africa better or worse than those of enslavement? Was slave society, although infinitely cruel, a means of survival more dependable for a group than the prospects in West African landscapes?

Notwithstanding the growth in numbers across the period, the most densely populated regions of western Europe were not, for the most part, the places of origin of significant numbers of emigrants to the Atlantic lands. In particular, parts of the Low Countries and of the Italian peninsula, urban as well as rural, supported population densities that grew and remained significantly in excess of those found in the major people-exporting countries in Iberia or Britain outside of London. Pre-eminently, Portugal saw an annual average of perhaps 2,400, mostly young men, emigrate to her imperial outposts around the world during the sixteenth century,[29] from a home population of perhaps 1.5 million c. 1530.[30] In practice, such early modern commentators who voiced concern about population sizes tended to do so because of their worries about unemployment and the rise of begging, rather than because of fears of undue pressure on land areas or resources. Indeed, progressive declines in yields from arable agriculture in southern Europe occurred in regions with dense urban populations, without provoking urgent calls for substantial emigration. As we have already observed, population movements within European societies were far greater than those from western Europe to the littoral.

Despite the enormous land area of the Atlantic littoral, immigrant populations were willing to concentrate to extraordinary degrees, where and when economic advantage encouraged them; at four hundred people per square mile, "In 1700 the human concentration on Barbados was four times greater than in England."[31] Although the single greatest resource, space was not necessarily the pre-eminent attraction of the North Atlantic colonial life, and by no means were all migrants land hungry, seeking to become independent freeholding farmers or proprietors. Land grants were certainly attractive to those with the skills to exploit them, but few migrants were willing to try farming without either some sort of relevant experience or control of appropriately skilled workforces, whether indigenous or slave. Occupational profiles in colonial communities quickly reproduced versions of the specialisms of the homelands, including the multiple and seasonal trades of Europe, to which the availability of land might be only incidentally significant.

Given the availability of considerable variety, we note that European settlers (with their slaves) did not always choose to reside in the most immediately hospitable environments around the Atlantic. The coastal jungles of the isthmus of Panamá were profoundly hostile, yet the importance of the traffic in bullion and goods from and to Peru sustained the settlement of Puerto Bello long after more tolerable alternatives could have been identified. Despite the harshness of the landscape in comparison with other parts of the region, Iberian settlers—admittedly in very small numbers—were willing to occupy the territory of what is now New Mexico, to which projects resistance amongst the indigenous peoples arose only after some 80 years of colonialism. Economic and political considerations could take precedence over propitious demographic circumstances, yet the inhospitable but valuable environments were not designated to be occupied only by the peoples of lowest status and least freedom to choose, criminals or slaves.

Life expectancy was not necessarily improved by emigrating to colonies. We have already remarked on the heavy mortality amongst the earliest West European settlers, and we have noted the continual and tragic loss of lives amongst slaves brought to the New World. In certain places and for certain categories of colonial inhabitants, however, the demographic prospects did become measurably better than those of the homelands. In New England, exceptionally, natural increase of earlier arrivals, augmented by newcomers, expanded the population far more quickly than in the English Caribbean. Over the seventeenth century, some 69 percent of English emigrants went to the West Indies, but fearsome mortality meant that, in Barbados, it took approximately 150,000 immigrants to produce a population of 20,000, whereas in Virginia, approximately 116,000 immigrants produced a population of 90,000. In general, however, colonial mortality rates could be comparable with those of societies in western Europe, particularly if one compared them with urban mortality.

Possibly one-quarter of the population of London perished in the plague of 1563, when the death rate was seven times higher than in normal years. Although 1665 became known as the year of the Great Plague, in fact proportionately more people died in the outbreaks of 1603 and 1625; together the epidemics of these years caused the death in London of up to 200,000 people. The outbreaks in Amsterdam in 1624, 1636, 1655 and 1664 are estimated to have removed respectively one-ninth, one-seventh, one-eighth and one sixth of the population. In Uelzen (Lower Saxony) the plague of 1597 carried off 33 per cent of the population, whereas a dysentery epidemic in 1599 killed only 14 per cent. Santander in Spain was virtually wiped off the map in 1599, losing 83 per cent of its 3000 inhabitants. The great "Atlantic plague" of 1596–1603, which gnawed at the coasts of western Europe, possibly cost one million lives, two-thirds of them in Spain alone. In France between 1600 and 1670 plague carried off between 2.2 and 3.3 millions. Mantua in 1630 lost nearly 70 per cent of its population, Naples and Genoa in 1656 nearly half of theirs. Barcelona lost 28.8 per cent of its population in the plague of 1589 and about 45 per cent in that of 1651. Marseille lost half of its people in 1720.[32]

Basic health care and public sanitation to protect the purity of water supplies, perhaps the two greatest contributors to demographic prosperity, were as haphazard and variable around the Atlantic as in western Europe, even though the pre-Columbian populations of Mesoamerica, for example, had sustained substantial urban concentrations without, apparently, recurrent catastrophic mortality. Endemic diseases amongst Europeans and their colonists included strains of malaria, influenza, as well as any number of waterborne infections. By comparison—and quite unforeseeably—the new risks to Europeans' health presented by the Atlantic environments were incremental rather than catastrophic. In health terms, nowhere around the Atlantic was declared too dangerous for European penetration, whereas as many as one in three Europeans arriving in Asia did not survive their first monsoon season.

What did distinguish the demographics of the littoral from those of the homelands was intermarriage across cultural and linguistic groups. Attitudes to what some characterised as miscegenation varied across the period and around the Atlantic. Amongst some groups of West European origin, so-called mixed marriages were those between Protestants and Roman Catholics, whereas in other circumstances, marriage between incomers (overwhelmingly men) and indigenous (women) were encouraged if accompanied by conversion of the latter to Christianity. Hostility towards unions between incomers and indigenous was perhaps most pronounced amongst the Anglophone settler societies of New England, in which the prejudice could be indulged because of the demographic prosperity enjoyed by the immigrants. In large part, attitudes to intermarriage were culturally specific, rather than responses to the particular demographic circumstances or relative opportunities to create new, mixed families and identities.

CULTURAL RESPONSES TO ENVIRONMENTAL FACTORS

In many of the indigenous cultures around the Atlantic and particularly in the Western Hemisphere, the practices of living in balance with nature were more advanced than were judged attractive or necessary in the views of early modern West European cultures. Nevertheless, in some parts of the Atlantic world, pre-Columbian agriculture was able to support substantial populations without provoking the worst Malthusian checks. There were also closer commitments than amongst many West Europeans to the idea that nature expressed divine views of life. Amongst some societies, there was already before the European invasions commitment to the capriciousness of gods that needed to be propitiated, so that catastrophes—through war, famine, pestilence—were divine judgements that destroyed morale and could be cited in longer retrospect as explanations of failure to put up more resistance. When European diseases destroyed populations, they did not destroy the capacity of indigenous agriculture to support larger numbers of people, nor were the numbers of incomers so great that they could effectively occupy all of the available agricultural land. In contrast with the reaction of the survivors of the European Black Death, agricultural labour did not become mobile and prosperous by exploiting the shortages of workers, nor was the availability of land exploited to raise consumption per capita. Instead, indigenous cultures began long and painful retreats in tacit acceptance of a subordinate status, whereas West European assertiveness was encouraged by each new advance and was resilient in the face of every reverse.

For the European conquerors and settlers of the North Atlantic, the most significant environmental factor they encountered was the scale. Within the experience of the early modern European mind—as also for the modern European visitor to the western lands—the seas, the rivers, the valleys, the mountains, all are larger, longer, broader, higher than most of those in the West European homelands. Yet the practical experience of these environments on the western side of the Atlantic was that the physical barriers of oceans, jungles, deserts, forests, and mountains were overcome not only by intrepid explorers, but also regularly thereafter by settlers and traders. In addition, the scale of the New World environments seemed to promise that to all practical intents their natural resources—animal, vegetable, and mineral—were inexhaustible in extent and usability, far beyond the limits of the European homelands. The natural environment ceased to be the major obstacle to endeavour, but instead became a resource on a scale far grander than anywhere in western Europe. Only on the smaller islands of the Caribbean were there clearly limits to the environments' riches, defined simply by the geographical extent of the land available for settlement. That there was always something more to be exploited, just over the horizon, became a presumption of the colonial mind.

The consequences of this different scale of perception were cumulative, in terms of the moulding of a distinctively North American cultural sensibility. It is difficult to suggest with confidence a date by which such a perspective was common amongst settlers of European origin, but we may characterise it as foreshadowing some commonplace features of a modern American sensibility: for example, an everyday indifference to distance when contemplating any journey or the presumption of achievability when pursuing any project—a can-do attitude to any undertaking. Lack of success in any project was no longer to be ascribed to the size of the challenge but to the weakness of the commitment to its achievement. Nothing was too difficult, too hard to achieve, if there were sufficient commitment to success. This sensibility also manifests itself in a struggle with the forces of nature on a much grander scale than commonly seen in western Europe or perhaps also in Africa. No environment is too hostile or uncongenial—too hot, cold, dry, or wet—if there are otherwise good reasons to inhabit it. This is particularly striking when we recollect that whilst the mainstay of the modern North American engagement with natural forces is technology—artificial heating, lighting, air-conditioning, drainage—such technology is of very recent origin. For some four hundred years of colonial settlement up to 1900, those of European origin did not possess the means to render their lives any more comfortable than the lives of their West European ancestors.

CONCLUSION

We now return to the questions with which we began this chapter. Were there significant or uniquely favourable environmental factors or circumstances that prompted or facilitated European settlement of the North

Atlantic? In practice, West European conquerors and settlers were never deterred by challenging environmental factors, at least in the Western Hemisphere. Depending on the vantage point one adopts, this may be interpreted as either a lack of significant environmental obstacles, or a greater determination on the part of conquerors and settlers to overcome such obstacles, than were encountered elsewhere in early modern European expansion around the globe. On the other hand, no West European society suffered from environmental problems on such a scale that they provoked either initial exploration or subsequent migrations of people. The environmental pressures of climate change, famine, or population pressure were not sufficient by themselves to make life in the early modern Old World overwhelmingly miserable enough to prompt migration across the ocean. Instead, unlike West Africa or parts of Asia, the Atlantic environment to the west, although not benign, was not overwhelmingly hostile, and this facilitated European enterprise in the region.

Once deployed across the Atlantic, West Europeans were able relatively quickly after first arrival to come to terms with the environments of their new settlements. In some places, they were able to transform an environment to one more to their liking, as in the creation of plantations or large-scale livestock farms. In others, they adopted just enough of the ways of the indigenous peoples to construct an ecological compromise between the familiar and the exotic. For their (and our) future, the vital lesson so quickly learned by Europeans was that, just as the indigenous peoples of the Atlantic had been mastered, so also the natural environments could be mastered, and with more profit than the Europeans judged to have been achieved from nature by the indigenous peoples.

Were there such or other circumstances that help to explain the relative weakness of resistance to European settlement amongst indigenous peoples? Before the Europeans arrived, with the exception of the inhabitants of the central valley of Mexico, indigenous peoples were by and large already at the limits of their environments' capacity to sustain them. Within a model of sustainable development, there were no incentives to upset the prevailing balances between population densities and ecologies. These balances, however, left the indigenous societies with no options when the arrival of Europeans, their animals and their pathogens, disrupted the native ecology. Some indigenous communities adapted to the ecological revolution and thereby sustained some of their traditional culture—the Dineh of what is now the southwest of the United States, adopted the animals of the incomers to become not only pastoralists but also the fearsome warriors called Apache by Hispanic settlers. Otherwise, those indigenous peoples who survived the crisis mortality of European diseases were absorbed into European models for the exploitation of the natural environment, using the Europeans' metal ploughs and axes to till the soil and clear the forests and the Europeans' livestock to revolutionise their diets.

Did such or other circumstances constrain the contribution of African peoples? West Africans were regarded by Europeans as well adapted to the climates, if not the whole environments, encountered in the Caribbean and southern parts of North America. If this were true, then West African peoples should steadily have displaced the Europeans by the arithmetic of superior rates of individual survival and collective reproduction. In reality, African slave emigrants were no better fitted physiologically to the New World environments than were West Europeans, as the population dynamics of free peoples of African origin in the New World suggest. Instead, the environment of climate, agriculture, and disease in West Africa permitted the demographic prosperity that fuelled the growth and maintenance of the Atlantic slave trade. That demographic prosperity was sustained because the annual export of human beings offset the intervention of Malthusian checks that would otherwise have limited population growth in West Africa. Famine was a function not only of poor harvests, but of too many mouths to feed. Horrifically cruel to individuals, the slave trade may have enhanced the prospects for survival of West African societies by keeping resident population numbers within the local agricultural productivity's limits of tolerance of the normal incidence of adverse climate and poor harvests.

Were there such or other environmental circumstances that help to explain or facilitate the eventual Anglophone domination of the North Atlantic? Amongst the European societies that pursued opportunities for colonial expansion around the Atlantic, as a proportion of their homeland population, more Anglophone colonists than those of other West European societies perceived their domestic circumstances to be sufficiently poor to motivate migration. Yet in their homelands, the Anglophone colonists did not suffer more or deadlier famines, nor greater numbers of natural climate disasters, nor more frightening plagues. We must therefore look elsewhere than the environment for explanations of the emergence of an Anglophone domination of the North Atlantic.

FURTHER READING

For: starting points in the established historiography of ecological transformation, see, for example, A. W. Crosby, *The Columbian Exchange: Biological and Cultural Consequences of 1492* (Westport, Conn., 1972), A. W. Crosby, *Ecological Imperialism. The Biological Expansion of Europe, 900–1900* (Cambridge, 1986/1993), and J. Weatherford, *Indian Givers: How the Indians of the Americas Transformed the World* (New York, 1988); a classic introduction to the study of climate's role in historical developments, see E. Le Roy Ladurie, *Times of Feast, Times of Famine: A History of Climate Since the*

Year 1000, trans. B. Bray (New York, 1971) or H. H. Lamb, *Climate, History and the Modern World* (London, 1982), and for a recent convenient synoptic account drawing on much of the recent scholarship, with limited technical material and some further bibliography, see B. Fagan, *The Little Ice Age: How Climate Made History, 1300–1850* (2000; reprint, New York, 2002)—whilst acknowledging the importance of climate effects around the globe, this account is generally focused on West European experiences, so see also the thought-provoking theses in G. E. Brooks, *Landlords and Strangers: Ecology, Society, and Trade in Western Africa, 1000–1630* (Boulder, Colo., 1993); more specific topical coverage, see, for example, E. G. K. Melville, *A Plague of Sheep: Environmental Consequences of the Conquest of Mexico* (Cambridge, 1994), R. H. Grove, *Ecology, Climate, and Empire: Colonialism and Global Environmental History, 1400–1940* (Cambridge, 1997), R. I. Rothberg and T. K. Rabb, eds., *History and Hunger* (Cambridge, 1985), K. F. Kiple, *Cambridge Historical Dictionary of Disease* (New York, 2003), and K. F. Kiple, *The Caribbean Slave. A Biological History* (Cambridge, 1986).

CHAPTER 7

1492–1607: From the Halls of Motecuçoma to the Lodge of Pocahontas

From the perspectives of contemporaneous as much as of modern observers, the creation of a Hispanic empire in the North Atlantic during the sixteenth century was simply awesome.

> When has it ever happened, either in ancient or modern times, that such amazing exploits have been achieved? Over so many climes, across so many seas, over such distances by land, to subdue the unseen and unknown? Whose deeds can be compared with those of Spain?[1]

As an observer on the winning side, Xerez was perhaps understandably enthusiastic about the achievements of his compatriots, but amongst the defeated and dispossessed, there was an equally profound appreciation of the enormity of the changes that overtook the societies and cultures of the Mesoamerican and African quadrants of the North Atlantic. Notwithstanding the extraordinary exposure to and interaction amongst societies and cultures all around the littoral, this period was, for all intents and purposes, the Iberian century.[2] Our efforts to understand this part of the story of the North Atlantic may perhaps be resolved into two broad questions: how did Iberian imperialism interact with the peoples it encountered, and was there something particular to the nature of Iberian imperialism that gave it the pre-eminence it so rapidly achieved?

Associated with these two broad questions, of course, there are numbers of dependent issues that we should explore. Although this became the era of the catastrophic collapse of the social forms, much of the culture and of the demographic prosperity of the indigenous peoples of the Caribbean and Mesoamerica, why, given the gross disparity of numbers and resources on each side at first contact, were the Iberian conquerors able to seize control of the North Atlantic lands from their indigenous peoples? Why were pre-Columbian peoples swept aside and so relatively quickly condemned to the margins of land, status, and power?

During this period also there began the enforced permanent transplantation of West African peoples to the Europeans' New World. Could this transplantation have been resisted? Alternatively, could African peoples have crossed the Atlantic independently and voluntarily joined in the exploitation of the western lands, and, if so, how would this have changed the trajectory of succeeding developments? Why were Africans so important in the development of the Iberian empire?

What, then, were the essential characteristics of the period of Iberian pre-eminence? Were these characteristics inevitable or inescapable, or uniquely attributable to the Iberian origins of the first European conquerors? Did these characteristics determine how the rest of the Atlantic story would unfold? Although from a West European perspective this was an Iberian century, a would-be monopoly from which other Europeans were to be excluded, why, given the attractiveness to other European societies of the rewards of the North Atlantic empire, were European rivals so ineffective in their challenges?

How may we assess the impact—or impacts—of the Iberian century on the other societies around the Atlantic littoral? We might attempt to compare the proportions of populations affected by developments in this period, with a scale ranging from entire populations changed beyond recognition, down to minorities experiencing effects limited to particular aspects of daily routine. In such terms and viewed from c. 1600, those proportionately most affected were the peoples in the Atlantic and Caribbean islands, and thereafter, in descending order, those in Mesoamerica, West Africa, and, least of all, in western Europe beyond Iberia. On the other hand, if we try to measure impacts by reference to absolute numbers of people touched in any way by these developments in the sixteenth century, we might reorder the sequence to be largest in western Europe, then Mesoamerica, West Africa, and, lastly, the islands. Whatever arithmetic we may try to employ, however, cannot fully capture the individual tragedies of millions—and triumphs of thousands—of people across the Western Hemisphere.

PEOPLES OF THE ATLANTIC

In the North Atlantic, the islands of Iceland, the Açores to the west of Portugal, Madeira, and the Canarias off the north-west coast of Africa, and the Caribbean archipelago were at least symbolically, if not always literally, the crossroads for the New and Old Worlds. By the early sixteenth century, the islands in microcosm portrayed two models of possible development, showing how far West Europeans might depart from the norms prevailing in their early modern mainland civilisation.

Chronologically speaking, the first model was that of the virgin land. Although discovered centuries apart, Europeans found Iceland, the Açores, and Madeira likewise uninhabited. Settlement was initially driven by a search for economic self-improvement, rather than strategic advantage or communication needs. Modest self-sufficiency was possible, but in each of these islands settlers devoted much effort to exploiting for trade the natural resources—in the first stages, respectively, fish, pasture for sheep, and timber. Notwithstanding distance, these island economies were developed beyond subsistence to some dependence on West European markets for the export of their products.

In the Canarias and Caribbean, a second model was adopted because of the crucial difference that these islands were already inhabited. Castilian "discovery" led to the attempted enslavement and subsequent progressive elimination of the indigenous inhabitants. In the Iberian peninsula, "aliens" were exploited, as in the *encomiendas* of post-Reconquest Granada; expelled, as with Jews from 1492; or forcibly relocated, as were *moriscos* after 1570. In these islands, *encomiendas* failed and eventually wholesale repopulation was effected by the settlement of West Europeans and West Africans, not by displacing the Guanches and Amerindians to remote or inhospitable locations within the islands, but by comprehensively superseding them. By no means only passive victims, the island peoples nevertheless failed either to match the violence of their conquerors or to compromise and integrate with them, but were instead subsumed by them. Much less than on the American mainland, there remains little modern evidence of a distinctive mestizo mentality to commemorate the crossing of ethnic and cultural boundaries in the islands by Amerindians and Europeans. In no other part of the North Atlantic experience were the consequences of European contact so proportionately devastating to aboriginal peoples, and nothing comparable would be seen elsewhere in the world until nineteenth-century Australia or twentieth-century Amazonia.

Along with ethnic went economic reconfiguration of the islands. In the Caribbean, once the early returns of precious metals diminished, Iberian settlers turned to the Portuguese plantation model, already copied in the Canarias. The indigenous peoples' limited subsistence agriculture mixed with hunter-gatherer techniques were superseded by more intensive forms of exploitation intended not only to feed the new residents but to support economic ties with Europe. The island landscapes were progressively transformed by clearance, livestock, and the creation of field systems to facilitate in some instances a plantation near-monoculture. Serving a European heartland, the islands conformed most nearly to Wallerstein's modern world system[3] in a truly colonial relationship: the subsistence needs of inhabitants often took second place to cash crops so that basic consumables were still imported to the islands at the end of the sixteenth century. Although "perfected" from the seventeenth century in the sugar plantation economies dominated by the English, this model of exploitation, including the use of West African slaves, was devised in the islands of the eastern Atlantic and transplanted to the Caribbean.

We have already noted that the earliest Iberian visitors to the Caribbean islands recognised amongst the peoples they encountered little or no evidence of lifestyles much above subsistence. The incomers applied tests of material culture, urban life, political organisation, and architecture (tests of the kind that Marco Polo, for example, had reported as being easily passed by societies in Asia) and quickly concluded that the indigenous peoples of the Caribbean were "primitive." As we know, these were by no means the first so-called primitive peoples Iberians had encountered: the Guanches of the Canarias had similarly failed the tests, but the Guanches had, for a time at least, fiercely resisted their invaders. Having failed to pass the incomers' tests for civilisation, the Caribbean peoples (the Kwaib—or Caribs—aside) also failed to mount effective resistance to the landings and settlements. They were thus doubly damned.

The indigenous peoples of the Caribbean were not unfamiliar with the threat and use of force, and with expropriation by their neighbours, but the pre-Columbian experience was of intermittent attacks, comparatively limited casualties, and rarely, if ever, permanent expulsion of a particular community from the territories it occupied. In part this reflected the low densities of population and their modest subsistence requirements, so that temporary flight might be as effective a defence against intruders as was armed resistance. Columbus's first expedition was met with mixed responses from the indigenous peoples, sometimes welcoming and on other occasions wary or hostile. Tragically for all concerned, the reaction of the local peoples to the establishment of the first Iberian settlement—Navidad, a stockade built from the timbers of the wrecked *Santa Maria*—was to destroy it and kill the 40 or so men of the garrison. Iberian expeditions had thereafter some licence to presume that they should be prepared to defend themselves.

For the most part, because the indigenous peoples failed effectively to resist them, the incomers had no incentive to compromise or reach some peaceful accommodation with the indigenous peoples. Admittedly, the Caribbean peoples entirely lacked the technologies of European warfare—ferrous arms and armour—but that had also been true of the Guanches and so did not itself render them incapable of inflicting casualties on the invaders. Indeed, the Iberians' relative neglect of the outer islands of the Caribbean reflected a judgement by the incomers that the Kwaib were a more difficult people to subdue than the perceived rewards would justify. Here, however, was the operative condition: in places where the rewards were calculated to be sufficiently large or easy to obtain (or both), the invaders would be ruthless, which approach was demonstrated in the campaigns to complete the conquest of what Columbus had named La Isla Española (Hispaniola),[4] in the revolt of the Tainos in the newly named Puerto Rico being "fiercely suppressed,"[5] and in the barbarity of the conquest of Cuba.[6] The indigenous peoples' understanding of war—that is, intersocietal violence as opposed to interpersonal violence—was significantly at odds with the approach of the Iberian incomers, for whom the objectives became occupation and systematised exploitation, rather than raids, and in pursuit of which there were apparently no limits to the level of violence they were willing to employ, perhaps as a response to being outnumbered. Avoidance by the indigenous peoples of further armed encounters with the incomers might, perhaps, have been a sensible response if it had been combined with flight to the interior of these tropical islands. Amongst most of the peoples of the Caribbean, however, the common response was neither resistance nor flight, but various degrees of collaboration.[7]

Collaboration was indeed what the incomers sought, whether achieved by the coercion usually employed by the settlers or by (occasional) application of crown policies with respect to the humane treatment and payment of native workers,[8] riddled as these policies were with contradiction. Notwithstanding the efforts of missionaries and of the settler-turned-Dominican, Las Casas, to protect indigenous peoples from the worst aspects of the *repartimiento* and *encomiendas,* the Caribbean peoples offered limited resistance on their own account, even before their populations were ravaged by disease and enslavement, and their morale was utterly undermined. It was as if the islands' peoples were almost complicit in their precipitant demise. Possibly, the peoples of the Caribbean were more intimidated by the material culture of the incomers than had been the Guanches and deferred to the technologically superior society. Perhaps it was the case that the indigenous peoples were by custom so socially fragmented that they were incapable of collective organisation to mobilise their numerical superiority and expel the invaders. As such, their discrete communities were vulnerable to defeat piecemeal by the Iberians, whose arms, armour, horses and war-dogs, generally guaranteed to the Iberians not only a local superiority of military force but also rapid success. Once defeated and thereafter presumably overawed by the threat of force, it would seem that the indigenous peoples seldom took opportunities for further resistance, either individual acts of sabotage, arson, or murder, or mass revolt. Indeed, the indigenous peoples were soon regarded as incapable of posing a serious challenge to the invaders: from the early years of island colonisation, the incomers were sufficiently confident of their own security from attack by the conquered to indulge in disputing the authority of those supposed to govern them, beginning with the Columbus family.[9]

In the absence of serious resistance, to be characterised as primitive could correlate as childlike, and thus in need of guidance, education, and care, which view was early adopted not only by missionaries, but also by some settlers. From the beginning of Iberian incursion, however, experience taught the incomers that the Arawaks and their neighbours were biddable, that they were unmindful of the "real" value of material (especially gold) objects, and it was these experiences that led to the fatal elision from "primitive" to "exploitable." With limited mechanical and animal aids, all efforts to create and maintain the ingredients of civilisation—permanent buildings, towns, farms—were dependent on human labour. The indigenous peoples were at first sufficiently numerous, apparently otherwise idle, and in need of educating in the ways of work and service. Christian Iberian societies generally subscribed to the common European view that the price of Adam's Fall included "Man" having to labour "by the sweat of his brow," but also that humanity was arranged in a hierarchy, in which some would command and others would serve. Whilst the Caribbean islands at the time of first contact might have had an Edenic quality to some of the incomers, civilisation required the mobilisation of labour and resources to create and sustain the material circumstances desired by individual settlers, for those circumstances to become at least equal to and preferably better than the circumstances to which they might have aspired in Iberia.

Such of the island peoples who survived the first 30 years of the Iberian invasions, became progressively subsumed in the emerging slave-owning society of plantation agriculture. Little of their culture or language was adopted by either of the new populations, of European or of African origin, and nothing of their traditional lifestyle.

The island experiences therefore came to represent the twin poles of a spectrum of European aims in the North Atlantic: occupation of empty territory or substitution of indigenous peoples. Subsequent to the settlement of the Caribbean islands, however, neither model was reproduced perfectly because the American mainland was neither entirely empty nor its peoples so comprehensively eliminated.

PEOPLES OF AFRICA

The first people from Africa to travel to the New World arrived with the Iberian conquistadores—not only as personal slaves but in some cases as comrades-in-arms—and they were perceived by the indigenous peoples of the Caribbean and America as "part of the invading culture."[10] Despite the official policy of the Catholic monarchy that there should be an Iberian monopoly of intercourse with the New World, interlopers from other European societies were early on the scene, engaging with the Hispanic settler communities to provide the goods and services in volumes that Sevilla either could not or would not deliver. By analogy with the behaviour of Europeans from outside Iberia, there were thus in theory no insurmountable obstacles—technological, commercial, or political—to the possibility that Africans themselves might pursue opportunities in the New World. Yet the overwhelmingly common form of encounter between the peoples of Africa and the developing Iberian Empire in the West was through slavery. Even though the principal European intermediaries in the trade were subsequently to come from northern Europe, from amongst the Dutch and English, it was Iberians who created the demand for African slaves in the Western Hemisphere and developed the means for their transportation. Herein, however, lay a contradiction.

Within the Iberian peninsula during the early modern period, successive monarchs and their ministers of church and state were concerned that they harboured in their midst potential members of what later Spanish history would call a "fifth column," people whose (disguised) loyalties might be to a foreign culture and power and who would, in certain circumstances, attempt the overthrow of Roman Catholic Iberia. Jews, Moors, and Protestants were successively figures within Iberian life who were to be persecuted, expelled, and, when necessary, exterminated. It is therefore at least surprising, if not most strange, that in seeking to establish their colonial empire in the Western Hemisphere the Iberians should have willingly become so reliant on imported peoples with profoundly alien languages and cultures who so quickly and permanently outnumbered their Hispanic hosts. If perceived aliens in Iberia were a serious threat to security, why introduce them to the New World?

The calculus of security in the New World, however, was fundamentally different from that in peninsular Iberia. First and foremost, the potential enemy in the New World was instantly identifiable by the colour of their skins, whereas within Hispanic society, the extent of the potential threat was difficult to measure because of the outward conformity of *conversos* and *moriscos*. Second, although slaves might escape to remote interiors of the New World, there was little or no prospect of them receiving direct military aid from their free compatriots: the Mediterranean coasts of Iberia, however, were thought exposed to the threat of invasion from Islamic North Africa in common cause with the *moriscos* within; hence, in the aftermath of the revolt of the Alpujarras their enforced resettlement across the whole peninsula away from the coasts. Third, expressed at its most cruel, slaves died—in large numbers, relatively quickly, as consequences of their treatment and of exposure to the western environment—so that at least in theory, control could be exercised over their numbers by limiting the quantities of new arrivals. Within peninsular Iberia, by contrast, the aliens were self-reproducing, and at times their numbers were feared to be growing faster than the so-called host communities. Fourth, as with the indigenous peoples, resistance amongst the enslaved to their masters was limited. Within our period, no substantial or sustained slave revolts occurred within the Iberian empire—indeed, on occasions, slaves were armed by their masters to help suppress the indigenous peoples—and the instances of individual acts of resistance—murder, arson, sabotage—were far outnumbered by the attempts at escape. Thus, the slave owners may have come to a presumption that the Africans not only could, but should, be likened to the "beasts of the field," over which God had given dominion to Adam: they needed to be taught obedience and occasionally to be restrained, but, despite their considerable numerical advantage, they were unlikely directly to challenge the power of their masters.

Taken as they were from diverse societies along the African littoral, and sometimes from deep within the continent, the members of the New World slave communities—communities manufactured by Europeans—might have little in common by way of language and culture. Their principal points of sodality were their shared experiences of transportation and slavery, and their designation by their Iberian masters as "not like us." Furthermore, they were also to be distinguished from the indigenous peoples of the Caribbean and mainland because, formally at least within the Hispanic empire, the indigenous peoples were free and could not (legally) be slaves, even if on a practical level of daily misery it was difficult to distinguish between Caribbean and African peoples. Unlike the indigenous peoples, those of African origin often had limited expression of shared identity outside of their enslavement. Within their captivity, they were forced to conform to the routines of labour and to a limited engagement with the language and culture of their masters, rather than in some common African culture. From relatively early on, and long before Europeans faced this challenge, Africans in the New World had to create new, shared identities, often through the medium of versions of their enslavers' cultures: forms of Iberian languages and of Roman Catholic observances, intermingled with such parts of broadly African heritages as they might recognise as in common. With the arrival of each draft of the newly enslaved (and mortality amongst the enslaved always encouraged regular replenishment) the cultural diversity amongst those of African origin in the Western Hemisphere was renewed, thus reinforcing a fractured sense of community amongst the enslaved that could not be overcome simply by invoking an identity "African."

Escape, rather than manumission, was the way out of slavery in the Hispanic New World.[11] Amongst those who did escape, there is little to suggest that attempts were made to return to Africa (either by seizing or hiring the means of transportation) or evidence of attempts from Africa to bring them home. Instead, from the earliest mass escape in Hispaniola in 1522, escaped slaves—*cimarrones,* later rendered by the English *ma-*

roons—created African communities within the interiors of the islands and on the mainland, called later by the Portuguese *mocambo*.[12] Even these free communities, however, did not seriously undermine the Iberian calculus of security, for they did not become bases from which slave liberation raids were mounted, nor did they become consistent allies for surviving indigenous peoples in wars of liberation, although on occasion they became short-term allies for European rivals to the Iberian powers. Instead, they became safe havens for the escapees and as such were sources of anxiety, but attempts to destroy these havens were intermittent and they were in effect tolerated by Iberian settlers, in contrast with the attitudes of later European slave-owning societies, particularly in the islands, that regarded the threat of slave revolt as a constant challenge.

The enslavement of Africans was the Iberian colonial remedy for the shortage of labour, but whereas the Hispanic version of this maintained the Africans in their enslaved condition, the Portuguese attitude could be in one respect significantly different: some Africans brought to Brasil as slaves might be freed. A custom developed of manumission by the terms of the master's will, by which mistresses of African origin—and their children—as well as loyal male slaves, joined a slowly growing number of other freed persons. Some of these bought their freedom using the tiny wages offered as incentives to productivity to those with special skills—craftsmen, foremen, herdsmen, farmers. By these means, people of African origin swelled the numbers of the free colonial populations, tending to seek waged labour in towns and becoming progressively acculturated to a colonial identity more European in character than African or indigenous.[13] In this, Portuguese colonial practice in Brasil merely replicated that of Portuguese settlers in Africa and in Asia. Notwithstanding the similar incidence of sexual and familial unions with African women and the consequent births of *mulatos*, Hispanic legal convention held that a person's status derived from the mother, so that a slave woman's children remained slaves, even if the father were of European origin and free. In such cases, a father might choose to obtain freedom for his children, but the greater numbers of people of ancestry that combined African with other origins arose from unions with indigenous or mestizo women, whose children were thereby legally free.[14]

Despite the considerable debate in sixteenth-century Castilian government circles about whether the indigenous peoples of the Western Hemisphere might lawfully be enslaved, no such debate was devoted to the question of the enslavement of Africans. Not even Las Casas applied the logic of his defence of the "Indians" to the case of the Africans. The absence of any meaningful consideration of the status of Africans as human and potentially Christian makes a striking contrast with the occasional troubled consciences and repeated claims of missionary zeal in the Iberian attitudes towards the Caribbean and Mesoamerican peoples. To an extent, the availability of Africans as a potential remedy for labour shortages created the opportunity to pursue the luxury of debate about the legal status of the indigenous peoples of the Western Hemisphere. For some Iberian minds, the central difference between these two groups of peoples may have been their respective relationship to the land of the Western Hemisphere. To legalistically minded Hispanic societies, prior occupation of territory provided the indigenous peoples of the west with a case prima facie of rights of ownership and, hence, legal identity. These rights might be ceded in appropriate circumstances or overtaken by conquest made legally justifiable by the refusal to embrace Christianity. Nevertheless, the indigenous peoples in the New World were in theory entitled to legal protections and rights. Africans brought to the New World, however, were by definition detached from any relationship with land that might carry with it legal rights or identity. Therein lay a further part of their attraction, for as chattels, they were available for purchase, sale, alienation, mortgage, and loan at interest, with complete flexibility. Notwithstanding their initial capital investment and ongoing maintenance costs, African slaves were an immediate remedy to the challenge of chronic labour shortage, and this simple commercial arithmetic no amount of moralising could undermine.

Africa's status as the principal reservoir of expendable labour for the development of the Europeans' vision of the New World derived from decisions made by Hispanic settlers and officials to imitate the Portuguese practice in their Atlantic islands. The geographical sources of these slaves, however, lay formally beyond the reach of Castilian traders, because West Africa was within the Portuguese sphere of monopoly as agreed in the Treaty of Tordesillas (1494). Furthermore, the littoral of sub-Saharan Africa in particular remained an ecological environment recognised as overwhelmingly hostile to Europeans. What allowed African slavery to develop in the Western Hemisphere was that from the beginning of the trade, it was conducted by intermediaries on behalf of the Castilian Empire—initially Portuguese and subsequently also French, Dutch, and English shipmasters and entrepreneurs. What made the trade effective, however, was the collaboration of slave raiders and traders amongst African societies in which slavery was well-established custom. Thus, African slavery became the first expression of economic interdependence across the Atlantic with an explicitly international dimension.

In this economic interdependence between Iberian settler communities in the Western Hemisphere and established African customs of slavery lay the explanation for the success (for the owners) of the enforced mass transplantation of millions of people from Africa to the New World. Iberian settlements consumed imported labour as fast as slave numbers could be replaced or enlarged, so that for the European intermediaries and African originators, profitable returns and continuing demand were virtually guaranteed. Generally denied the possibility of manumission and any significant place as free members of the settler societies, imported Africans had to choose between miserable survival and escape to the hostile interior. Without the Africans' labour, the Iberian Empire might have remained in economic isolation from the rest of the Atlantic.

PEOPLES OF THE AMERICAN MAINLAND

How did the Iberian invasion affect the indigenous peoples of the mainland? For themselves, the conquistadores told stories of great heroism in the face of almost impossible challenges, both of physical geography and the armed numerical strength of their indigenous opponents, leading to the subjugation of the millions of Amerindians, preparatory to their conversion to Roman Catholicism. In retrospect, the Mesoamerican survivors' accounts of their downfall laid emphasis on their prospective doom foretold in prophecies and stories, coinciding with key points of identification between what the traditional stories prepared the pre-Columbian peoples to expect and what arrived from the ocean, so that their present oppression was but one stage in a story unfolding over eternity. For a modern reader, neither version seems convincing: the numbers and firepower of the attackers seem insufficient to have overwhelmed indigenous peoples, and explanations rooted in the collapse of the will to resist amongst superstitious Amerindian élites are unappealing in today's less credulous era. Steel, guns, horses, and germs are all part of the story of the Iberian conquests, but the central question for the historian remains this: why was there not more effective indigenous resistance?

First of all, we should note that these accounts reflect a preoccupation with the story of Cortés and the dramatically sudden overthrow of the politicomilitary power of the civilisation of the central valley of Mexico, so often in the modern age called Aztec but more properly called Mexica. The conquest of the Mexica was, in effect, the displacement of one form of exploitative regime—admittedly indigenous to the continent—with another, ultimately controlled by outsiders but initiated by and reliant on the cooperation and active support of substantial portions of those Mesoamerican societies seeking to escape the Mexica *imperium*. From the perspective of Cortés's Mesoamerican allies, his arrival could be welcomed as an opportunity and his cooperation as military ally sought by purchase. Elsewhere around the littoral of the Caribbean and Gulf of Mexico, by contrast, the indigenous peoples were largely reacting to initiatives taken by the Iberian incomers.

Early but intermittent reconnaissance of the mainland was not seriously pursued until the expeditions that left Hispaniola in December 1509.[15] The fate of these may be said, in retrospect, to be more characteristic of this age of adventure, than would be the subsequent Cortés expedition. Despite significant resources—relative to the contemporaneous Iberian population of the Caribbean and comparable to those of the Cortés expedition—and clear mission objectives to establish settlements and exploit the gold believed to be on the mainland, the expeditions sustained high casualties from navigational hazards, exhaustion of their supplies, and armed resistance from the peoples they encountered. To be shipwrecked, starved, or killed by the natives remained the more likely fates of expedition members than to become rich and retire to the mother country. The founding of the first permanent European settlement on the mainland, at Santa María la Antigua de Darién (1509), was at the time but meagre compensation for these otherwise disastrous attempts to continue the expansion of the Castilian Empire in the manner seen in the Caribbean islands.

These encounters demonstrated to the Iberians that there were societies on the mainland that were more "civilised" than those of the islands, whilst the peoples of the mainland acquired early exposure to the contradictory characteristics of the incomers, by turns friendly, greedy, or violent, powerful in war but incapable of living well off the natural environment and vulnerable to natural hazards of the flora and fauna. A later account, describing the early contacts with Yucatán, may be taken to illustrate this confusion, and is worth quoting at length.[16]

SEC.III

It is said that the first Spaniards to come to Yucatan were Gerónimo de Aguilar, a native of Ecija, and his companions. These, in 1511, upon the break-up at Darien resulting from the dissensions between Diego de Nicueza and Vasco Núñez de Balboa, followed Valdivia on his voyage . . . to San Domingo, to give account to the admiral and the governor, and to bring 20,000 ducats of the king's. On the way to Jamaica the caravel grounded . . . [and] was lost with all but twenty men. These went . . . in a boat without sails, . . . and were at sea for thirteen days. After nearly half of them had died of hunger, the rest reached the coast of Yucatan. . . .

These poor fellows fell into the hands of a bad cacique, who sacrificed Valdivia and four others to their idols, and served them in a feast to the people. Aguilar and Guerrero and five or six others he saved to fatten. These broke their prison and came to another chief who was an enemy of the first, and more merciful; he made them his slaves, and his successor treated them with much kindness. However, all died of grief, save only Gerónimo de Aguilar and Gonzalo Guerrero. Of these Aguilar was a good Christian . . . and finally escaped on the arrival of the Marquis Hernando Cortés, in 1519.

Guerrero learned the language and went to Chectemal. . . . Here he was received by a chief . . . , who placed in his charge his military affairs; in these he did well and conquered his master's enemies many times. He taught the Indians to fight, showing them how to make barricades and bastions. In this way, and by living as an Indian, he gained great reputation and married a woman of high quality, by whom he had children, and he made no attempt to escape with Aguilar. He decorated his body, let his hair grow, pierced his ears to wear rings like the Indians, and is believed to have become an idolator like them.

During Lent of 1517 Francisco Hernández de Córdoba sailed from Cuba with three ships to procure slaves for the mines, as the population of Cuba was diminishing. Others say he sailed to discover new lands. Taking Alaminos as a pilot he landed on Isla de las Mugeres, to which he gave this name because of the idols he found there, of the goddesses of the country, . . . The building was of stone, such as to astonish them; and they found certain objects of gold, which they took. Arriving at Cape Cotoch they directed their course to the bay of Campeche, where they disembarked. . . . They were well received by the chief and the Indians marveled [sic] at seeing the Spaniards, touching their beards and persons.

. . . At Campeche they learned of a large town nearby, . . . there they found a chief . . . , a warlike man who called his people together against the Spaniards. Francisco Hernández was much disturbed seeing in this what must happen; but not to show a less spirit he put his men in order and had the artillery fired from the ships. The Indians however, notwithstanding the strange sound, smoke and fire of the guns, attacked with great cries; the Spaniards resisted, inflicting severe wounds and killing many. Nevertheless the chief so inspired his people that they forced the Spaniards to retire, killing twenty, wounding fifty, and taking alive two whom they afterwards sacrificed. Francisco Hernández came off with thirty-three wounds, and thus returned downcast to Cuba, where he reported that the land was good and rich, because of the gold he found on the Isla de las Mugeres.

These stories moved . . . [the] governor of Cuba, as well as many others, so that he sent his nephew Juan de Grijalva with four ships and 200 men. With him went Francisco de Montejo, . . . the expedition sailing on 1 May, 1518.

. . . On this voyage they discovered New Spain, Pánuco and Tabasco, where they stayed for five months, and also tried to make a landing at Champotón. This the Indians resisted with such spirit as to come out close to the ships in their canoes, in order to shoot their arrows. So they made sail and departed.

When Grijalva returned from his voyage of discovery and trade . . . , the great captain Hernando Cortés was in Cuba; and he on the news of such a country and such riches, conceived the desire of seeing it, and even of acquiring it for God, for his king, for himself, and for his friends.

For the indigenous peoples, therefore, any encounter with the Iberians would soon reveal the incomers to be men—admittedly not quite like other men—who needed food and drink, took sick and died, could kill and be killed. The incomers possessed technologically superior arms and means of transport, but these need not be decisive if the encounters became violent, not least because their numbers at any one time or place were never insurmountable. Despite the reverses experienced by their expeditions, however, the incomers were persistent. The incomers' recurrent attempts to probe the societies of the mainland suggested to indigenous peoples that, instead of armed resistance that risked extensive collateral damage to the homes and farms of the indigenous peoples, some form of accommodation might need to be reached with the incomers if the pre-

Columbian patterns of settlement, trade, and political authority were to be sustained. In defining the precise form of any accommodation, the ability of Mesoamerican élites to exploit the interplay of war, alliance, and payment of tribute in negotiation with the incomers might be determinative, provided that these élites could quickly acquire a usable understanding of the motives and objectives of the incomers.

For mainland societies—those that were settled, urban, agricultural with complex political and cultural systems—the arrival of small parties of Iberians could present opportunities to expand the domestic cultural and spiritual capital of the indigenous leadership, who would act as the intermediaries between their people and the novel ways and possessions of the incomers. The success of these encounters would be measured, from the perspective of the indigenous leadership, by the speed with which the incomers either moved on, or became willing contributors to the social and ceremonial lives of the indigenous peoples. As the earliest—peaceful—contacts between Pizarro's expeditions and the Inca Empire would later show, for example, indigenous élites were capable of quickly assessing the challenge or opportunities of contact with the incomers before deciding their response. The immediate lessons were that the Iberians were preoccupied with certain limited types of material goods, principally gold and silver, and were unwilling or unable to provide for their own subsistence. These characteristics made them vulnerable: they could be bought off or starved out.

Two factors undermined this kind of calculation. First and foremost, diseases from the Old World had devastating impact, repeated in successive generations, on the indigenous peoples, whereas the incomers—as carriers—in comparison suffered relatively light mortality. Exposure to these diseases did not require prolonged or firsthand encounters with Iberians, and their effects would long outlast the Iberians' departure from a region. The terms of engagement, therefore, were dramatically revised to undermine the significance of the numerical superiority of the indigenous peoples. In addition, and more quickly than had been the case in the islands, were the Iberians' efforts to convert indigenous peoples to some form of Roman Catholic Christianity. To themselves and the audiences at home, the missionaries and soldiers stressed the barbarous paganism and the credulity of the indigenous peoples. The depth of the challenge to pre-Columbian societies was measured by the revelation of the determination of the incomers not only to strip them of their material assets but also to deny them the continued observance of their spiritual and ceremonial values.

Catastrophic mortality combined with dependence on agriculture left indigenous peoples unwilling to challenge the incomers' expropriations of their resources and labour. The indigenous peoples who escaped expropriation were those who had little or nothing to plunder; for example, the semi-nomadic peoples of what is now northern Mexico, Arizona and New Mexico, or the peoples of the lowland jungles of Central America. For these societies, the hostility of their environment to the Iberians could help sustain indigenous autonomy, but nothing could shield them from European diseases.

By this account, the story of the conquest of the Mexica Empire stands out—not as the exemplar of the story of the conquistadores, but as the spectacular exception that nevertheless became the idealised version of the Iberian encounter with the mainland societies. The Mexica Empire was undermined before the full impact of the Europeans' diseases was experienced, and it was brought low by the first case, on a grand scale, of the alliance between incomers and indigenous dissenters.

SEC.IV

Hernando Cortés sailed from Cuba with eleven ships, the largest being of 100 tons burden, . . . He took along 500 men, some horses, and goods for barter, having Francisco de Montejo as a captain and Alaminos as chief pilot. . . .

With this fleet and no further equipment he set sail. . . . They arrived at Cozumel on the north, where they found fine buildings of stone for the idols, and a fine town; but the inhabitants seeing so great a fleet and the soldiers disembarking, all fled to the woods.

On reaching the town the Spaniards sacked it and lodged themselves. Seeking through the woods for the natives they came on the chief's wife and children. Through an Indian interpreter named Melchior, who had been with Francisco Hernández and Grijalva, they learned it was the chief's wife, to whom and the children Cortés gave presents and caused them to send for the chief. Him on arrival he treated very well, gave him some small gifts and returned to him his wife and children, with all things that had been taken in the town; and begged him to have the Indians return to their houses, saying that when they came everything that had been taken away from them would be restored. When they were thus restored, he preached to them the vanity of idols, and persuaded them to adore the cross; this he placed in their temples with an image of Our Lady, and therewith public idolatry ceased. . . . [17]

By this account of his arrival in Yucatán, we see Cortés acting in a manner consistent with his predecessors' expeditions, mixing violent expropriation with gestures of peace, accompanied by the enforcement of a kind of Christianity. With such a small force, notwithstanding the horses and firearms, Cortés could not have been expected to achieve any more than other adventurers mounting a reconnaissance in force, or than was later achieved by his subordinate Montejo in his efforts to conquer Yucatán.[18] The vital difference in the Cortés expedition was what happened next.

. . . Cortés . . . reached Tabasco. Here among other presents and Indian women which those of Tabasco gave to him was one who was afterwards called Marina.

She was from Xalisco, a daughter of noble parents, stolen when small and sold in Tabasco, and later sold in Xicalango and Champotón, where she learned the language of Yucatan. By this she was able to understand Aguilar, and thus God provided Cortés with good and faithful interpreters, through whom he acquired knowledge and intimacy with Mexican matters. With these Marina was well posted, having mingled with Indian merchants and leading people, who spoke of them daily.[19]

In the view of one historian, the conquest of the highland empires of the Americas by Iberians was consistent with longer historical trends of the regions, that of successor empires.[20] Indeed, the so-called victories of the tiny armed expeditions of conquistadores were made possible by the nature of the command and control exercised by the Mexicas over their subject peoples. Mexica tribute and exploitation were levied not directly on the mass of neighbouring societies but on their élites. At the time of Cortés's arrival, there was amongst these élites sufficient resentment of the burdens of Mexica rule that Iberian promises of specialist military assistance outweighed fears of retribution for unsuccessful rebellion, so that for the Tlaxcala people and others, the enemy were the Mexica, not the incomers. Fighting, when it occurred, was vicious and bloody, and in combat the possession of steel blades and armour—far more than guns and horses—gave Cortés's soldiers a military effectiveness disproportionate to their numbers. Without their indigenous allies, however, they should have been slaughtered, as was demonstrated in the Iberian casualties in their night-time fighting retreat from Tenochtitlán (1520).

Before 1519, the Mexica exploited a loose hegemony bound together by tribute in which "Aztec supremacy was enforced . . . by the terror of mobile armies and punitive raids."[21] As such, the Mexica *imperium* was easier to challenge than if it had been founded on dominion and direct government. Once challenged, however, the key to the conquest of the Mexica were the repeated miscalculations by the Mexica leader, Motecuçoma, about the intentions and vulnerabilities of the insurgents. His initial willingness to offer gifts and negotiations to Cortés might be interpreted as Motecuçoma taking advantage of early contact to gather intelligence about the incomers, combined with a testing of the loyalties of the Mexicas' subject peoples through their responses to the new arrivals. The massacre of the Cholulans, however, surely put beyond doubt that the Cortés expedition could pose a military threat, disproportionate to its small numbers. Overconfidence in his numerical superiority combined with personal curiosity, rather than awe at the prospect of meeting a god on earth, may explain Motecuçoma's decision to permit Cortés (and, by this point, his considerable body of allies) to enter the capital city and take up residence. Until his death, Motecuçoma disabled effective armed resistance to Cortés, who—aided by his interpreter and sometime mistress,

Marina/La Malinche—capitalised on the opportunities to expand his alliances amongst the discontented subject peoples of the Mexica empire.

With the death of Motecuçoma, armed resistance by the Mexica population quickly expelled the invaders and their allies from the city and, if the pursuit had been maintained, should have been capable of the total destruction of the Iberian expeditionary forces. What saved the Iberian invaders was the adherence of their native allies, who preferred collaboration in the prospective overthrow of the Mexica *imperium* in the expectation of peaceful coexistence with Cortés, to the certainty of retribution that would follow a restoration of Mexica power. At this point, disease devastated the Mexica people, not so much by the mortality amongst the population as a whole but by removing the new, fighting leadership of Cuitláhuac. The subsequent siege and street-by-street battle for Tenochtitlán was a military triumph for the coalition of Mesoamerican manpower and Iberian techniques (more than technology), welded together by Cortés's use of the political intelligence mediated by La Malinche.

Whereas it might be too much to say that the Mesoamerican peoples connived at their own downfall, this interpretation of the evidence for their resistance to invasion suggests that they cooperated in—or in some cases did not seek assiduously to resist—the overthrow of their indigenous rulers. Having secured this outcome, however, Cortés's indigenous allies rapidly ceded to the Iberians the place of pre-eminence that they had only recently denied the Mexica people. Subsequently, the indigenous peoples offered only limited resistance to their cultural conquest by mendicants. How may we explain this rapid surrender?

From the purely material point of view, the exploitation of indigenous labour and land called by the invaders *encomienda* did not (at least in the early years) challenge the social structures and patterns of commerce of the indigenous peoples, not least because the numbers of Iberian settlers and *encomenderos* were relatively small, and so they remained dependent on the traditional leaders of indigenous society to mediate their demands. The surrender of objects fashioned from the gold and silver that the incomers prized so highly was a tragedy to art, but not yet to lives of those forced to work in mines. Once the Mexica Empire had been overthrown, the *encomenderos* simply replaced one exploitative élite with another. Unlike in the islands, existing agricultural practice and patterns of settlement were largely preserved. Tribute, an established part of Mesoamerican life, continued to be collected for the benefit of an élite.

In this respect, the Castilian conquest of Mexico resembled the Norman conquest of England: a tight-knit force of military specialists seized political control in a *coup de main*, substituting a new ruling élite without immediately tearing down the fabric of the conquered society, thus compromising with everyday life in just enough ways to undermine the resentment that might have turned into prolonged resistance. These arrangements began to be transformed from the 1540s, under the twin pressures of growing demand for labour, particularly in mining, and rapidly declining Amerindian populations in Mesoamerica. Had there been no other changes in circumstances, the latter development could to some extent have been offset by changes in agricultural practice and the extension of pastoralism. The *encomienda* system was in any case under assault by the crown's New Laws, intended as much to restrict the licence enjoyed by overmighty subjects as to spare the burdens on Amerindians. The demand for unskilled labour in the newly discovered silver mines, for example, highlighted the significance of demographic collapse on a scale modern thinking attributes largely to epidemic disease. It is at least plausible to suppose that the indigenous peoples also chose not to reproduce. From a pre-Conquest population estimated at 25 million, by 1548 this had fallen to perhaps 6.3 million, to under 3 million in 1568, 1.9 million in 1580, to perhaps 1.25 million in the early 1600s, when the "white and near-white population was increasing steadily and may already have reached 100,000."[22] By the middle of the sixteenth century, the marginalisation of the material interests of the indigenous peoples was already complete.

It was one thing to throw off a set of murderous Mexica rulers in favour of a new exploiting élite; it was quite another to comply with the hispanisation of culture. What might have seemed in 1521 as the overthrow of a tyrannical regime in Tenochtitlán progressively developed into first compromise with and then subversion by a new common language and system of government and justice, introduced by the invaders. The new departure for the indigenous peoples was the effort of missionaries to promote Christian observance, which seemed to meet with ready success or at least outward compliance with the hybrid form of Roman Catholic worship that sought where possible to appropriate indigenous cults and needed to temper the element of human sacrifice in the crucifixion. By and large, however, there appeared for now to be more continuity than change in the Amerindian experience of everyday life.

The life experiences of the indigenous peoples were by no means consistent across the whole region. The north remained untamed and resistant until c. 1600; the peoples of the Inca Empire resisted for several years after the initial invasion; an absence of direct resistance need not mean an absence of opposition, through dissimulation, feigned ignorance, artificial compliance, manipulation, flight, theft, acquiescence;[23] and there were eventually areas designated as reservations for indigenous peoples— *congregaciones*—in Mexico and Guatemala.[24] Nevertheless, the incomers themselves reported, "As the Mexican people had signs and prophecies of the coming of the Spaniards and the end of their power and religion, so also did those of Yucatan some years before they were conquered by Admiral Montejo."[25]

Did the indigenous peoples invent or "discover" myths and prophecies of invincible invaders to explain their defeat after the fact, retrospectively to heighten the significance of divine agency to provide themselves an alibi for nonresistance? Perhaps we may instead see the career of La Malinche as exemplifying the confused relationship between indigenous and invader: sexual and family relationships between indigenous women and incomers were common enough in the Iberians' empires in Africa and Asia to encourage accommodation between the customs of each society, whilst allowing only partial access to the others' world to disguise the personal motives of the intermediaries.

A "SPANISH" EMPIRE?

Even a superficial review of the catalogue of expeditions, founding of settlements and volumes of maritime traffic re-emphasises the rapidity, extent, and variety of Iberian engagement with the Atlantic world. The sustained scale of this engagement, relative to the human and material resources of the Iberian peninsula, is the more remarkable when we consider its wider context. During the sixteenth century, Iberian empires were also being founded in South America and in the Pacific. On the contemporaneous European scene, this was the period when Iberia became most heavily committed to military struggle abroad in pursuit of the political and religious objectives of her new Habsburg rulers. Yet this period also saw the progressive compromising of cultural contacts between Iberian societies and those in the rest of Europe, at just the same time as there was initiated a sustained exposure to and interaction with cultures and societies outside of Europe.

We should from the first be wary of using misleading, shorthand labels to refer to the peoples who created Iberia's Atlantic world. To describe the empire and its creators as "Spanish" may be convenient, but it is not entirely accurate: Spain was a unitary state only in the sense that from 1516, one man wore the crowns of all of the constituent polities, as king of Castilla and León, of Aragón, and from 1580, the king of Portugal also, with each of the other states that had fallen into the dynastic empire of the Habsburgs.

From its beginnings, the Atlantic enterprise was dominated by Castilians.[26] Because Isabel the Catholic had been the chief supporter of the early Atlantic expeditions, it was perhaps not surprising that she drew on her own servants and courtiers, principally her chaplain Juan Rodríguez de Fonseca, to oversee the Castilian crown's interests in the early settlements and attempts at exploitation. In addition, she obtained formal papal confirmation of Castilian monopoly—the bull *Inter caetera* (1493) assigned to the crown of Castilla all lands and non-Christian peoples in the seas beyond the line one hundred leagues west of the Açores. After Isabel's death in 1504, technically the crown and its "empire" were inherited by her daughter Juana, the Mad, although Fernando wrested effective control from his daughter's Habsburg in-laws until his own death in 1516. In the period of the regency of Cardinal Cisneros (1516–17), Fonseca was stood down from his responsibilities for the Indies, possibly as a consequence of the cardinal's concern about the maltreatment of the indigenous peoples as reported by Las Casas and his distaste for Fonseca as a worldly prelate.[27] With the arrival of the new Habsburg monarch as Carlos I, however, Fonseca returned to prominence in the determination of crown policy towards the Indies until his own death in 1524. By then, Sevilla had become secure as the Iberian headquarters for the exploration, exploitation, and maintenance of the Castilian western enterprise as the home of the *Casa de la Contratación de las Indias*, established there by royal decree in 1503, whilst its governance reposed in the *Consejo de las Indias* "which emerged between 1511 and 1519 as a standing committee of the Council of Castile, and which was constituted as a separate organ of government in 1524."[28]

Fernando made no serious attempt to enlarge the circle of Iberian society from which access to the Indies would be given. Despite, for example, the entrepreneurial resources of Barcelona that might have increased the logistical support for whilst spreading the financial risks of expeditions, Fernando maintained the distinction between the westward, Atlantic enterprises of Castilla and the eastward, Mediterranean interests of Aragón. It is not clear to what extent this was deliberate policy on the part of the crown or an accidental consequence of Fernando's interests being directed elsewhere. He may have calculated that the risk of failure in the Atlantic could not compare with his conviction that success—military and diplomatic victory as well as great profit—lay more certainly within his grasp in the Italian states. While its returns were still as modest as they were in Fernando's lifetime, he may have judged that the Atlantic enterprise could be a drain on Castilla alone.[29]

Two men may perhaps be held to represent the twin poles of the Castilian interpretation of how to respond to the opportunities for colonial empire in the Western Hemisphere: Nicolás de Ovando and Bartolomé de Las Casas. Both arrived on Hispaniola in 1502, Ovando as "the first fully fledged governor . . . belonging to the royal bureaucracy,"[30] and Las Casas as one of the adventurers seeking land and profit. Ovando brought experience of government and settlement of frontier zones within Iberia, and he vigorously pursued the establishment of three foundations for colonialism: the imposition of crown authority on settlers and natives alike (confirmed after his tenure by the establishment of the *audiencia* of Santo Domingo); the establishment of towns as the preferred mode of occupation (as demonstrated in the *villas* founded in 1504–5); and the promotion of Hispanic, Christian, family life as the foundation of permanent settlement and individual prosperity, rather than permitting a passing traffic of profiteers to "get rich quick" and return to the homeland. In addition, he ruthlessly suppressed what remained of independent indigenous communities to secure labour for the colonists. By the end of Ovando's governorship, the material circumstances of the Caribbean empire promised improved living standards for colonists, over those of the homeland.

Las Casas, in contrast, became progressively dismayed by what he observed as (and initially participated in) the merciless exploitation of the indigenous peoples. His decision (ultimately) to reject the material in favour of the spiritual world was not particularly unusual for the period, but his forthright championing of the cause of the indigenous peoples was remarkable for the extent to which he promoted what became the Black Legend of the Iberian conquest of the New World. His efforts to arouse a sense of shame amongst his contemporaries coincided with crown policies, at least for a while, and he perhaps made permanent the tension in colonial enterprise of all European societies, between the methods of the settlers and the aspirations of their homeland governments. His concerns, however, had limits: although tonsured probably in 1501, he continued to profit substantially from the colonial conquests and *repartimientos* until renouncing his (substantial) worldly goods in 1514; he withdrew from the world to monastic seclusion for 10 years until 1531; he did not readily associate his concerns for the Amerindian peoples with the contemporaneous experiences of African slaves.

For the 30 years following Columbus's first voyage, whether by design or neglect crown policy allowed a predominant Castilian interest in the Atlantic enterprise to become entrenched, not only in the crown's bureaucracy but also in the complex of commercial interests that provided the necessary financial capital; technical underpinning in terms of ships, weapons, and trade goods; and personnel for exploration and settlement. From its early days, therefore, the Atlantic enterprise was characterised by monopoly: of access (through Sevilla), of authority and the administration of justice (through the creation by royal licence of *audiencias*),[31] and of exploitation (through the *Casa de la Contratación*). This monopoly aimed to exclude other Iberians who might seek to question Castilian jurisdiction almost as much as it tried to exclude other West Europeans, and in so doing Castilla's ruling elite in retrospect perhaps missed the earliest opportunity to promote a common Iberian imperial vision, based on shared burdens and rewards in the expanding Atlantic territories.

The Habsburg succession to the crowns of both the Catholic monarchs was initially fraught with difficulties, and for a time, open revolt amongst townspeople—*comuneros*—of Castilla. Notwithstanding their Burgundian upbringings, however, both the Holy Roman Emperor Charles/Karl V—Carlos I of Castilla and Aragón—and his son Felipe II chose to identify themselves with Castilla as the heartland of their far-flung domains. As legitimate, hereditary rulers of polyglot, multicultural polities, they both took seriously the various coronation oaths to respect the established laws, rights, and privileges of their subjects in each of their territories. Perhaps because of their respect for such *fueros*, under both monarchs the policy of monopoly of access was sustained, even though in hindsight either might have hoped to reap political benefit from the inauguration of a shared imperial project, with a greater participation of all of their subjects—for example, those in the Low Countries—in its creation and in the sharing of its rewards. Even under the Habsburgs, the Atlantic empire remained largely a Castilian project. It has been estimated that before 1559, of the perhaps 150,000 Iberian emigrants to the New World, 35 percent were from Andalucía and more than 50 percent from Extremadura, the two Castillas and León.[32] Of these, although there were early examples of "those who had cause to fear the Inquisition: Jews, *moriscos, conversos,*"[33] crown policy generally aimed to exclude any whose loyalties might be suspect.

While Carlos I reigned, the Atlantic was in effect merely one, relatively minor part of the king-emperor's responsibilities, and he made only limited efforts to associate subjects other than Castilians directly with the enterprise. The *Augsburger* house of Fugger was granted mining rights in Santo Domingo and Nueva España, although these could be construed as extensions of the Fuggers' long-standing role in the mining of mercury in Almadén (Castilla la Nueva) and silver in Guadalcanal (Andalucía). From 1528, however, the house of Welser was granted leave to undertake the settlement of what is now Venezuela, whither the first German settlers in the New World were transported.[34] These grants were not, it seems, intended as first steps towards an imperial project shared with Carlos's other European subjects, but rather as part of the repayment to the families that had lent cash to secure the imperial election of 1519 and subsequently advanced funds for war with France. Thus, the American grants were a Habsburg gift, not an Iberian one, reflecting the extent to which this monarch could exploit his sovereign rights in one domain to serve his personal interests in another.

Felipe II found no occasion to revise his father's privileging of the Castilian perspective, notwithstanding his filial preoccupation with preserving his Burgundian inheritance. The attachment of the Low Countries to his Iberian inheritance was, from a geopolitical perspective, a questionable decision even allowing for the importance of the ties with the Castilian trade fairs, because many of the strategic and other, economic considerations might have pointed to these lands becoming part of the Holy Roman Empire and the German-speaking dominions of Felipe's uncle and co-heir, Ferdinand. Sentiment above all dictated the assignment of the Burgundian patrimony to the son, Felipe, although the status of Antwerpen as the finance capital of Europe would be a bonus to a king confronting, until the 1559 peace of Câteau-Cambrésis, an aggressive France, and despite a treaty in 1562, continuing threats from the Ottoman Empire.

From his accession until c. 1580, Felipe encountered trials and challenges both within and without Iberia on a monumental scale. The financial burdens particularly of war provoked crown bankruptcies in 1557 and 1575, with debt restructuring followed by chronic shortages of cash and credit. The need to raise funds for defensive war prompted *El Prudente* to try to exploit the resources of more of his domains, which contributed to crisis in the Low Countries and intensified his fiscal demands—and dependence—on Castilla. Also through these years the succession was in doubt, notwithstanding his four marriages, because in 1568, Felipe's heir, Don Carlos, was imprisoned at his father's order to die in mysterious circumstances seven months later, thus adding further to the political uncertainties of the reign. Despite his devotion to his religion, Felipe was for long at odds with the formal head of the Roman Catholic world, with major political differences with the Papacy symbolised by the imprisonment of Archbishop Carranza (1559–66). At the same time, however, the king's militant and intolerant Roman Catholicism that led him to strengthen the remit of the Inquisition and prohibit his Iberian subjects from studying at foreign universities, also contributed to the causes of the revolt of the *moriscos* (1568–70), leading first to their bloody suppression and then to their enforced dispersal across Iberia.

Outside Iberia, war or the threat of it dominated policy. With the Ottomans, it was more often a story of failure—Djerba (1560), Oran (1563), Cyprus (1570–71), Tunis (1573–74)—than it was one of heroic survival (Malta in 1565) or even victory (Lepanto, 1571). Felipe's attempts to tax more heavily his subjects in the Low Countries, to which constitutional conflict was added militant Calvinism, might have been retrieved, but perhaps Felipe's most fateful decision was to reject a personal tour of the Low Countries to appeal for loyalty in favour of the duke of Alba's policy of repression. The introduction of Castilian-led troops to the Low Countries in 1567 saw a civil war become a war of independence and thereafter prompted Felipe to deploy the resources of Castilla across the whole of western Europe, beginning at precisely the moment when Castilla's American empire had, at last, most to give. The more that Felipe attempted to draw on the resources of his disparate territories, the more he came to rely on his faithful servants from Castilla and the silver from their American territories. Indeed, it was only in 1596 that Felipe formally opened the Americas to emigrants from all over Spain.[35] Nevertheless, Felipe's reign saw the securing of the Iberian hold on the islands of the Caribbean and the mainland territories of the Americas: "The 'taming of the Americas' during the second half of the sixteenth century was unquestionably Philip II's greatest achievement."[36]

This is not to argue that the conquest was made secure without effort or cost, but in comparison with the manpower and money deployed by the crown in defence of its dominions and interests in Europe and the Mediterranean, the costs of acquiring the empire in the Atlantic had been relatively small, and from the mid-1540s, it was clearly profitable. Despite the enormous geographical extent of Iberia's Atlantic empire and the relatively small numbers of the empire's population who fully shared Hispanic languages and cultures, there is little evidence to suggest that the Atlantic enterprise itself placed unmanageable strain on Castilla. Emigration to the Atlantic empire was not the cause of the rural depopulation decried by *arbitristas* and other commentators in the 1590s.

Furthermore, amongst all the crown's difficulties a striking characteristic of the century was the relative absence of rebellion or crises in the Atlantic territories amongst its Iberian settlers. Hispanic colonists might trade illicitly with other, unlicensed Europeans, as a way of obtaining otherwise scarce commodities—including slaves. They did not, however, seek to throw off their government by or their allegiance to a crown in Madrid. The greatest challenge to the crown was perhaps that posed by "the five violent and ungovernable"[37] Pizarro brothers and their conquistador rivals in the 1540s, principally over the extent of and control in the defeated empire of the Incas and the other peoples of the territories to the west of 65°W, to which the uncompromising attempt to impose the New Laws provoked direct conflict with the viceroy.[38] The centrality of plunder in the aims of these Iberian rivals was, however, reflected in the wars and murders they perpetrated on each other, until the viceroy Pedro de la Gasca defeated and executed Gonzalo Pizarro in 1548. Despite the subordination of the American empire to Habsburg imperial projects in Europe, there were no serious challenges to the crown from amongst its Iberian subjects in the islands or American mainland, no clamour that a larger portion of the wealth of the Americas be spent where it was mined, no attempt to use the bargaining chip of bullion to extract political concessions, such as settlers' assemblies or popular accountability. The free air and frontier mentality of the Americas did not, for Hispanic populations in this period, engender a demand for rights of political participation or that there be no taxation without representation.[39]

Fear, either of the indigenous peoples[40] or of repression by the crown's limited local armed forces, seem inadequate explanations of the relative absence of calls for political rights amongst Iberian peoples in the islands and Americas. Given the striking contrast with the contemporaneous demands for rights and respect for ancient custom—and privilege—voiced in the other kingdoms of Iberia, particularly Aragón, as well as amongst the subject peoples in the Italian peninsula and the Low Countries, the explanation seems to lie in the emergence of a general and enduring satisfaction with the political status quo amongst, at the least, Hispanic societies in the North Atlantic. This satisfaction may have been founded simply on the experience of successive immigrants to the New World that their economic circumstances were likely to be improved by the move. Material improvement, if not prosperity, more than compensated for any diminution of participation in local political decision making relative to that enjoyed in the old country.[41]

Felipe II's achievements in the Atlantic included the promotion of a generally willing adherence to orderly government, directed in a legal framework by the crown in Madrid. Even allowing for the compromises on enforcement struck by local officials and characterised by the phrase *obedezco pero no cumplo*,[42] neither crown government nor the Holy Office was generally seen as threatening either the material prosperity or social standing enjoyed by most *criollos* in colonial societies. As with apartheid in twentieth-century South Africa, discrimination on the grounds of race and culture could encourage in the poorest settler of European origin a sense of superiority over all of the other cultures amongst whom he lived, and a sense of loyalty to an ideal of Hispanism for which Iberian discrimination against *conversos* and *moriscos* had already rehearsed the vocabulary for its expression and a machinery for its enforcement. In its essentials, therefore, the so-called Spanish empire was racist, and its racism became characteristic of all subsequent *imperia* in the Atlantic.

Nevertheless, this racism was not without its Hispanic opponents, and the subject was one for intense debate throughout this period. If the Atlantic empire was essentially racist, it was equally legalistic, and from its early days jurists pursued the question of whether Castilla's *imperium* should be founded on right of conquest or on an imperative to bring Christian salvation to heathen peoples. Isabel the Catholic was opposed to the enslavement of indigenous peoples in the New World, and from 1510, particularly the Dominicans pursued the case for care and conversion. The debate before Carlos I between Sepúlveda and Las Casas at Valladolid in 1550 was a climax in this controversy, in which the crown had already committed itself to protecting the rights of indigenous peoples in the New Laws (1543). The importation of West Africans as slaves, however, had by this date become viewed as an economic necessity as the indigenous populations were already in catastrophic numerical decline.

In summary, between 1492 and c. 1600 a monopoly of access licensed by the crown laid across the Atlantic a veneer of Castilian language, culture, and law at the expense of the indigenous peoples, in settlements characterised by exploitation, racism, and political loyalty to Madrid.

TOO LARGE A WORLD?

After Columbus, searches for a route to the Orient continued, not only in Balboa's spectacular crossing of the isthmus of Darién and the first

European contact with the Pacific Ocean (1513), but also in the first expedition to circumnavigate the globe, led out from Cádiz by Fernão de Magalhães—the Portuguese known to Anglophones as Magellan—in 1519. The priorities in these years were to chart the extent of the New World, and to lay claim to as much of it as possible by establishing outposts to pre-empt other Europeans. Even by the standards of the day, however, these expeditions were not particularly large, and their size was only partly a function of the availability of suitable ships for their journeys. Funds for expeditions were in short supply, hence also men, equipment, and provisions. Lacking adequate manpower to garrison newly discovered territories, the legalistic part of the Castilian mind sought a virtual occupation of the land by charting the places to which its people travelled, and the making of maps became a means by which to demonstrate sovereignty. On these maps was played out part of the struggle for precedence in the naming of places, a struggle that continues in our own era in the choice between, for example, Harare and Salisbury, or Malouines, Malvinas, and Falklands.

If one of the greatest achievements of Columbus's contemporaries was to overcome the psychological challenge of crossing the Atlantic, for the following generation of adventurers it was the apparently limitless extent of the mainlands bounding the western edge of the ocean that posed the supreme test. Five thousand kilometres of ocean might seem empty and featureless, but the interiors of these western continents were filled with rivers, mountains, plains, swamps, forests, and deserts, each vastly bigger than the landscapes with which they were familiar in Europe. Balboa stared out over seas with no horizon, which proved to be the Pacific Ocean; Ambrosius Dalfinger thought to do the same but found himself instead on Lake Maracaibo.

For more than 50 years, expeditions in and beyond the islands and the Mesoamerican mainland continued to reveal more and more of the scale of the Iberian achievement and the challenge of geographical extent. For the populations of the pre-Columbian era, communications were maintained in part by the density of their settlements, for example, in Mexico, so that distance could be overcome by relays of human runners. With the dramatic decline in total human numbers, population densities fell sufficiently for distance to be a challenge even in the regions at the heart of settlement. What, then, were the strategies by which the Iberian conquerors and settlers tried to come to terms with the vastness of these lands? First and foremost, the incomers sought to overcome size by fundamentally changing the ecology of the Americas.

Horses gave the incomers the speed and mobility to try to tame the challenge of distance in those regions inaccessible by sea or river. The isolation of settlements and communities, still considerable by modern standards, was broken by the use of animal transport capable of covering several times the distance a man, even a Native American, could travel in a day. From the earliest days, populations of feral horses spread across the continent beyond the frontiers of Hispanic settlement and thereafter irrevocably altered the cultures—and warfare—of the indigenous peoples of the Great Plains and what is now the south-west United States. Along with horses, mules were introduced as the principal beasts of burden, the importance of which grew in direct proportion to the decline of the indigenous population from amongst whom porters could be recruited or impressed. Mule trains linked the Pacific and Caribbean coasts, and the central valley of Mexico with both. By the mid–sixteenth century, these trains were also carrying goods from the regular and growing Manila-Acapulco-Lima trade, thus helping to maintain communications in the first truly global empire.

As if the world were not enough, Felipe II's annexation of Portugal (1580) took his empire to yet grander extent, in Brasil, Africa, India, and the (real) Spice Islands. Although secured initially by military occupation of Portugal, in a manner reminiscent of his accession to the crowns of Castilla and Aragón, Felipe swore to respect the rights and privileges of his new subjects. These undertakings significantly eased his acceptance amongst the Portuguese nobility; for their part, Portuguese merchants and settlers gained access to the whole of the Iberian Atlantic—and its silver. At this point, Felipe's empire seemed poised to secure control of the sea routes to and from western Europe, the bulk of the territory of the New World, and a powerful role in a global economy that would trade American silver for Asian spices to the profit of Iberia.

For a moment, inspired by Cardinal Granvelle, Felipe might have transferred the seat of imperial government from Madrid to Lisboa, and thereby symbolised a reorientation of the crown and empire beyond the interests of and reliance on Castilla to share its burdens of government and defence.[43] Instead, Felipe subordinated the potential of his global empire to reiterate his commitment to his European interests: the suppression of Dutch nationalism, the defeat of militant Protestantism, and the control of French territorial ambition. Felipe's enhanced naval power with established global reach was deployed not, for example, in further extending Iberian control of Asian maritime trade, but against England, in successive Armadas from 1588. The system of trading privilege and monopoly within the Iberian Empire brought commercial benefits to Portuguese merchants and settlers, rather than to the wider population of Iberia. Eventually, when the balance of advantage seemed to have swung away from membership of an Iberian Empire, the Portuguese would seek to reassert their independence in the war beginning in 1640.

By the end of the sixteenth century, Castilla had become at once the privileged component and yet one of the chief victims of the empire, the chief reservoir of manpower and taxation whilst suffering most from the draining imperial responsibilities, the most demanding of which were not in the North Atlantic but in Europe. At the same time, the North Atlantic territories were not explored as opportunities for development but as assets to be exploited. Yet even with the seat of actual as well as formal government an ocean away and a growing self-sufficiency in many everyday respects during the period to 1600, the Latino population of the Americas chose to maintain their professions of loyalty to and dependence on Iberia. That there were material benefits in so doing is not to be denied, but these were neither so substantial nor so irreplaceable that they outweighed the connections based in sentiment. Those people who crossed the Atlantic mostly chose to stay in the west, whereas those born in the New World with any Hispanic parentage thought themselves as much the subjects of their king as those who had never left Murcia or Valladolid. The evidence that individuals and families crossed and recrossed the ocean in some numbers suggests that the links could be as much domestic as symbolic. Significantly for their Iberian monarchs, they maintained a loyalty greater than that shown by those other subjects of the same king, in Antwerpen or Eindhoven. Despite enormous distances, Iberian imperialism in the Atlantic thrived on a shared (Hispanic) language and culture.

EL DORADO: THE CURSE OF BULLION?

In the years between 1492 and 1520, for those crossing the ocean the rewards of the Atlantic territories lay at least as much in the hope of easy access to the riches of Asia as in any material prosperity to be derived from occupation of Caribbean islands. Early expeditions sent home some few items made from precious metals, but it was the conquest of Mexico that fulfilled the wildest dreams of those who believed that out west there was treasure to be seized from "primitive" but fabulously wealthy natives, an ideal powerfully reinforced by the conquest of Peru. Plunder became a credible objective of exploration and settlement, confirming a model of "get rich quick" imperialism. Even after the first period of extraordinary despoilation of the mainland peoples, plunder remained a plausible objective—and one adopted by the Iberians' European rivals in the Atlantic—because of the exploitation of precious mineral deposits from the 1530s, and spectacularly with the large-scale exploitation of the deposits at Potosí (in modern-day Bolivia) from 1545 and Zacatecas (Mexico) from 1548.

One may only speculate about the history of early modern Europe had these riches been used to invest in the domestic economy of Iberia or in cementing economic ties between Iberia and the other states of Felipe's inheritance. Like the citizens of a twentieth-century Middle-Eastern state made suddenly wealthy by oil, Felipe's subjects might have enjoyed previously unimagined material prosperity. Instead, by the end of Felipe's reign, Castilla was already suffering the ravages of rural depopulation, inflation, and poverty.

To its Habsburg monarchs, and thence to its Castilian governors and administrators, the Atlantic possessions became a vitally important source of cash which could be exploited without the political risks associated with attempts to tax the resources of the other parts of their dominions. As bullion came to be the single most important product of the Iberian Atlantic, so the policy towards the Atlantic territories became increasingly dominated by the need to exclude from the Atlantic other Europeans as interlopers, traders, or rival settlers.

CONQUEST AND CONVERSION: MODELS OF EMPIRE

At each end of this period, the coincidence of the fall of Granada with the start of the American enterprise, and of the expulsion of the *moriscos* with the Twelve Years' Truce, symbolised an Iberian identification of militant Roman Catholicism with territorial ambition. In between, the hispanisation of Iberia and its empire was carried forward in developing concepts of identity, race, and cultural relativism amongst the occupiers and occupied, juxtaposed with religious imperatives to conquest and conversion. In this, the centralism of the Castilian project—the direction of the empire from Madrid in matters of governance and from Sevilla for commerce—contrasted with the political and particularist difficulties with all other parts of the Habsburg Empire.

In retrospect, we may suggest that in sixteenth-century Iberia, the crown pursued a process of state-building through the extension into local communities of royal justice, taxation, mobilisation of military manpower and *matériel*, and the encouragement of a nobility increasingly tied to the crown's endeavours. Across Europe, this phenomenon has been explained as the response of monarchs to the spiralling costs of warfare, and it is observed that it almost invariably led to domestic confrontations between a traditional political world of consultative assemblies and customary rights, with a new model of bureaucratised, centralised government and declaratory law.

In the North Atlantic, however, the Castilian crown confronted what was, from the contemporaneous Iberian perspective, a true tabula rasa, an arena within which the indigenous peoples had no pre-existing rules, rights, or privileges to obstruct or impede the deployment of idealised models of government and exploitation. With no native or customary rights to be respected or accommodated, within its new territories the Castilian crown was at its most free to innovate and integrate in government and exploitation, and across the Atlantic, Castilla could reify the model of government that most suited the practical and theoretical preferences of its administrators and lawyers. By taking the opportunity to create a model government outside of Iberia, the crown might avoid confronting the most serious problems of its government within the peninsula—problems that were early and so violently illustrated in the revolt of the *comuneros*. Ironically, the creation of an Atlantic empire prolonged the life of the regionalist mentality and constitutionalist diversity of Iberia, beyond the period when other emergent early modern European states were challenging their own versions of these characteristics.

Was this effect conscious or intended by the crown? Did the Castilian crown or its servants deliberately seek to create polities beyond the frontiers of Iberia to escape what they perceived as the restrictions inherited from former ages? Were the territories of the Atlantic empire governed in the ways their administrators wished they could rule in Iberia? There is, in fact, little to support a view that the Iberian Atlantic was conceived of as a laboratory for testing or refining methods of government for the homeland: the evidence for innovation in the administration of government, justice, or commerce points to the export from, not the import to, Iberia of models and principles, in rather the same way that Iberian cities founded in the Atlantic world were built on the rational, mathematical model of the gridiron, whereas not even Madrid was built or aggrandised according to this plan—in contrast with some pre-Columbian cities of Mesoamerica.

In essence, the Atlantic lands were "discovered" by accident, seized to pre-empt other European rivals, and exploited for the benefit of the non-Iberian, European projects of Habsburg monarchs. America was a side-show in the thinking of hispanised kings who were actually foreign to Iberia whilst they fought Protestants in the German lands and secessionists in the Low Countries. Castilla's élite, however, through successive generations, chose to support the imperialist aims of their monarchs, and not simply once the royal capital had been fixed at Madrid (1561). Castilian soldiers, bureaucrats, and nobles willingly served their monarchs both in Europe and the Atlantic in a relationship that was, if not initially then very quickly, symbiotic: the infant "Spanish" state developed rapidly in response to a need to manage the imperial project which in turn supported an unnaturally bloated but semi-privatised bureaucracy. At home, the prosperity of a few was the reward for service to the crown, not for enterprise.

THE IBERIAN ACHIEVEMENT AND THE CHALLENGES TO MONOPOLY

We should now revisit our initial question: how did Iberian imperialism interact with the indigenous peoples it encountered?

With deliberate and conscious cruelty, occasionally mitigated by missionary activity, the effectiveness of both approaches derived in part from the combination of collaborationism amongst some indigenous peoples and passivity on the part of others: of the minority who did resist, they could literally be outgunned. Herein lay the root cause of the tragedy of the indigenous peoples of the mainland, but even if a model of peaceful co-operation had been devised, the impact of European disease on the indigenous peoples of the islands and American mainland would nevertheless have fundamentally altered the demographic and hence social history of these regions. Into the resulting partial vacuum, sufficient numbers of people from Iberia were unwilling to venture, and an empty Western Hemisphere might have resulted. This emptiness would have been more profound if the Iberians had taken the path, later adopted by the English, of limiting or avoiding liaisons with indigenous peoples; instead, the opportunity to develop a mestizo culture would probably have been taken in any case as a response to the population deficit.

The additional factor was African slavery, and we may ask why there was not a greater importation of free or time-limited indentured labour to encourage exploitation, in collaboration with an expanding transatlantic African commerce. An answer lies in African societies' readiness to accept immediate returns on exports of peoples—profits of slaving—rather than invest in the larger, longer terms needed to support African enterprise. African societies were not sufficiently motivated to pursue the Atlantic opportunities on their own behalf because prospective returns were insufficiently attractive when compared with the likely investment of capital, resources, and people. A lack of scruple on the part of Iberians about enslaving Africans is not a sufficient explanation: circumstances permitted indulgence of this kind of thinking rather than its creation, but Iberian projects created precedents that other Europeans followed and from which sufficient Africans themselves profited that they collaborated. The contradiction in Iberian thinking about slavery for non-Christian Africans, when compared with non-Christian Americans, marked the limits of the Iberian missionary zeal.

Was there something distinctive about Iberian imperialism that gave it early pre-eminence? On balance, this seems untenable: any advantages of a geographical position nearer the oceanic wind tracks seems insufficient, the population of Iberia was not pressing on the limits of resources or land, and there were relatively limited numbers of emigrants to the Atlantic world. Instead, Iberia's undeniable pre-eminence was merely the result of being first in the field, and its greatest achievement, that its empire lasted relatively unchallenged for so long. In the view of one distinguished expert, the fact of the empire's creation was itself remarkable, rather than any debate about reasons for its decline:

no unified nation-state but a political framework which worked for a while; no "modern" centralization of power, but a widely diffused ethos and habit which made obedience come easily; no bonanza but a modest measure—by the standards of the time—of fiscal productiveness; no heroic prowess, but a dogged ability to keep armies in the field and fleets at sea; no uniformity of culture, but a disposition to peaceful change; no peculiar virtues and vices, but some special merits—in particular, a relatively large educated elite with values which favoured technical innovation and creative arts. At the same time, the paradox at the heart of the subject abides: the fragility of the achievement is always apparent, its durability always impressive.[44]

At what point and for what reasons did the pre-eminence of Iberia begin realistically to be challenged? Was the seventeenth-century so-called decline of Spain an inevitable consequence of false expectations generated by America? Or did it derive from the failure of the count-duke of Olivares to persuade enough of his fellow subjects of Felipe IV to embrace the ideal of a shared empire?

In reality, the sixteenth century was not the high-water mark of Iberian influences on the development of new societies in the New World. The Iberian century created a new consciousness of the Atlantic as a highway, not a barrier, exemplified in the regularity of the fleets despite the burdens of war and rivals to empire. From an Iberian perspective, the period began the successful extension and maintenance of Iberian, particularly Hispanic societies and culture, throughout the early modern period and into the modern era, at the expense of indigenous forms that were absorbed, hispanised, or both. There was the establishment and maintenance of political control from Madrid—if not always economic power—in a voluntary empire with persistent commitment of—admittedly modest—resources from the crown. This became an imperial model to be envied, emulated, and challenged by other European powers, so that Iberia set the pattern for the history of the North Atlantic until 1776, when the revolutionary change came from an alternative, white Anglophone tradition.

FURTHER READING

For: helpful and concise ready reference on specific subjects, see S. A. Bedini, ed., *Christopher Columbus and the Age of Exploration: An Encyclopedia* (1992; abridged and reprinted, New York, 1998); a recently updated analytical narrative of the whole of our period, see P. Bakewell, *A History of Latin America*, 2nd ed. (Malden, Mass., and Oxford, 2003); a detailed account of the first settlement, see K. Deagan and J. M. Cruxent, *Columbus' Outpost Among the Taínos. Spain and America at La Isabela, 1493–1498* (New Haven, Conn., and London, 2002); analytical and textual criticism of some of the leading accounts of contact, see B. Pastor Bodmer, *The Armature of Conquest: Spanish Accounts of the Discovery of America, 1492–1589*, trans.

L. L. Hunt (Stanford, Calif., 1992); the experiences of the incomers, see J. Casey, *Early Modern Spain: A Social History* (London, 1999), P. E. Pérez-Mallaína Bueno, *Spain's Men of the Sea: Daily Life on the Indies Fleets in the Sixteenth Century*, trans. C. R. Phillips (Baltimore, Md., and London, 1998), I. Altman, *Emigrants and Society: Extremadura and America in the Sixteenth Century* (Berkeley, Calif., 1989), J. F. Schwaller, *The Church and Clergy in Sixteenth-Century Mexico* (Albuquerque, N.Mex., 1987), and A. C. Van Oss, *Church and Society in Spanish America* (Amsterdam, 2003); a detailed scholarly account of the conquest of Mexico, see H. Thomas, *Conquest: Montezuma, Cortés, and the Fall of Old Mexico*, (New York, 1995); contacts to and from the wider empire, see R. Pieper, *Die Vermittlung einer Neuen Welt. Amerika in Nachrichtennetz des Habsburgischen Imperiums, 1493–1598* (Mainz, 2000); a perspective on the experience of the indigenous peoples of the mainland New World, see J. Wilson, *The Earth Shall Weep. A History of Native America* (London, 1998); S. Schroeder, ed., *Native Resistance and the Pax Colonial in New Spain* (Lincoln, Nebr., and London, 1998), J. I. Israel, *Race, Class and Politics in Colonial Mexico* (Oxford, 1975); a collection of links to diverse sites, mostly in English, on 15th- and 16th-century European voyages and voyagers around the globe, see "Discoverers Web: The Age of Discovery," http://www.win.tue.nl/cs/fm/engels/discovery/#age.

CHAPTER 8

1607–1697: La Nouvelle-France, New England, Nieuw Nederland, and Nya Sverige

If we may conveniently label the century or so following Columbus's first transatlantic expedition as that of the Iberian monopoly, we may perhaps portray the seventeenth century as, for West Europeans in the North Atlantic world, the period of diversification, capitalism, and the first age of globalisation. At the same time, however, there were further millions of victims of European imperialism, chiefly amongst the indigenous peoples of Mesoamerica, to whom were now added more of the peoples on the continent to the north. Beyond these victims, there was further significant growth in the rate at which peoples were forcibly transplanted from Africa: numbers of slaves being shipped annually across the Atlantic may have averaged 9,500 around 1600, to reach perhaps 36,100 around 1700.[1] The North Atlantic world thus remained united for a plurality of cultural groups by their common experiences of settlement, exploitation, and suffering.

In this chapter, we explore these themes of diversity and common experience. Within these themes, however, perhaps the greatest interpretative challenge for historians is the question of timing, "Why then?" Put another way, given that amongst European societies there was a widespread knowledge of the existence of the Atlantic world from c. 1500 and a common sense of ambition to profit from exploitation, why did Europeans other than Iberians make so little headway in establishing settlements in the Atlantic world before c. 1600 and so much headway after that date? At the same time as we try to understand what happened during the seventeenth century, we shall also contemplate what might have, but did not, happen. In particular, we shall reflect on such alternative scenarios as a resurgent Hispanic imperialism, the emergence of colonial multilateralism, French hegemony, a greater resistance amongst indigenous peoples, and wars of independence. In this period, perhaps more significantly than in the centuries immediately before and after it, what did not happen and why is as important as what did happen for our understanding of the transformation of the North Atlantic.

DIVERSITY

From a West European perspective, by c. 1700 the societies of the North Atlantic world were significantly more diverse than was the situation c. 1600. This diversity was exemplified in language, religious practice, attitudes to race, social structures, and in the physical environment such as the layout and architecture of towns and cities. From 1603, Samuel de Champlain led the way to French colonisation of Canada, with Québec founded in 1608. In 1607, English settlers founded Jamestown and from 1612, settled in Bermuda. Dutch traders maintained a year-round presence at Fort Nassau, then Fort Orange (now Albany, New York) from 1614, on the Essequibo River (now Guyana) in 1616, and settlers founded Nieuw Amsterdam (now New York City) in 1625, where in 1643 a French priest reported eighteen languages were in use.[2] In the Delaware valley and originally staffed by Dutch renegades, Nya Sverige was refounded in 1643, with Finnish and Swedish families. Other Scandinavian, German Protestant, and Jewish as well as Dutch families settled in Nieuw Nederland. Amongst the smaller islands of the eastern Caribbean, English settlements were established from the 1620s, on St. Christopher/St. Kitts (1624), Barbados (1627), Nevis (1628), Montserrat, and Antigua (1632); French settlers shared St. Kitts with the English (from 1627), and began to occupy Guadeloupe and Martinique (secured by 1638); and Danish agents occupied St. Thomas. Although English attempts to establish bases on the mainland of South America were not successful (from 1611), Dutch traders set up bases on Curaçao (1634), St. Martin, and St. Eustatius (1641). Thus, the political and cultural geography of the Europeans' North Atlantic, so clearly Hispanic in 1600, by 1650 was fragmented in polyglot rivalry.[3]

This was, of course, not the first period in which attempts were made by other Europeans to intrude on the Iberian North Atlantic monopoly, but it was the first period in which these attempts met with any appreciable success or permanence. After 1600, we may propose, it was not so much that the Iberian Empire had suffered a diminished capacity to exclude them, as it was that these rivals attained a level of technical[4] competence sufficient to give their colonial-imperial enterprises improved chances of survival and success. In effect, practice made perfect: between

c. 1600 and c. 1635, a number of West European societies developed work-able technical means that were enough for the establishment of viable overseas settlement by meeting the challenges which confronted all of them—namely, communications, demographic sustainability, economic viability, and defence.

A number of elements, each necessary but none of itself sufficient, con-tributed to this technical breakthrough. Most difficult to quantify was the element of psychological fillip, the boost to self-confidence, of surviving as independent states the long and exhausting wars with the Iberian su-perpower. Awareness of risk had itself been altered by the years of war, for not only had societies in western Europe confronted and survived the challenge of foreign invasion, there had also been in the last years of the sixteenth century a succession of harvests so bad that people had starved to death in the streets, and in the opening years of the seventeenth century plague had carried off yet more people, particularly on the eastern littoral of the North Atlantic.[5] By comparison with the threats of invasion and conquest by Felipe II, transoceanic enterprise may have seemed to em-body only moderate dangers.

More easily quantified, there was a peace dividend for north-west Eu-rope's maritime powers. Although formally allied in their common fear of the Iberian empire, Henri IV of France secured peace at the Treaty of Vervins (1598), James VI of Scotland and I of England made peace at the Treaty of London (1604), and the Dutch republic made a Twelve Year Truce (1609). In none of these cases did a separate peace bring the Catholic monarchy much relief or advantage in those of its struggles that continued. For Iberia's opponents, however, the measurable peace dividend included reservoirs of military and naval expertise otherwise surplus to requirements, reduced opportunities for enrichment or ennoblement through war, and enlarged state machinery for raising taxes and mobilising resources, all of which might potentially be exploited to establish colonies.

A third set of elements was related to material circumstances and ex-pressed principally in the consequences of a growth in populations, notwithstanding the demographic challenges of war, disease, and poor harvests. During the sixteenth century, West European populations recov-ered from the low points following the Black Death to create growing num-bers of the rural poor so that "By the late sixteenth century most villages had sizeable numbers—and often a majority—of land-poor and landless households."[6] The impoverishment of rural populations prompted a search for waged employment, migration to growing towns in search of oppor-tunity, an expansion of arable farming, more commercialised agriculture, and contributed to price inflation.[7] Migration within a kingdom could be-come emigration beyond it, if other circumstances permitted.

With European politics more or less stabilising after 1600, any entrepreneur willing to risk modest outlay but looking for large returns quickly had to find alternatives to privateering, profiteering in military supplies, or dealing in contraband goods. A century and more of Portuguese and Castilian maritime enterprise had demonstrated proof of concept of North Atlantic colonialism, and the circumnavigation of the globe by, for example, Francis Drake (1577–80), demonstrated that the Iberians could not enforce a monopoly on either oceanic access or marine technology. Contemporaneous with but not necessarily consequent on the moves to peace in western Europe, there was a surge of investment in maritime commercial enterprise that capitalised trade and settlement around the globe. These enterprises were sponsored by joint stock companies which, although by no means novel forms of organisation, nevertheless, attracted larger scale investments than their predecessors: the English East India (1600), the Virginia (1606 and 1609) Companies, and Ulster Plantation; the Dutch Vereenigde Oost-Indische Compagnie (1602) and a West-Indische Compagnie (proposed from 1614 and chartered in 1621); the Compagnie de la Nouvelle France (1627); and the Danish east and west India companies.

In contrast with the policies of the previous half century, however, was the extent to which governments were now willing to support these companies politically and diplomatically against rivals at home and abroad. These companies enjoyed state support through their charters of monopoly rights over commerce to secure profits and to support economies of scale. Again, such charters were not innovations and indeed imitated the long-established practice of their Iberian competitors. In comparison with other forms of enterprise, there were low entry costs, participation by speculators was just as likely to succeed on the small scale as on the grand, and access to opportunities was not a function of relative state power. Scots, Swedes, Portuguese, and English, subjects of the smaller states, vied on roughly equal terms with Dutch, French, and Hispanic subjects of the more populous and rich states. Notable for their continued absence as direct participants although they remained heavily involved in the capitalisation of Iberian projects, were the merchant communities of the Italian peninsula: profit from North Atlantic enterprise need not require expeditions by one's own compatriots.

This proliferation of West European societies' engagement with the North Atlantic world reflected, in part, a surge of commercial and political confidence in the ability to contend with the Iberian pathfinders in their worldwide expansion. Iberian enterprise having set the examples and precedents, other West Europeans sought opportunities in the gaps in the Iberian Empire, rather than in frontal assaults on the established Iberian colonies. Along the West African littoral and amongst the Caribbean islands, there remained significant opportunities for the establishment of outposts from which to compete and, as occasion demanded, collaborate with the Iberians, as well as with other West Europeans. On the North American mainland, the Iberian presence was virtually nonexistent. Despite the inflated hopes, nothing comparable with the indigenous empires of Mesoamerica was found by the new insurgents, but that probably improved the prospects for their success: large indigenous communities able to mobilise sizeable armies and to deny local resources to the latest incomers would have significantly raised the costs (in terms of manpower and firepower) needed to establish outposts. This is not to say that the indigenous peoples were indifferent to the new arrivals: Kwaib peoples of the Caribbean maintained the resistance they had for long shown to the Iberians, and mainland peoples had to be persuaded to collaborate by trades in metalwares and firearms. In any event, relatively small groups of settlers were able to establish workable colonies, without the benefit of expropriated indigenous labour, provided that they could early identify tradable commodities: fish, furs, sugar, and tobacco. Except for the peculiar case of English refugees of conscience—Puritan or Roman Catholic—the speed and size of return on the investment were important to the long-term viability of these outposts, but the success of some rather than others did not rely only on the factors at play in the colonial context.

Through the early years of wider European settlement in the North Atlantic, amongst the islands as well as on continental North America, until perhaps the beginnings of the Revolt of Portugal and the Revolt of the Catalans (1640), there was no compelling reason to suppose that these new ventures would not meet the same fate as their predecessors of the sixteenth century—collapse through inadequate planning and support, in the face of hostile environments and indigenous peoples—even without the possibility of expulsion by the armed forces of Madrid. Dutch, French, Swedish, and Danish endeavours were roughly comparable with each other and with those of the English, for size, competence, capitalisation, engagement with the indigenous peoples and environments. Surveyed around the mid-1630s, it would not have been easy to predict that some or other of these colonial projects would—or would not—succeed.

We should note that there was not necessarily in the early seventeenth century a simple or commonly shared understanding of colonial success. Territorial acquisition was not yet—as it would to some extent become for later-nineteenth-century Europe—the measure of great power status. Volumes of trade and value of commodities were increasingly perceived as important ingredients in any rise to great power status, as the Europe-wide envy of the Dutch republic blended with emergent theories of what in retrospect we identify as mercantilism. Early modern Dutch prosperity, however, was built on unglamorous but reliable endeavours: domestic agricultural productivity, skilled manufacturing and finishing trades, and the maintenance of food supplies from the Baltic (grain) and North Seas (fish). By comparison, the total value of colonial enterprise was always useful but not essential to Dutch society. In any calculation of expected returns, for most West European societies colonial settlement was more likely to be a necessary inconvenience in the pursuit of riches rather than an objective for its own sake.

The creation of colonies of permanent and self-sustaining settlement was not the prime objective of early-seventeenth-century European enterprise. Rather, colonies might be deemed necessary as points of access to other sources of valued commodities for onward trade in western Europe, and this proposition lay at the heart of the establishment of European outposts along the West African littoral, as well as amongst the societies of the Indian ocean and Asia. This approach was also adopted in the New World by all of the contending West European societies, except the English.

In retrospect, we may suggest that the great discriminator in the calculus of establishing successful—that is, permanent and self-sustaining—colonial settlements in the Western Hemisphere, was the extent to which there were more profitable and attractive prospects closer to the homeland. Simply put, for the English in the early seventeenth century, there were fewer and less attractive opportunities in western Europe than were perceived to exist by their European colonial rivals. Colonial endeavour could bring spectacular rewards, relative to the investments and for the benefit of a small number of participants, but in the pursuit of large and sustained returns, opportunities in western Europe were at once closer and potentially greater.

Notwithstanding the securing of peace terms amongst the West European governments around 1600, within a few years of the treaties, the politicomilitary rivalries were renewed—with enthusiasm. In 1610, Henri IV of France was preparing for war in alliance with Protestant German princes against the Habsburgs, when his assassination threw domestic French politics into turmoil. Continued politicoreligious tensions amongst the central European states, seeking to inhibit the Habsburg imperial power with which purpose other European governments connived, led to the start of what became the Thirty Years War (1618–1648). In succession, the Iberian, Dutch, Danish, Swedish, and French governments subsidised allies amongst the central European states before intervening directly in warfare that spread out over much of the continent and became subsumed in wider struggles: wars of independence (by the Dutch, Portuguese, Catalans), imperial expansion in Europe (by Danes and Swedes, against each other as well as in the German lands), and European hegemony (between the Habsburg Empires and the French).

During this period of extended European war, colonial enterprise from these West European states did not cease, but neither did it substantially increase. Colonial campaigns were not yet perceived—other than by the Dutch—to be effective means to pursue major objectives of the participants in the European war, and although the "wealth of the Indies" received by Iberia remained an object of envy and concern, the most spectacular (and strategically effective) coup of the period was not the seizure of significant colonial territory but an act of grand theft—the capture of the treasure fleet at Matanzas (northern Cuba) by a Dutch fleet commanded by Piet Hein (1628). For the most part, the commitments of manpower and *matériel* to operations in European theatres of war were more, and more likely to be, productive in terms of territorial and political gains, particularly if the fiscal burdens were underwritten by other states (such as France) or were offset by plunder and expropriations in the territories in which combat was pursued.

Only the monarchy in Britain stood aside from these struggles, at first because of the pacifism of James VI and I (which saw him seek to act as intermediary in re-establishing peace), and then because of the lack of financial resources to allow military intervention to be taken seriously, in the case of Charles I. Certainly, the poor military performance of the English forces sent to France in the 1620s did not suggest that here was a potential ally capable of changing the balance of power on the continent, although the English navy in the Channel was a force that might significantly affect the ability of the Iberian monarchy to maintain its maritime link with the Low Countries. In the 1620s and 1630s, opinion amongst the politically active in English society was often resentful of the lack of action on behalf of international Protestantism, which combined with fears for the reformed faith at home. Some of this resentment spilled over into volunteers serving in the armies of the Dutch, German, or Swedish states; for others, resentment moved them to emigration to the New World to set a clearer example of the life of the godly community: "as a city set upon a hill," in the words cited by John Winthrop.

We may observe that, as was powerfully demonstrated in the 1640s and 1650s, English society did possess the resources to mount major military and naval operations, leading to colonial conquest: in Scotland and Ireland. If, therefore, the English state had intervened in the Thirty Years War, we may speculate that it might have played a role akin to that of the Swedish monarchy: a smaller state with disproportionately effective military power, subsidised by its richer allies and seizing opportunities to create its own empire in northern Europe. Swedish society, however, was not so divided within itself on ideological grounds as was English society, which may have made it more likely that the English state would have suffered the fate of the other, lesser central European players, and become a dependent of either the Habsburgs or the French.

In retrospect, we may suggest that it was of crucial significance in the development of English colonial endeavour in the New World that, unlike the other West European states with maritime colonial ambitions, the English were not drawn into major war, until the 1640s. For 20 years or so, whilst other West European societies were pursuing continental struggles, English society remained largely at peace (notwithstanding political and religious controversy) as it exported settlers to territories over which there were limited disputes with European rivals. English domestic circumstances, whilst not utterly impoverished, provided only limited opportunities for some individuals to pursue social advancement or religious preference. Consequently, numbers of emigrants were sufficiently large in these early years—proportionately much larger than the numbers from other West European societies, although still a tiny fraction of migration in Britain as a whole—to permit English colonial populations to attain critical mass: new arrivals and natural reproduction made some colonial settlements self-sustaining, and the probability of personal enrichment encouraged a continuous flow of new arrivals to the colonies with higher mortality. When Britain was overtaken by catastrophic civil war in the 1640s, the campaigns were fought without intervention by other European powers, whilst the colonial settlements were sufficiently well established to survive with reduced contact and immigration from the homeland. The English state that emerged in the aftermath of civil war, in the 1650s, was utterly different from that of the prewar era: not only did it conquer its immediate British neighbours, it quickly reasserted control of Anglophone colonies and became a sought-after ally of the major European powers.

Certainly, the Thirty Years War in Europe was hugely destructive and expensive for all those societies engaged in it. It did not, however, reach over the Atlantic to be fought out in lands and seas far distant from the centre of the conflict, because the potential gains in colonial campaigns were not immediately supportive of political aims in Europe. With the significant exception of the efforts by the English state, against the Iberian colonies in the 1650s and the Dutch from the 1660s, it was not until c. 1700 that the war aims between European states were pursued across the Atlantic: eighteenth-century experience was crucially different in this respect. From the 1660s until the 1690s, the states of western Europe replaced more or less general war with a succession of shorter, more targeted campaigns in pursuit of the aims they had refined in the earlier conflict—territorial expansion around the Baltic and along France's eastern frontiers and naval supremacy in European waters. Around the North Atlantic, meanwhile, the development of settlement and exploitation (as contrasted with plunder) was pursued, along with the diversification amongst the societies from which settlers were drawn to bring peoples, both involuntarily and willingly, from all across western Europe—and Africa—to Caribbean and American settlement. The growth in numbers of settlers in Anglophone colonies (augmented by an early openness to immigration from other parts of Europe) continued to outpace population increase in settlements governed by other European states, making the populations of European origin ruled by English colonial governments second in size only to those of the Iberian colonial empire.

MERCANTILISM, CAPITALISM, GLOBALISATION?

Already in the London of the 1660s, a man like Samuel Pepys might enjoy as his morning draught a cup of chocolate (from Jamaica), fortified with sack (dry white wine from the Canarias). When he went to the Royal Exchange for news of maritime commerce, he could take coffee (from Mocca) in Covent Garden, to which he added sugar (from the Caribbean), before discussing the state of trade in spices and textiles imported from Asian societies. He might enjoy sweet potatoes and perhaps a tomato (originally from the New World) with his dinner of salt cod (from the Grand Banks), and round off the meal with a pipe of tobacco (from Virginia). Pepys took pleasure in the commodities of the Atlantic and wider world, by no means all of which came from territories owing allegiance to the king of England, the restored Charles II. Never a man to shy away from enthusiastic comment about any of life's experiences, Pepys seems rarely to have been moved by the extraordinary range of commodities that were available to him at prices which he, still a relatively junior civil servant in the 1660s, could afford. Whether or not they were conscious of it, Pepys and his contemporaries participated in a globalised economy that connected them to oceanic commerce, plantation agriculture, slave ownership, and colonisation—not only in the Anglophone but also in the whole mercantile experience of early modern Europe. From the mid–sixteenth century, bullion imports from the Iberian New World had, by increasing money supplies faster than growth in commodities, contributed to monetary inflation across Europe. In the seventeenth century, what has been called the gastroeconomy of the North Atlantic conquered the European diet (although not necessarily to the same extent at all levels and in all societies), as expressed in the exotic agriculture of the everyday, such as the wonder crops, potato and maize; in the newly plentiful narcotics, sugar and tobacco; and in the new staples, tomato and Grand Banks cod.

Colonial—and, more important, commercial—rivalries around the North Atlantic were accompanied in the seventeenth century by emerging doctrines of economic competitiveness, even though the realities were that West European trading economies became increasingly interdependent. In this period, however, amongst those few thinkers who gave serious consideration to economic affairs, prevailing assumptions included the belief that international trade was an activity of finite—and fixed—volume and value. Although the term "zero-sum" was unknown in seventeenth-century Europe, the concept was believed to apply to trade such that a state might increase its share and value of international trade only at the expense of other states participating in such commerce. If trade were an expression of a state's wealth and power, then each state should seek to maximise its share of the finite cake. The Dutch republic seemed to demonstrate that a society deriving wealth by trade could overcome limitations in its natural resources. Lacking state machinery to enforce policies, the period was inevitably characterised by discrepancies between intentions and attainments. Immature capitalism coincided with growing state aspirations to influence economic development, and a form of globalised European commerce was an unintended consequence of frustrated monopolies and open competition in trade and war.

In our enquiries about the transformation of the North Atlantic, however, we may be struck more forcefully by the convergence of personal experiences, rather than the impact of "isms."

EXPERIENCES IN COMMON

Whilst we note the diversification of cultures and languages amongst Europeans seeking permanent settlement around the North Atlantic, we may also observe that they were united by the common denominators of colonialism's challenges. In the absence of significant technological advances in this period, competing European societies met these challenges in more or less the same ways. Over time, the colonial experience for all of these societies was perhaps more similar, and therefore more likely to encourage a common outlook, than were the experiences and attitudes that divided them one from another. In turn, as experience of Atlantic colonialism spread across European societies along with the exotic fruits of those contacts—tobacco, chocolate, maize, potatoes—regional differences could be eroded.

First and foremost, colonies all relied on the maintenance of communications with European homelands to allow for continued immigration, commerce, and cultural reinforcement of identities that so often aspired to remain distinct from, rather than enriched by, the cultures of the indigenous peoples. Next in importance, they all pursued demographic sustainability, often by attempting to recruit family groups to migrate from the homelands rather than by actively promoting intermarriage with indigenous communities. Third, the attractiveness of colonial emigration was in part dependent on fostering economic viability for the new settlements, which would provide demonstrable material incentives to incomers in standards of living at least equal to, but preferably better than, those on offer in the homeland. Last, but not least, physical security—effective defence against raiders from outside or against rebel dependent peoples, slave or indigenous—had to be credible for settlers, particularly families, to be willing to stay. Notwithstanding competition and irrespective of the societies from which they originated, European colonists confronted the same challenges—communications, demographic sustainability, economic viability, and defence—so that there was perhaps more in the experiences of ordinary people across the North Atlantic that united them than there was to divide them: e pluribus unum?

Beyond these common issues amongst European incomers, however, there were other significant forms of experience that were shared around the North Atlantic. Extreme violence against the non-European peoples around the North Atlantic continued as it had during the sixteenth century. First contact with indigenous communities might be characterised by peaceful trade or tolerance, but this initial stage was recurrently superseded by contempt for indigenous customs and recourse to violence as part of the expropriation of land, labour, and resources, adding to the tally of victims of colonialism. It should, however, also be recalled that murderous rivalry amongst Europeans was already established as a feature of the early modern Atlantic world, graphically illustrated by such events as Menéndez's massacre of the French settlers in northern Florida in 1565, or Drake's sack of Santo Domingo and Cartagena in 1585–86. Beyond the sufferings of the indigenous peoples, the seventeenth century saw substantial growth in the numbers of involuntary migrants—principally slaves from Africa but also some of European origin—transported across the North Atlantic. Only rarely do we find amongst Europeans forthright criticism of the violence of colonial endeavour: it was useful in England in the 1650s to remind a public that the Iberian Empire was built on vast cruelty and to commemorate this in one of the first operatic performances in London, but this was merely propaganda in time of war rather than a declaration of a crusade to relieve suffering.[8]

Misery for the many and prosperity for the few would remain the predominant character of the European presence around the North Atlantic, in the seventeenth century as much as in the sixteenth.

THE ROADS NOT TAKEN

When we began, we noted that for the seventeenth century, it may be as interesting to reflect on the developments that did not arise as it is to ponder how the North Atlantic story actually unfolded. This was a century, after all, in which the extraordinary seemed to challenge so much that had been presumed beyond dispute. In retrospect, we count as forward steps in the progress of knowledge: Galileo's viewing of the surface of the moon, Harvey's account of the circulation of the blood, Descartes's geometry, Huygens's pendulum clock, Guericke's creation of a partial vacuum, Leibniz's calculating machine, Newton's laws of motion, and Leeuwenhoek's studies of the microscopic world. In the world of affairs, the supremacy of the shogunate and the closing of Japanese society to outside contacts, the establishment of the Manchu dynasty, the public trial and execution of a king for "crimes against the people" in England, the climax and beginnings of the fragmentation of the Moghul empire, an Ottoman siege of the Habsburgs' Viennese capital—each of these developments meant for those involved a "world turned upside down." Our understanding of the actual transformation of the North Atlantic may be enriched by limited speculation on the possible alternative outcomes.

Hispanic Resurgence

Conventionally, it has been argued that the seventeenth century saw the eclipse of the Iberian Empire as the global superpower, through the struggle of the Thirty Years War and in the rise of France, symbolised by the Peace of the Pyrenees (1659).[9] At first sight, it may be tempting to describe the North Atlantic world as changing in the same rhythm, with a proliferation of new, non-Hispanic colonies in the Caribbean and North America transforming an Iberian monopoly into competitive pluralism. Before accepting this proposition, however, we should recall that in many respects, the Iberian Atlantic Empire continued to grow and flourish through this period.

New settlers from Iberia continued to cross the North Atlantic during the 1600s in numbers which, although they contributed to the general decline in the peninsula's population, sustained the growth of an Hispanic population of the empire. Perhaps as many as 5,000 people a year left for the New World during the seventeenth century, for the most part fleeing economic decline in Iberia.[10] Culturally Hispanic populations in the empire grew over the century, not least because of the expansion in numbers of mestizo peoples, who aligned themselves more with the culture and language of the rulers rather than those of the ruled. That total populations within the empire may not have grown as significantly reflected a continuing decline in the numbers of the Pre-Columbian peoples. Even these populations, however, slowed their (previously catastrophic) rates of decline.

Overall, the prosperity of the Iberian Empire also continued to grow, as reflected, for example, in the value of goods passing through Sevilla, even if much of the trade profited foreigners elsewhere in Europe. For the crown in Madrid, of course, of most importance was the value of the bullion imports, which though at times less than the peaks of the late sixteenth century, nonetheless remained by any definition substantial. The consequences of this for state finances and Madrid's ability to project military power across Europe were considerable, although this was not the only measure of the colonial economy. Amongst the colonists, there developed a greater self-sufficiency in the commodities of ordinary consumption that had previously been supplied from Iberia, and a growing volume of trade was conducted with interlopers: Dutch, French, and English.

The empire also grew territorially, at least with respect to the frontier of settlement on the continental mainland, which continued to be pushed north and west, where new settlements continued to be founded. Admittedly, Hispanic rule, if not always settlement, was ousted from a number of Caribbean islands—for example, Jamaica (1655)—but these territories were by no means as significant to lose as either the new rulers hoped or with nineteenth-century hindsight they appeared to be.

Although the loss of these islands gave imperial rivals strategic bases for potential further operations, this potential was largely unfulfilled in the seventeenth century. In the first place, the new European insurgents were as much rivals to each other as to the Iberian Empire and devoted significant proportions of their still-limited resources to multilateral conflict. Second, no serious attempts were made to dislodge the Iberian hold on major territories on either the mainland, for instance, Florida, or the strategic islands of the eastern Atlantic, for example, amongst the Canarias. Instead, by and large the newcomers sought to establish themselves in those parts of the New World that were not already colonised by Iberians. On the mainland, perhaps the most directly challenging to the Hispanic empire was the Scottish attempt to settle on the Darién isthmus (1698–1700) in, as it were, the interstices of the empire, as the Dutch also tried to do in Surinam. What defeated these efforts, even with the expressed mission to raid and plunder the "Spanish Main," was the hostile climate and unprofitable agriculture that had already deterred Hispanic settlement in Darién since the early days of the conquistadores. In contrast, some serious damage was done to the richest parts of the Iberian New World by the stateless buccaneers, but in this the buccaneers did not discriminate or target: the Hispanic territories were simply numbered amongst their many victims, which included settlements and ships of all the European states.

If we apply to the Hispanic North Atlantic our four tests or challenges—communications, demographic sustainability, economic viability, and defence—we find that the responses already adopted in the sixteenth century were by and large maintained after 1600. The flota continued to provide the principal link across the ocean, and horses and mules, rather than wheeled road traffic, maintained most land communication. Populations continued their shift towards a numerical, as well as political, dominance of Hispanic language and culture. The domestic colonial economies, at least on the mainland, were largely self-sustaining and capable of exporting significant volumes of material to the rest of the empire, in the Americas, Europe, and Asia. Defence remained an important item of government expenditure, in cash, manpower, and *matériel*, but was largely successful, or rather, was not particularly challenged, in preserving the territorial integrity of the empire from either indigenous resistance or external invasion.

The decline of Spain was therefore a European phenomenon rather than a global experience. From this perspective, the founding of Jamestown, despite the eventual eighteenth-century Anglophone "triumph," should in no way be described as sounding the death-knell of the Iberian power in the North Atlantic world. Jamestown did, however, exemplify the extent to which the century-old claim to an Iberian monopoly of access to the Atlantic world was unenforceable, and that whereas claims by prior occupation would largely be respected by Europeans from outside Iberia, claims by title alone would not. This was simply a consequence of geography and the availability of military resources. In the 1560s, the Castilian colonial power had exterminated the French expedition to settle in Florida, which had a deterrent effect for some years. Subsequent sixteenth-century expeditions by French or English would-be settlers endeavoured to keep out of such relatively easy reach of the conquistadores by exploring along the St. Lawrence Valley and the Chesapeake, respectively.

Perhaps the most probable development would have been some reassertion of monopoly by those communities that were predominantly Hispanic in language and culture. The combined populations of Hispanic communities around the North Atlantic c. 1700 still outnumbered by a significant margin all others of European origin, so by this measure alone Madrid had the potential to expel rival settler communities and reestablish at least the semblance of Iberian monopoly. Indeed, these territories did not yet support the numbers of population they probably had c. 1500, so there remained potential for resurgence in the demographic and hence economic prosperity of the Hispanic North Atlantic. At the same time, amongst the surviving communities of indigenous origins in these areas, resistance to Hispanism, whether military or cultural-religious, had largely disappeared, by retreat either physically to the geographically most inhospitable and inaccessible regions or mentally to the secret places of ancient "superstitious" worship. The Hispanic and Roman Catholic victory in this *Kulturkampf* was, to all intents and purposes, complete. Despite, however, the richness of its military-imperial heritage with which to mobilise men and *matériel* to help to overcome the limits of natural and taxation resources, the Iberian Empire of Carlos II lacked the leadership necessary to pursue a reassertion of monopoly. Corruption in Madrid, both political and moral, left the North Atlantic communities to consolidate their positions largely within existing frontiers, instead of adventuring in the manner of their conquistador predecessors. Perhaps the clearest evidence that what the empire lacked was leadership rather than capacity was seen after the extinction of the Habsburg line, in the efforts and achievements of the successor Bourbon/Borbón dynasty.

Colonial Multilateralism

Practical considerations could, from time to time, encourage collaboration amongst the otherwise rival West European settler groups. The most obvious but perhaps unfortunate illustration of this was the internationalism of the buccaneer communities, particularly in the Caribbean. Otherwise, on the small scale, Anglo-French condominium in St. Kitts from the 1620s was motivated by their common fear of the indigenous peoples and of the Iberians being greater than their resentment of each other. Such recognition of mutual interest, whether against the indigenous peoples or the Iberian power, was never much in evidence in the North Atlantic, and in this we may perhaps see missed opportunity.

Instead, the settler communities continued to cultivate their ties of kinship and culture with their homelands and thereby reinforced a fragmentation of the colonial experience into competing imitations on the small scale of European societies. Despite the common challenges and experiences of colonial life and a reliance for a number of years on Dutch merchant shipping to maintain contacts, there was maintained an essential loyalism to metropolitan cultures of origin and identity of economic interest, leading to the emergence of transatlantic cultures in which individuals might move back and forth across the ocean, more readily than across colonial frontiers. In this respect, however, the experience of the colonies ruled by the English did vary; from the later seventeenth century, we see significant numbers of settlers of non-English origin appearing in the Anglophone colonial settlements by migration, rather than as a consequence of conquest. The presence of Scots-Irish, Scots, German, and French immigrants to formally English colonies was an example that other would-be colonial powers might have emulated.

L'Amérique Française

As we have already observed, Eurocentric historiography has for a century or more pursued the characterisation of the seventeenth century as the period of the decline of Spain in contrast with the rise of France. Such a perspective may reasonably prompt us to consider whether there was for French society a comparable story in the North Atlantic. After all, the ingredients of French *grandeur*—rich domestic resources of people, economy, and (within constraints) state power—might have been expected to have enabled French colonialism to fulfil its potential in the Atlantic. The interpretative challenge, however, is to explain why, despite the significant expansion of French territory and influence in Europe between 1600 and 1700 and the claim to vast territories particularly in the interior of North America, the French hold on Atlantic enterprise was, in fact, so tenuous.

Despite earlier enterprises across the Atlantic—encouraged by François I and the attempt to establish settlement in Florida in the 1560s—French engagement with the Atlantic by 1600 remained largely confined to various forms of plunder—by fishing, licensed piracy, or trade in furs. This was explicable as yet one more consequence of the murderous internecine conflicts labelled by historians the French Wars of Religion. Having emerged from prolonged civil war and religious strife with a new dynast on the throne, the French state c. 1600 might perhaps have sought to reknit the torn fabric of French society by avoiding further dangerous engagement in European politics in favour of a common pursuit of North Atlantic exploration, conquest, and colonisation. Arguing for such pursuit was an established capability in transatlantic seafaring (symbolised by Breton fishermen at the Grand Banks), surplus military capacity (the ending of civil wars and the expulsion of the invading armies of Felipe II), a growing population (perhaps 16 million c. 1600), a pool of talented explorers (exemplified by Samuel de Champlain), and men willing to evangelise amongst the "heathen" peoples native to the Atlantic littoral. In addition, the French crown was served by a succession of ministers blessed with imagination combined with political (if not always economic) realism— Sully, Richelieu, Mazarin, Foucquet, Colbert, Vauban—even in periods when her monarchs were of limited capacity. Across the century, at the behest of these ministers, royal government declared itself supportive of a succession of companies and associations established to mobilise manpower and resources for Atlantic enterprise, in African trade as well as in the Western Hemisphere. There was thus, in principle, no lack of willingness at the highest levels of French government to promote transatlantic enterprise.

By comparison with other European societies in this period, France may have lacked the most sophisticated means to mobilise financial resources enjoyed by the Dutch, but the French state did enjoy substantially larger tax revenues than most others. Likewise, although the French navy was usually outnumbered by those of the Dutch or of the English, from the 1620s the state invested in the development of a blue water navy. In common with the North Atlantic efforts of all European societies outside of Iberia, French expeditions looked to occupy some or other of the Caribbean islands for their utility as bases for raiding the established Hispanic settlements and for their potential as sources of tropical agricultural luxuries, as well as those remote corners of the western continent least likely to provoke counterattacks ordered by Madrid or Lisboa. Piracy, plantation, and pelts, a combination familiar to contemporaneous Dutch and English adventurers, was pursued with equivalent profit by Frenchmen.

By 1700, French colonialism in the North Atlantic could point to an impressive list of achievements, from a starting point as low as that of any other European society outside of Iberia. Indeed, in some respects, French enterprise was more successful than many in reaching early accommodation with some of the indigenous peoples of the North Atlantic, especially in the North American interior. In particular, the cultivation of alliances with the Hurons significantly extended the reach of French territorial claims beyond those of Dutch or English mainland colonialism. At the same time, France could also look to the established profits of "her" sugar islands, particularly Martinique, and the potential returns from the occupation of the Mississippi delta.

There remained, however, a fundamental contradiction between French territorial claims and the security of her colonial possessions, as the consequence of the tiny numbers of French settlers. Like Dutch enterprise, French expeditions failed to generate sustained interest amongst people at home, sufficient for them to be willing to settle permanently in the Western Hemisphere, whether in the Caribbean, the St. Lawrence, or the Mississippi delta. Recurrent efforts to transport the destitute or condemned criminals underscored the unattractiveness of the destinations, and the prohibition on Huguenot migration denied the French Atlantic Empire a direct equivalent to the Pilgrim Fathers. Even the effectively limitless supply of land provided insufficient of a draw to a society weighed down by partible inheritance.

This is not to say that the numbers of those willing to migrate to the French Atlantic Empire were substantially lower than those who had been willing, for example, to migrate to the Hispanic settlements. Iberian migration, at perhaps 1,000 people per year during the sixteenth century, compared with French numbers at their best, except that, of course, Iberian migrants had a century's head start. In addition, Iberian migrants from the early sixteenth century had expropriated the labour and agricultural surpluses of the indigenous peoples so that simple subsistence was less of a challenge in the Iberian settlements, and African slavery filled the void of the catastrophic decline in indigenous populations. Like the English and Dutch, French settlements in the Caribbean copied this formula, but for French Canada there was no plantation crop suitable to the northern environment, and the lower densities and limited agricultures of the indigenous peoples allowed them more easily to evade enslavement than the peoples of Mesoamerica. As with the English, for the French the creation of a self-sustaining colonial society depended on emigration from Europe to reach a critical mass to allow the economies of scale needed for the division of labour, specialisation of function, and consequent social diversity. Hispanic communities were ideologically committed to the creation of towns sustained by the expropriated product and labour of indigenous or African peoples, and they generated sufficient surplus to pay for imported items, both basic and luxury, not least because of the output of bullion. English settlements attracted emigrants in sufficient numbers to allow early differentiation of employment into farmers, craftsmen, merchants, and even lawyers, despite the lack of a high-value export commodity. French mainland settlements in the north, however, remained locked into subsistence agriculture, depended on imports for basic commodities, and relied principally on the fur trade to fund the transatlantic commerce. The Louisiana projects, although potentially sources of plantation agricultural products to rival the English, failed to attract sufficient numbers of settlers to sustain growth.

In the absence of substantial emigration to her Atlantic empire, French ambitions were condemned to outrun the realistic prospect of her colonial population attaining sufficient critical mass. This judgement, however, is to read backwards from a knowledge of what eventually came to pass: from the perspective of 1700, French enterprise around the North Atlantic looked at least as propitious as that of the English. Over the century as a whole, however, the French crown, and to an extent French society, pursued European opportunities in preference to all of those potentially available around the Atlantic.

Peoples of the Great Spirit

By c. 1600, the indigenous peoples of much of the Caribbean had been largely wiped out, and those in Mesoamerica had lost their overwhelming numerical superiority over the Iberian incomers and their descendants. Further to the north, Native Americans at this point still had some choice in how their relationships with other West Europeans might be characterised. By c. 1700, however, Native Americans had begun progressively to lose their freedom to choose between purposeful resistance, peaceful coexistence, or remorseless retreat to the interior. Social and cultural forms amongst the peoples of North America differed significantly, amongst themselves as much as between them and the societies of Mesoamerica. Yet their fates appeared to be the same even though this outcome was by no means inevitable. Why was there no native American resurgence to rid the continents, North and South America, of the incomers, or to confine them to the coastal strips where they could be sustained directly by their navies?

Expressed at its simplest, indigenous peoples did not presume that Europeans came with hostile intent and consistently underestimated the greed and ambition of the incomers. As with some of the peoples of the Caribbean and of Mesoamerica, the incomers could be welcomed as potential allies in local disputes or as sources of novel trade goods and technologies. Hostility could be a learned response, rather than a reflex. Furthermore, in large measure what divided the indigenous peoples of continental North America—their languages, cultures, material wants, rivalries—was generally greater than their willingness to collaborate in sufficient numbers over sufficiently long periods successfully to oppose the incomers. With some notable exceptions—for example, the confederacy of the Five, later Six Nations—European incomers generally overcame indigenous communities by deploying, by turns and as occasion required, trade goods, firearms, alliance, disease, or massacre. This is not to say that leaders amongst the indigenous peoples did not recognise the extent of the threat to their communities posed by Europeans, but their ability to mobilise coordinated and consistent resistance was often compromised by the willingness of some amongst indigenous communities to collaborate with the invaders. Whatever Pocahontas, for example, conceived of as her role in the unfolding relations between her people and the new English settlers, she was no Malinche—whether a woman determined to exact her own kind of revenge on a whole society by whom she and her people had been wronged or an ambitious and opportunistic manipulator of others' greed. Rather, Pocahontas may symbolise the willingness of some Native American peoples to compromise with the incomers, without achieving recognition and respect for their original identity, because of the attractions of the extraordinary material culture of European societies.

The diversity of the peoples of North America both prolonged their resistance and increased the likelihood of their defeat. Each community encountered by Europeans presented the incomers with the full range of options—trade, alliance, war—and each community was as vulnerable to the diseases of the incomers. At the same time, the enormous land area of the continent always provided a last resort for an embattled indigenous community: retreat to the interior. Indigenous communities were made and remade as the frontiers of European settlement advanced from the ocean and waterways, and the survivors of disease and war were assimilated into societies further inland.

For those communities that sought to compromise with the incomers, indigenous cultures were recurrently challenged by missionary work or subverted by the goods and foodstuffs of the settlers. Clashes over rights of access and contending notions of justice provoked fighting and opportunities for settlers to accuse their hosts of betrayal. After years of attempts to live side by side, armed resistance might achieve short-term success, as in King Philip's War or the Pueblo uprising in what is now New Mexico, but such setbacks to colonialism generally prompted vicious retaliation, rather than permanent evacuation, by European forces that had already established secure colonial bridgeheads from which they were extremely difficult to dislodge. By 1700, however, it was not yet a foregone conclusion that indigenous resistance would fail to halt the incomers.

Wars of Independence

Over the course of the century, occasion and opportunity arose for some amongst colonial populations to question the substance of the political and economic ties with the homelands. In addition, political and wartime upheavals in Europe from time to time undermined the capacities of home governments, so that separation—independence—of colonies might have been achieved, to be sustained by freer trade with the merchants and colonists of rival European societies. Beyond any disputes between colonists and homeland governments, there were bodies of stateless free agents at large—buccaneers—who had the means and the motives to overthrow colonial governments in favour of independent, pirate states, akin to those of the North African corsairs.

Amongst English settlements, disputes with home governments arose over control of trade—as much for revenue purposes as for the assertion of sovereignty—from 1625 and intermittently through the 1680s. Disputes over religious practice from the 1630s led some immigrants to create their own, separate colonies, as in Rhode Island. The fall of the Stuart monarchy in 1649, prompted some colonies to proclaim their allegiance to the exiled king, Charles II. Pirates operated out of Jamaica from the 1650s, with their power in local government symbolised by the career of Henry Morgan, appointed lieutenant governor in the 1670s. Resentment of colonial government provoked support for Bacon's Rebellion in Virginia (1676).

These experiences represent the gamut of the possible amongst colonial communities in the seventeenth century and were at least potentially available to the colonists of any of the European societies engaged in North Atlantic enterprise. Yet when offered choice, colonists tended to confirm their formal allegiances to their homelands. In the most spectacular case, although the Dutch conquest of north-east Brasil lasted almost 25 years, their eventual expulsion—largely by colonial efforts—was not followed by a declaration of independence but by restitution of all the ties with Portugal.[11]

That this was so may reflect a preference for cultural affinity over political autonomy, in another manifestation of a reluctance to recognise that the shared experiences as colonists around the North Atlantic, gave settlers more in common with other colonists of whatever origin than they might have with the people of their homelands. On the other hand, in large measure, decrees by homeland governments could apply in colonial settings only with the compliance or tacit consent of the colonists. As we have observed before, homeland governments were unwilling to deploy substantial armed forces permanently to their colonies, not least because of the expense, and so the capacity of governments to coerce their colonial populations was markedly less than their capacity to enforce policies in the homelands. In some cases, formal representative bodies mediated the will of the homeland government to the circumstances of colonial life, but even in those communities in which there was no such formal provision, cooperation was the only way to implement policies. Time and again in the English settlements, for example, compromises had to be worked out between the programmes of governments that ultimately would not risk alienating and thus potentially losing the allegiance of colonists, and the practical circumstances of colonial communities that still aspired to recognition as members—at a distance—of the homeland society.

Only the buccaneers, in reality, represented an alternative social and political identity.[12]

CONCLUSION

For West Europeans, the seventeenth century set the precedent for the free movement of people across the globe—and perhaps determined the model—for the millions of nineteenth-century emigrants. Almost all West European societies with access to the sea pursued attempts to found settlements across the North Atlantic. The numbers of European settlers willing to venture their lives and fortunes across the ocean increased dramatically over the numbers in the 1500s, with a corresponding diversification of social forms, cultures, languages, and religious observances set up in the New World. Whereas European contacts with Asia had to this date involved only limited numbers of West Europeans, few of whom settled permanently as tolerated guests amongst powerful host societies, the North Atlantic became the busy highway by which more or less accurate facsimiles of the many West European societies were established overseas. Copying Iberian practice, this was true colonialism with other Europeans successfully maintaining their social, economic, and political ties with a motherland across enormous geographical distances. By the end of the century, transatlantic travel and settlement had become, if not commonplace, unexceptional.

Viewed from 1697, it was not apparent what configuration of forces amongst the contending societies of the littoral might emerge in the North Atlantic. Amongst European societies, at least, we may discount the extremes that, for example, a new era of world peace would emerge as commercial prosperity displaced war as the chief pursuit of states, or that the Papacy would successfully sustain its hoped-for pan-European alliance against the Ottoman Empire.[13] It is to what happened next that we turn in chapter 9.

FURTHER READING

For: a widely available account of the Dutch experience, see C. R. Boxer, *The Dutch Seaborne Empire, 1600–1800* (London, 1965); a recent account of the English experience, see D. M. Loades, *England's Maritime Empire. Seapower, Commerce and Policy, 1490–1690* (New York and Harlow, 2000), K. Morgan, *Slavery and Servitude in North America, 1607–1800* (Edinburgh, 2000), B. Lenman, *England's Colonial Wars, 1550–1688* (New York and London, 2001); on the impact of the English willingness to permit asylum for refugees, see M. C. Baseler, *"Asylum for Mankind." America, 1607–1800* (Ithaca, N.Y., and London, 1998), esp. chapters 1 and 2, and on politics between colony and homeland, see R. M. Bliss, *Revolution and Empire. English*

Politics and the American Colonies in the Seventeenth Century (New York and Manchester, 1993); the Iberian experience, see H. Kamen, *Spain's Road to Empire* (New York and London, 2002); a recent summary account of early modern imperialism as globalisation, see G. Raudzens, *Empires. Europe and Globalisation, 1492–1788* (Thrupp, England, 1999), S. Schroeder, ed., *Native Resistance and the Pax Colonial in New Spain* (Lincoln, Nebr., and London, 1998) and D. J. Weber, ed., *What Caused the Pueblo Revolt of 1680?* (New York, 1999).

CHAPTER 9

1697–1763: Rule Britannia?

Our final chronological section reflects on the forms and consequences of the struggles for imperial dominance between European states sufficiently sophisticated to mobilise resources for worldwide conflict. From the perspective of c. 1700, Louis XIV's France might seem best equipped to seize the initiative, but strategic attributes—population, tax base, bureaucracy—do not alone seem sufficient to have determined the outcome of a struggle for the North Atlantic.

In 1697, the Peace of Rijswijck between Louis XIV and William III left the contending alliances of France and England ranged in a rough equilibrium of forces in western Europe, across the North Atlantic, and in the Indian subcontinent. The rivalry between European states was not extinguished by the Peace, but their struggle for military and diplomatic pre-eminence had been focused on the European continent, to which their North Atlantic territories were largely subordinate elements. The naval war between France and the Anglo-Dutch state had been gruelling,[1] but such fighting as had occurred on land beyond Europe had been relatively limited in scale and made little or no difference to the outcome of the war or to imperial-colonial frontiers.[2]

The indigenous peoples of the Atlantic littoral beyond Europe had not been mere spectators in these conflicts; indeed, in North America much of the fighting had been between the local allies of English and French colonists. No seriously challenging attempts were made, however, by indigenous peoples to exploit the opportunity of European rivalries and reassert native independence. This may be understandable in respect of indigenous peoples within the Iberian North Atlantic Empire, because by c. 1700 they had been in large measure superseded by mestizo communities, acculturated to membership of a transoceanic Hispanic society that they generally embraced. It is less clear, by contrast, why West African and North American peoples did not more effectively exploit the rivalries amongst the interlopers of European origin. For many amongst these indigenous peoples, extensive contact with Europeans had not yet led to conquest and occupation, but contact had exposed them to European technologies of travel and warfare for over a century, surely time enough to acquire these means of resistance. Instead, West African and native North American societies were subverted by the material culture of their European, sometime friends, persuaded first to collaborate with and progressively to surrender to European control.

In contrast with the stasis of 1697, the Peace of Paris in 1763 left the British Empire of George III as a power of almost unprecedented extent and economic resources, with a global reach. In the absence of Atlanticist ambitions amongst African or Asian imperial powers, Britain's main rivals were still Europe's other great powers, but by 1763 these powers had been defeated in their colonial empires as much as they had been matched in western Europe. In the North Atlantic world, Britain and her colonial forces had conquered Canada: in the treaty, France lost all of her North American territories to the east of the Mississippi and a string of Caribbean islands, and Spain lost Florida. Thus, the whole Atlantic seaboard of North America became part of a British Empire that also controlled the bulk of maritime trade across the ocean. What had been an Iberian monopoly and might have become a French one, was instead established as an Anglophone lake. Out of such a period of urgent competition by force of arms and economies, the far from inevitable outcome was that, by 1763, an industrialising Britain could assert pre-eminence over the whole North Atlantic, only to clash subsequently with the emergent, newly self-confident societies rooted in the American continent. This paradox returns the reader to the challenge of the introduction: why did the Anglo-American model of empire displace its competitors?

We now explore these developments through themes that, of necessity, interacted and that we may regard as having been of equal significance. We may characterise each of these developments as necessary but not wholly sufficient for the outcome of an Anglo-American supremacy. The order in which they now appear is thus one of convenience rather than priority. We first consider the role of great power dynamics on the European continent, including the changing role of the lesser European states, and the effects of domestic stresses on the colonial powers. Second, we reflect on the significance of contemporaneous developments of colonial life, in society and economy but also the absence of political challenge or colonial revolt. Third, we consider the reactions of and interplay with indigenous peoples.

GREAT POWER DYNAMICS IN EUROPE

Although Britain may be said to have emerged from the wars with Louis XIV's France as a European great power, Britain was by no means *the* European great power. In terms of population, all the peoples of the British isles (even if they could be presumed all to be loyal to the Anglo-Hanoverian state) numbered perhaps 8 million, in comparison with the possibly 20 million of France and the possibly 7 million of the newly united Spanish monarchy. Beyond these, by 1715, traditional imperial-colonial rivals, the Austrian Habsburg Empire contained perhaps 20 million and the Russian Empire perhaps 14 million people, and both empires had enlarged their territories and their ambitions during the years of war. The manpower and direct taxation resources of each of these states, once mobilised, made them formidable rivals, potentially capable of brushing aside any of the second-rank powers of Europe—Swedish, Dutch, or Prussian.

From c. 1700, the geopolitical balance amongst European states had material significance for the first time in our story of the transformation of the North Atlantic. This was largely manifested in two developments that contrasted with the previous two centuries of European insurgence: the progressive withdrawal from formal Atlantic engagement of the smaller European states, and, in place of the notion of "no peace beyond the line," the inauguration of an era in which there was a more explicit demarcation between times of peace and times of war.

The Minor Players

As we saw in the previous chapter, an important characteristic of European engagement with the Atlantic in the seventeenth century was the participation in war, trade, and settlement of people drawn from across the wider European continent, under the flags and (loosely) the sovereignty of states of all sizes. Scots, Swedes, Danes, Portuguese, and English, subjects of the smaller states, vied on roughly equal terms with Dutch, French, and Hispanic subjects of the more populous and rich states to establish their own settlements. By contrast, the period after 1700 saw in our story a progressive decline in the importance of projects sponsored by the smaller states—in effect, the end of a role for minor players—in favour of a rivalry confined to the more populous and richer powers. This transformation from open to closed competition arose largely from developments within Europe itself, rather than any relative increase in the difficulty of Atlantic enterprise. Entry costs to colonialism were no more or less prohibitive than in the earlier period: the effort to find people willing to participate, capital to invest, and shipping to sustain any enterprise were comparable with the earlier period. The terms of trade in such enterprises, however, had altered as a consequence of the increasing availability (and lower unit prices) of the principal consumer prizes from the Western Hemisphere—sugar, tobacco—which perhaps diminished the commercial-mercantilist incentive for the smaller states to establish their own territories in the areas of supply.

That there was from the end of the seventeenth century a revised arithmetic of engagement was perhaps symbolised by the effort in and failure of the Scottish enterprise at Darién (1698–1700). The project attracted substantial public interest and support in Scotland, notwithstanding fear of Jacobite resurgence and perhaps encouraged by poor harvests and the consequent growth of poverty. The project was seen as giving expression to ideals of Scottish independence and international presence as a colonial power, and the project prospectus promised rich returns from a combination of plantation agriculture, an *entrepôt* for Atlantic-Pacific commerce and state-licensed piracy. Although the location chosen for the settlement had been abandoned by Iberian colonialism, that was not of itself a warning of likely failure, but the technical challenges of climate and cultivation proved too great for the Hibernian colonists, and neighbouring Hispanic colonies launched a succession of task forces to destroy the Scottish settlement whilst English forces in the Caribbean denied the Scots aid. For cautious Scots investors seeking early and strong profit, the newly founded Bank of England offered better returns.[3] For individual Scotsmen and their families seeking better prospects away from the homeland, there were welcomes in the newly reconquered Ireland of William III and in the Middle Colonies of English North America.

By 1700, it seemed clear that for new colonial enterprise to flourish, either the eventual returns had to be even bigger to be sufficiently attractive to outweigh the financial loss needed to establish a lasting settlement, or the state had to underwrite the enterprise with cash and military presence. The Swedish crown, although still an energetic imperial power around the Baltic until the early 1700s, ceased to pursue transoceanic enterprise as the disputed succession to the Swedish throne after Karl XII (r. 1697–1718) combined with domestic tensions to undermine imperial ambitions, whilst a powerful rival emerged in the form of a Russian Empire, inspired by Tsar Pyotr I the Great. Even Dutch colonial enterprise underwent a change, with a renewed concern about homeland defence and in alliance with Britain against France, coinciding with a shift in investment to *rentier* capitalism with better rates of short-term returns.

It might be tempting to seek an explanation for this withdrawal by the minor players as in some way a function of critical mass—that states below a certain threshold of population and wealth, or exhausted by war, were newly disadvantaged in the competition for trade and settlement in the eighteenth-century Atlantic. Such an explanation, however, cannot account for the contrasting trajectories of Portugal and England.

By the last third of the seventeenth century, Portugal had successfully regained her independence from Madrid and had expelled the Dutch from sometime Portuguese territories in South America. The settlement and exploitation of her territories around the Atlantic were potentially set to flourish, as she still possessed a few strategic points on the West African littoral from which to participate in the Atlantic slave trade, and tropical and semitropical plantations from which to export sugar or tobacco. Possessed of a small population, dominated by great landowners and rigidly authoritarian in its brand of Roman Catholicism, Portugal might have been expected to pursue common causes with Louis XIV's France, to protect herself from Madrid's ambitions or the predatory Dutch. Instead, Portugal sought and sustained military and commercial alliance with England—even in the period of the English republic—a connection reconfirmed by the marriage of a Portuguese princess to the restored Stuart king, Charles II. The alliance was reinforced in the war for the Spanish succession and cemented in successive trade treaties from Methuen onwards. Portugal's sustained imperial trajectory demonstrated that relatively small size of homeland or population was not an inherent disadvantage; ambition and focus on areas of particular importance could allow colonial projects to continue.

At the same time, there were loosenings of nationalist restrictions on potential settlers, so that (preferably Protestant) Germans, Scots, and French, for example, were permitted to settle in the North American colonies of Britain, in which there were already Dutch and Swedes. The Scots-Irish did not seek to establish a sovereign independence but preferred instead to exploit the opportunities opened to them in the aftermath of the formal Union of 1707. Whereas the numbers of non-English emigrants from Europe to the British-controlled territories in the Atlantic made a significant contribution to the growth of their (white) population, there were no comparable movements to the French and Spanish empires. Emigration to the Bourbon/Borbón Atlantic from Europe did not cease, but little or no effort was made to encourage recruits from outside of France or Iberia, and the numbers of emigrants of European origin failed to grow as rapidly as those to the English colonies. Attempts to recruit German Roman Catholics to settle in Louisiana, for example, were not only on a small scale but were notably unsuccessful.

Peace and War Distinguished

The years of war that ended with the Peace of Utrecht reaffirmed the inability of any power to secure decisive military superiority over its rivals in Europe, and the costs in lives and treasure to learn this lesson may have encouraged politicians and their monarchs to seek a "peace dividend" as their peoples and economies sought to recover. Between 1713 and 1756, there were periods of comparative peace in the North Atlantic—in striking contrast to the recurrent warfare on the European continent—between the leading West European powers. Substantial effort was devoted to the suppression of piracy, an activity that had for long been a form of licensed or private enterprise warfare. In the North American interior, although there was strategic rivalry between French and English colonial enterprises in the Ohio valley, these were largely pursued by proxy, through allies amongst the indigenous peoples.

Domestic Stresses

Each of the major European states, however, was confronted by powerful domestic constraints, some of which were consequences of warfare, some of which arose as internal forces sought to take advantage of war's distractions. All the major European states had undergone substantial challenges—political and material if not always military—for which peace would provide a vital relief. In Britain, in 1688–89, the legitimate dynasty had for the second time in 50 years been overthrown by open, armed revolt, now assisted by foreign invasion. The immediate consequence was again a series of civil wars within the British Isles, from which the conquest of Ireland from 1690 and the formal union with Scotland from 1707 granted a kind of stability. That the transition to the Hanoverian dynasty in 1714 was not similarly bloody was not for lack of attempts to subvert it, and a Jacobite counterrevolution remained a possibility until at least 1746. In many respects, the Hanoverian state relied on its economic development, pre-eminently the growth of domestic agricultural productivity and international commerce, to draw the sting of political subversion amongst its ordinary subjects, just as it deployed bribery to secure compliance amongst its politicians. War was to be avoided by the Britain of the first two Georges and Walpole, in order not to expose the regime to further domestic unrest arising from war taxation.

In France, loyalty to the dynasty was sorely tested by the demands and defeats of war between 1688 and 1713, which provoked popular resistance (although neither as dangerous nor on the scale of the popular rebellions of earlier in the seventeenth century). These travails came on top of the economic and social consequences of the departure of perhaps 500,000 Huguenots after the revocation of the Edict of Nantes (1685). Even in peacetime, the state seemed to betray its people, as in the collapse in ignominy of the public finances as managed by the Scotsman John Law (1720). On the other hand, state sponsorship of commerce and industry in the manner of Colbert continued to encourage moderate prosperity for some, even as the particularism of the regions hampered the state's efforts to develop an infrastructure of roads and canals. The structural weakness of the French economy was perhaps symbolised by the recurrent *entraves*, the grain riots in which popular direct action asserted a "moral economy of the poor," in a period when such phenomena were disappearing in Britain.

In the unified state now properly designated Spanish, the Bourbon/ Borbón succession was achieved only at huge expense of blood and treasure, and the suppression of the ancient liberties of Catalunya and Aragón. Felipe V secured the crowns of Spain at the price of much of her European empire but oversaw the introduction of significant reform of government and institutions such that, from 1716, a truly Spanish monarchy was created. Population growth was recovering in the early eighteenth century, but only to restore the numbers of the late sixteenth century. Recurrent pursuit of imperial and dynastic projects in the Italian lands from 1717 was not necessarily clearly in the best interest of Spanish peoples but demonstrated that Spain remained a European great power. Meanwhile, colonial enterprise advanced at a modest pace.

By contrast, the Dutch state after the death of William III (1702) and the treaty settlements of 1713–15, suffered population stagnation and heavy taxation that eroded incentives to colonial enterprise. The loss of the southern Netherlands to French occupation and then Austrian sovereignty, was accompanied by peace terms that favoured British trade in the Spanish Empire. In place of the aggressive colonialism of the earlier seventeenth century, Dutch enterprises consolidated their activities to draw profit from the extensive commerce within Asia, and between Asia and Europe via southern Africa. A decline in enthusiasm and interest, rather than a decline in capability, seems to have been at the heart of the issue.

Whatever colonial opportunities were recognised as existing, amongst the European colonial powers there were grounds for proceeding with caution. New imperial powers—the Austrian and Russian Empires, as well as smaller but militarily effective states like Brandenburg-Preussen— could not be presumed to be disinterested in projecting their power and interests beyond Europe. Elsewhere around the globe, Europeans were not the only societies with the potential to create empires. Chinese imperial power extended to the north and east, to frontiers with the Russian empire and the Indian subcontinent. Russian expeditions began to explore the north-west rim of the Pacific, as well as expanding their territory in central Asia. The dissolution of the Moghul Empire in northern India provided opportunities for new centres of power to arise in the subcontinent. That none of these powers, however, sought to intervene in the Europeans' enterprises in the North Atlantic could not have been presumed.

A COLONIAL LIFE

Notwithstanding the almost Homeric achievements of British and colonial armed forces during the French and Indian/Seven Years War (1756–63), this transformation of the North Atlantic to an Anglophone lake was not the result of war alone. Rather, between the end of the seventeenth century and the middle of the eighteenth, the North Atlantic world changed in social and economic character in ways which gave a greater permanence to the settlement of 1763 than would have been derived from military endeavour alone, or from diplomats' pen strokes on a map. Around 1700, the Atlantic world was still largely a reservoir of raw materials, hemmed in by hostile peoples and environments, which was drawn on for the benefit of European economic development. By c. 1763, particularly in Anglophone North America, it was already becoming a complex consumer society, bourgeois and entrepreneurial in outlook, well-practised in the exploitation of natural and human resources to participate in a transoceanic commercial economy, for which the resistance of indigenous peoples might be an inconvenience but never an impediment.

In the space of one lifetime—for which Benjamin Franklin (1706–90) may stand as representative—Anglophone North America was transformed to become the pre-eminent region of the Western Hemisphere. This pre-eminence was expressed through the growth and changing nature of its population, through its economic development, and through its changing place in the geopolitical balance amongst the European imperial-colonial states. Franklin's life experiences may serve to illustrate these developments to us.

Franklin was born in Boston, which in the early 1700s had a population of perhaps 9,000. As such, whilst it was amongst the smallest urban settlements in the English-speaking world, it was yet amongst the largest in the Anglophone North Atlantic. Barely two hundred miles from frontiers of settlement with the indigenous peoples, in 1675–76, it had been threatened by the fighting with indigenous peoples, called by the settlers King Philip's War. During Franklin's childhood, the principal trades of the community had been with the Caribbean colonies and Britain, exporting such as fish, wheat, horses and lumber, and importing all kinds of manufactures, mostly in ships built and owned in the colony. New England merchants and shipping provided vital services for the Caribbean sugar islands, but by no means stood to overtake them in the value of their commerce.

Nevertheless, growing trade between North Atlantic colonies of all kinds and western Europe was carried largely in British-owned (and crewed) ships. Annual transatlantic crossings by British ships grew from about 500 in the 1670s to 1,500 by the late 1730s. A growing positive balance of trade between Britain and her North American colonies from the mid–eighteenth century encouraged the colonists to seek to recoup their deficits through trade with the rest of the North Atlantic, and into the Mediterranean. The volume of marine traffic crossing between British and North American ports by midcentury already far exceeded that attained during Iberia's imperial zenith, as did the value of the goods transported in both directions, once bullion was excluded from the calculation. Marine insurance rates reflected the confidence with which voyages were undertaken, and the turnover of bills of exchange between British and North American-based merchants emphasised the fluency of commerce across the ocean. There persisted the long-time aim that other nationalities be excluded, but this proved as impossible to enforce, as it had for the Iberians against the likes of John Hawkins.

Franklin's father was in the print business, and Ben was apprenticed as a printer, an occupation reflecting the demand for printed materials in an already very literate society. When Ben left Boston for Philadelphia in 1723, the city inhabitants numbered perhaps 11,500, reflecting the continued natural increase and immigration. The rate of growth of populations of European heritage in the English-ruled colonies exceeded those of other empires. The Anglophone empire sucked in people from Scotland, Wales, and the German-speaking lands, bringing further religious—that is, Protestant—diversity that made uniformity unenforceable. By contrast, religious revivalism in the English-speaking world would take some inspiration from the Great Awakening. Population movement to the Americas and the Caribbean continued to reflect the appeal of settlement, just as the relentless advance of the perimeter of land settlement across the continent demonstrated that, from a European perspective, there was room for all-comers. Yet Franklin was critical of the numbers of German-speaking settlers in Pennsylvania.

It was in Philadelphia that Franklin became successful as printer, symbolised by his marriage in 1730. That he could pursue such a trade indicates the high degree of specialisation in occupations made possible in a complex, urban, literate community. As entrepreneur and journalist, he catered to a colonial taste for plain and honest values, and *Poor Richard's Almanac* made him annual profits, from 1732. He embraced deism and became a Freemason, both symbols of the independent mind, and exemplified his enthusiasm for the practical informed by science for profit by inventing the Philadelphia stove. He affected the style and manners of a simple man, whilst pursuing political intrigue as a lobbyist for his colony's interests in the imperial capital. He had already spent time in London in 1724, and so participated in the metropolitan transatlantic culture of the English-speaking Western Hemisphere, before taking up residence there in 1757. His intellectual stature was celebrated by membership of the Royal Society (1766).

He became an advocate of self-government; of colonial higher education leading to the foundation of the first institution to enjoy the title of University in Anglophone North America; he praised meritocracy and self-help; his son became the governor of New Jersey (1762), by royal appointment. Such a life would seem to be as much as a man might hope for—until a revolution.

Franklin, of course, was neither a typical colonial in his career nor singular in his views, and we should recall the very different kinds of colonial societies that existed contemporaneously beyond his Philadelphia. Slave-owning, plantation agricultural capitalism with pseudo-aristocratic style and Anglican religion, the Virginian Byrd and Lee families, could also characterise the Anglophone colonial life. This contrasted again with the continued push of the frontier of settlement in the interior, and along which Regulator movements, could confront the forces of government. Yet within this diversity of opportunity, expressed through a variety of forms of government and social hierarchy, there was promoted a common currency of social and political discourse in a vocabulary shared with the homeland. Franklin's Anglophone world was not characterised by political harmony: disputes amongst colonial governments, between individual colonies and London, between established settlers and newcomers, between newcomers and indigenous peoples—these were likely to have perpetuated a role for London as mediator and arbitrator, precisely because of the capital's wider, imperial perspective of the common interest. Mutual economic benefit and defence, particularly for as long as rival colonial powers were active in the New World, tied the diverse colonies to a common sovereign. Rebellion against specific policies could be contemplated, but rebellion to separate from the homeland was not to be countenanced until a fundamental change overtook a North American colonial understanding of the meaning of membership of the empire.

INDIGENOUS PEOPLES

The indigenous societies of the Caribbean and Mesoamerica had already disappeared or been subsumed in the demographic turmoil of the post-Columbus century of epidemic and settlement. Their cultures had been incorporated into an emerging hybrid of Iberian Christian hidalgismo and mestizo peasant agriculturalism, either to be remade in imitation of Jesuit Catholicism or to be persecuted as ideologies of resistance. They were inevitably integrated into the Atlantic economy as the principal consumers of Africa's chief export—people—or as leading providers of the agricultural raw materials that fed emergent industrialisation in the Anglophone littoral. The economic and social reforms of Carlos III's Spain did not extend to his American dominions, which were increasingly dependent on British capital for investment and British purchasers for their commodities. Brasil, although more open to the possibility of interethnic cohabitation than other parts of the European-ruled western continent, nevertheless subscribed to the Atlantic economy on much the same terms as the Hispanic empire.

Africa was already contributing its people and treasure to the Atlantic economy at the rate of tens of thousands per year from 1700. This growing traffic represented significant income to the indigenous slave traders and community leaders of West Africa, so that African participation in the ocean's commerce was not dependent on substantial numbers of European settlers, either for its initiation or perpetuation. At its crudest, West African societies had surplus commodities for which the sustained external demand generated for the providers a premium that they ploughed back into their domestic economies. The larger the volumes of slaves traded, the greater the income of the intermediaries, as demand in the West for new slaves grew ahead of the supply. In the absence of an indigenous rebellion against the trade, it continued until some in European societies turned against it.

Only in the North American interior did the indigenous peoples continue to exercise some autonomy in their dealings with European incomers. To that extent, it was perhaps in the strategic interest of, for example, the Six Nations, that the rivalries between the French and the English in the Ohio should not be resolved by victory of either side. The ability of these indigenous peoples to choose their own fate was already compromised by the depredations of disease, but their military and political independence relied on the perpetuation of colonial conflict.

CONCLUSION

The Seven Years War was the climax of the processes of change that confirmed the North Atlantic as an Anglophone lake: the military victory of Britain derived from an industrialising economy with growing population, which mobilised resources of war more effectively than her neighbours or rivals. Yet the war came about because of the perceived threat of France—in Europe, in Asia, in India, as much as in the Western Hemisphere. A period of peaceful coexistence had been attempted by the policies of Prime Minister Walpole and the Regent Fleury, but both had gone from office in the early 1740s, and war in Europe and the interior of North America had quickly followed. In France and Britain, renewed political will sought a definitive clash of empires.

Between 1756 and 1763, the European powers contended for preeminence on a worldwide scale, and Britain emerged triumphant, apparently beyond the reach of its rivals. The Atlantic and India constituted the major prizes for those powers with the naval forces and imagination to project their ambition beyond the Rhein and the Elbe. Of the great empires of the Eurasian landmass—Austrian, Ottoman, and Russian—only Catherine the Great's stood as potentially as powerful, with her reserves of population and material resources but limited outlets to the world's oceans. The Ottomans, whose expansionism in the fifteenth century had been one of several factors in West European maritime ventures, by the mid-1700s could barely maintain their Balkan frontiers.

This was, however, by no means the end of colonial rivalries around the North Atlantic and in North America. Spanish colonialism continued to expand its frontiers, with further explorations and new regional governments in Texas (1718), Sinaloa (1734), Nuevo Santander (1746), and California (1767). Certainly, Spain lost Florida, but Louisiana was ceded to Spain in the peace of 1763, with New Orleans returned to French rule. Russian reconnaissances in the Pacific alarmed Madrid as much as London. Perhaps the least expected turn of events after 1763 was a rebellion by some of Britain's western colonies.

FURTHER READING

For: the struggle between the powers, see D. McKay and H. M. Scott, *The Rise of the Great Powers, 1648–1815* (New York and London, 1983); the colonial experience in British territory, see D. H. Fischer, *Albion's Seed: Four British Folkways in America* (New York, and Oxford, 1989), as well as M. K. Geiter and W. K. Speck, *Colonial America: From Jamestown to Yorktown* (London, 2002; New York, 2003); for the wider colonial story, see A. Taylor, *American Colonies* (New York and London, 2001); one biography amongst many, see R. W. Clark, *Benjamin Franklin: A Biography* (New York and London, 1983); the wars, see W. R. Nester, *The Great Frontier War: Britain, France, and the Imperial Struggle for North America, 1607–1755* (Westport, Conn., and London, 2000), S. Brumwell, *Redcoats. The British Soldier and War in the Americas, 1755–1763* (Cambridge, 2002), J. Brewer, *Sinews of Power: War, Money and the English State, 1688–1783* (Boston, Mass., and London, 1989), and F. Anderson, *Crucible of War: The Seven Years War and the Fate of Empire in British North America, 1754–1766* (New York and London, 2000).

Conclusions and Prospects

We began our consideration of the early modern North Atlantic with two, related questions that may be said to encapsulate some central aspects of the transformation of the region. Why was an Iberian imperialist Catholic agrarian aristocracy superseded by an Anglophone constitutionalist Protestant capitalist republic as the dominant force in the Western Hemisphere? Why is the American Declaration of Independence written in the language of Shakespeare, and not the language of Cervantes?

These questions presume that it was the choices of West Europeans, above all, that provoked the transformation and influenced its eventual outcome. Over the intervening pages, however, we have added to these questions with reflections on the circumstances that encouraged West Europeans to pursue exploration and exploitation around the North Atlantic. We have pondered ways in which indigenous peoples of the North Atlantic littoral, in West Africa and the Western Hemisphere, were drawn into the transformation—to some extent willingly if not entirely knowingly—and contributed their blood, sweat, and tears to the making of new social and cultural contexts. We have also reflected on the instruments of transformation, technical and technological aspects of early modern European culture, and the extent to which Europeans took precedence in the North Atlantic because of their possession of tools and equipment—ships and guns, above all—that magnified the Europeans' powers beyond their numbers of participants.

Beyond this, we have pondered the proposition that central to the transformation of the North Atlantic to a region dominated by Europeans lies a succession of coalitions, of exploitative and asymmetrical alliances with indigenous peoples from which people of European origin emerged as chief beneficiaries. Within the framework of those successive coalitions, further transformation was effected by the superior returns to English alliances with interests—commercial and military, native and colonial— than those obtained by the first societies to exploit the North Atlantic, the Iberians. This was not, however, "manifest destiny" but was a consequence—one of several possible outcomes—of a coincidence of factors in the 1620s and 1630s: an England at peace whilst much of Europe was at war; a reservoir of migrants seeking to settle permanently overseas in preference to enrichment and return; a lack of coordinated resistance to and often collaboration with the incomers, amongst the indigenous peoples in the territories that became New England and the Middle Colonies, allowing the establishment of self-sustaining bridgeheads on the continent; the development of large-scale addiction amongst European consumers to the narcotics, tobacco and sugar. In these developments in the first half of the seventeenth century, there was a turning point—although not an absolutely conclusive one—in the subsequent transformation of the North Atlantic.

Within early modern English and subsequently British society, expectations of living standards and the definitions of relative poverty moved upwards, so that aspirations of emigrants continued to exceed the capacity of colonial societies readily to meet them all. Hence, newly arrived settlers, and those who had served out their indentures, and the children of earlier arrivals, all sought to extend the frontiers of settlement and profitable cultivation, into the continental interior, whilst their tastes for the comforts of home encouraged lively trade with the homeland and on to the rest of Europe. The Iberian Empire, meanwhile, continued the story of its first century, and poured its treasure into imperial endeavours within Europe.

But it's more complicated than that.

It is, of course, an impossible task to summarise the story of the challenges and changes of nearly three hundred years, involving millions of lives across thousands of kilometres, in a few short paragraphs or a single volume. In making a selection of ideas and issues to include in this account, huge areas of importance have been set aside. There is, for example, too little reference to the experiences of women from all societies of the littoral, and none at all about children. This is largely a history of the technical context and aspects of the transformation, with stresses on economic, social, and political aspects, rather than a rounded account including close consideration of religions and cultural developments, or the details of art, architecture, and law. To use an outmoded terminology, it has been about foundations rather than superstructures. It leaves unconsidered other vital questions.

Reviewing the triumph of the peace of Paris (1763), was a revolution in

1776 (and in other parts of the New World from the 1820s) an inevitable consequence of the growth of economic independence and hence military self-reliance, or was it lodged in the development of divergent models of political rights and identity? North America was inevitably multicultural and multilingual, inhabited even in the early modern period by the "hyphenated Americans," so in what circumstances did the WASP preeminence become secure? If the history of the emergence of a predominant Anglophone social and political model is manifested in a modern worldwide interest in learning English, how will that interest in Anglophonia respond to the challenge in the United States represented by the current and future growth of Latino culture and social models? If we reflect on this linguistic point—the evident displacement of Spanish by English by the eighteenth century—we may confront the Churchillian "history of the English-speaking peoples" triumphalist teleology, in favour of recognising the extraordinary achievement, against the odds, of the Anglophone era. Yet what has changed over time from Latino to Anglophone may revert, and with what consequences: is a Hispanic, Roman Catholic sensibility more attuned to communitarianism, whereas capitalist individualism is innately competitive? Although the growing significance of the Pacific Rim in the global economy need not represent an insurmountable challenge to North America or to Europe, does it represent a further prolongation of arrested progress in Africa, or does it intensify the need to recognise alternative models of development?

History is a story, but it is also a study, a questioning, probing and analysing of what we know about what happened.[1]

Notes

INTRODUCTION

1. J. Cummins, *The Voyage of Christopher Columbus: Columbus' Own Journal of Discovery Newly Restored and Translated* (New York, 1992), pp. 93–94.

2. The Declaration of Independence, reprinted in *The National Experience*, 2nd ed., ed. J. M. Blum (New York, 1968), p. 851.

3. This was the claim of the admiral himself in his letter to his employers, the Catholic Monarchs (4 March 1493), when he described one of his landfalls: "que yo pensé que no sería ysla, salvo tierra firme, y que sería la provinçia del Catayo." M. Zamora, *Reading Columbus* (Berkeley and Los Angeles, Calif., 1993), p. 181.

4. For further discussion of this topic, see chapter 7, this volume.

5. Although San Salvador is the traditional first landfall, the expedition did not put ashore there. At least one reconstruction (computer-generated) of the voyage further supports an identification of where Columbus went ashore as Watling Island; P. L. Richardson and R. A. Goldsmith, "The Columbus Landfall: Voyage Track Corrected for Winds and Currents," *Oceanus* 30 (1987), pp. 3–10.

6. Indeed, it has been suggested that "the Atlantic is a purely European construct," not otherwise known to the peoples of the littoral; J. H. Eliott, "Atlantic History: A Circumnavigation," in *The British Atlantic World, 1500–1800*, ed. D. Armitage and M. J. Braddick (Basingstoke and New York, 2002), p. 234. For a brisk, broadly conventional narrative account of the history of European engagement with the ocean from antiquity to the present, however, see P. Butel, *The Atlantic*, trans. I. H. Grant (London and New York, 1999).

7. In the phrase of Bernard Bailyn quoted by E. H. Gould, "Revolution and Counter-Revolution," in *British Atlantic World*, Armitage and Braddick, p. 208.

8. J. Selden, *Mare Clausum* (London, 1635); described as "a monument of misplaced ingenuity and learning" for attempting to prove the English crown's sov-

ereignty over the seas around the British Isles by G. Davies, *The Early Stuarts 1603–1660*, 2d ed. (Oxford, 1979), p. 217.

9. For an illustration of the development of historians' understanding of the subject, see K. G. Davies, *The North Atlantic World in the Seventeenth Century* (Minneapolis, Minn., and London, 1974), with its largely European perspective, to contrast with discussion of aspects of recent debate on the varieties of Atlantic history, in Armitage and Braddick, *British Atlantic World*, pp. 15–27.

10. Styling themselves Zapatistas, thereby drawing on a more recent heritage of resistance.

11. Whilst acknowledging the importance of contemporaneous historical developments in Asia, the detailed study of their interrelationships with the early modern Atlantic is the subject of another book; for a readable, scholarly, thematic account amongst the several available for this period, see G. V. Scammell, *The First Imperial Age. European Overseas Expansion, c. 1400–1715* (London and Winchester, MA, 1989); for a briefer, recent résumé of the subject, see G. Raudzens, *Empires: Europe's Globalisation, 1492–1788* (Thrupp, England, 1999); for a stimulating introduction to some reappraisals of these wider issues, see J. Black, *Europe and the World, 1650–1830* (London and New York, 2002).

12. F. Braudel, *La Méditerranée et le monde Méditerranéen à l'epoque de Philippe II*, 2nd rev. ed. (Paris, 1966): inspirational text of the *Annales* school and a "classic" but, *pace* Mark Twain, still worth the read and available in English translation.

13. A. J. P. Taylor, "Accident Prone, or What Happened Next," quoted by K. Burk, *Troublemaker. The Life and History of A. J. P. Taylor* (New Haven, CT, 2000), p. 408.

14. For those seeking further guidance on historical method and explanation, of the many texts available a brief but stimulating introduction to the topic is provided by K. Jenkins, *Re-thinking History* (London and New York, 2001). That this matters is demonstrated by the challenge of the Holocaust deniers, taken up, amongst others, by B. Southgate, *History: What and Why? Ancient, Modern, and Postmodern Perspectives* (London, 2001).

15. For a recent meditation on this, see P. Gigantès, *Power and Greed. A Short History of the World* (London, 2002).

16. For one analysis of this in practice in England, see J. T. Rosenthal, *The Purchase of Paradise. Gift Giving and the Aristocracy, 1307–1485* (London and Toronto, 1972).

17. Perhaps most entertainingly presented in R. H. Tawney, *Religion and the Rise of Capitalism*, reprint (Harmondsworth, 1975), but for a more contemporary perspective, see also R. H. Roberts, ed., *Religion and the Transformation of Capitalism* (London and New York, 1995), especially pt. I, "Revising the Classics."

18. For a summary account, see S. Digby, "The maritime trade of India" in *The Cambridge Economic History of India*, ed. T. Raychaudhuri and I. Habib, Vol. 1, c.1200–c.1750 (Cambridge, 1982), pp. 125–59; and in greater depth, K. N. Chaudhuri, *Trade and Civilization in the Indian Ocean* (Cambridge, 1985).

19. See, for example, A. Schottenhammer, ed. *The Emporium of the World: Maritime Quanzhou, 1000–1400* (Leiden, 2001).

20. D. Landes suggests, however, that accumulation and the legal protection of property through inheritance is a distinctively European characteristic; see *The Wealth and Poverty of Nations* (London, 1999), pp. 32–35.

21. See, for example, T. T. Allen, *Mongol Imperialism: The Policies of the Grand Qan Möngke in China, Russia, and the Islamic Lands, 1251–1259* (Berkeley, CA, 1987).

22. For a recent summary account, see A. Kappeler, *The Russian Empire: A Multiethnic History,* trans. A Clayton (Harlow, 2001), pp. 21–59.

23. Although by no means would it be argued that imperialism is a distinctively European ambition; see, for robust comment on this, Landes, *Wealth and Poverty,* p. 425.

24. For a further discussion, see chapter 2, "A Note on Medical Practice," and chapter 6, "Population," this volume.

25. For a further discussion, see chapters 1 and 2.

26. H. Cortés, the fifth letter, 3 September 1526, in *Letters from Mexico,* trans. and ed. A. Pagden (New Haven, CT, 1986), p. 446.

27. This point is made briefly by Scammell, *The First Imperial Age,* pp. 77–80.

28. The conventional west European calendar of the Common Era will be employed for all dates, with the year start adjusted to 1 January. For those events for which the distinction is significant between the Julian and Gregorian calendars (New and Old Style), or between Christian and other usages, both forms are used.

29. Quoted by B. Simms in his review of *Interesting Times: A Twentieth-Century Life,* by E. Hobsbawm, *Times Higher Education Supplement* (London), 6 December 2002, p. 27.

CHAPTER 1: SETTING THE SCENE

1. B. Cunliffe, *Facing the Ocean: The Atlantic and Its Peoples* (Oxford, 2001).

2. For an entertaining account of the reconstructed transatlantic crossing from Ireland, see T. Severin, *The Brendan Voyage* (London, 1978).

3. For further discussion of this, see chapter 6, this volume.

4. Cited by S. Özbaran, "Ottoman Naval Policy in the South," in *Süleyman the Magnificent and His Age: The Ottoman Empire in the Early Modern World,* ed. M. Kunt and C. Woodhead (Harlow, England, and New York, 1995), p. 62.

5. It was from Malindi, in modern-day Kenya, that the Gujerati, Ibn Majib, piloted da Gama to Calicut.

6. In using the term *Mexica,* rather than *Aztec,* I follow the usage commended by H. Thomas, *Conquest. Montezuma, Cortés, and the Fall of Old Mexico* (New York, 1995), p. xix.

7. See T. Mackintosh-Smith, ed., *The Travels of Ibn Battutah* (1958; reprint, London, 2003).

8. G. Parker, *The Military Revolution* (Cambridge, 1989), p. 83.

9. This is the reason suggested by J. Glete, *Warfare at Sea, 1500–1650* (London, 2000), p. 76.

10. Notwithstanding Menzies's belief that the Chinese fleet reached the western seaboard of North America; G. Menzies, *1421: The Year China Discovered the World* (London, 2002), published in the United States as *1421: The Year China Discovered America* (New York, 2003).

11. On the use of the names of the constituent polities of Iberia, rather than the term "Spain," see chapter 7, "A 'Spanish' Empire?"

12. See the journeys down the west African coast commencing in 1270.

13. For a recent scholarly biography, see P. Russell, *Prince Henry "the Navigator"* (New Haven, CT, 2001).

14. It was perhaps the shock of the new discoveries that helped to encourage the scientific spirit of the early modern period.

15. Aspects of this problem of perception are further explored in L. J. Ramos Gómez, *Cristóbal Colón y los indios taínos* (Valladolid, Spain, 1993).

16. For an interesting discussion of the likely superior mission intelligence of the Portuguese, see J. H. Parry, *The Age of Reconnaissance, Discovery, Exploration and Settlement, 1450–1650* (London, 1963; reprint, 1973), pp. 178–80.

17. G. Raudzens, *Empires: Europe and Globalization, 1492–1788* (Thrupp, England, 1999), p. 28.

18. The first expedition consisted of 3 ships and 90 men; the second of 17 vessels and 1,200 men; H. Kamen, *Spain 1469–1714* (Harlow, England, and New York, 1983), pp. 54, 55.

CHAPTER 2: GOING THERE AND GETTING BACK

1. Derived from sources quoted in C. Cook and J. Stevenson, *The Longman Handbook of Modern European History, 1763–1985* (London and New York, 1987), p. 216.

2. For the Caribbean, see figures cited as "White" by S. L. Engerman, "France, Britain and the economic growth of colonial North America," in The *Early Modern Atlantic Economy*, ed. J. J. McClusker and K. Morgan (Cambridge, 2000), pp. 238–39. For the mainland, see the figure cited as "White" in table A.1. of M. R. Staines and R. H. Steckel, eds. *A Population History of North America* (Cambridge and New York, 2000), pp. 694–95.

3. H. Kamen, *Spain, 1469–1714* (Harlow, England, and New York, 1983), p. 158.

4. F. Fernández-Armesto, *Civilisations* (London, 2000), p. 468.

5. Kamen, *Spain*, p. 158.

6. G. Parker, *The Military Revolution. Military Innovation and the Rise of the West, 1500–1800* (Cambridge and New York, 1989), p. 76.

7. Fernández-Armesto, *Civilisations*, p. 468.

8. B. Cunliffe, *Facing the Ocean* (Oxford and New York, 2001), p. 105, describing the regular convoys from the Italian trading cities to England in the fourteenth century. For an introduction to the question of journey times in Europe, see F. Braudel, *The Mediterranean and the Mediterranean World in the Age of Philip II*, 2nd rev. ed., vol. I, trans. S. Reynolds (London and New York, 1973), pp. 355–63.

9. "When Spanish navigators opened two-way communications across the Pacific in the late sixteenth century, it normally took three months to get from Acapulco to Manila and six months back," Fernández-Armesto, *Civilisations*, p. 468. In the words of Parry, "Spaniards were the only Europeans who regularly crossed the Pacific: one or two big ships each year traversed, in thirsty scorbutic squalor, the immensity of open water between Acapulco and Manila" and because of the sailing conditions, these journeys made no landfalls in between; J. H. Parry, *Trade and Dominion. The European Overseas Empires in the Eighteenth Century* (London, 1971; reprint, 2000), p. 237.

10. See, for example, prices in seventeenth-century England quoted by R. S. Dunn, *Sugar and Slaves* (New York, 1973), p. 205.

11. For more detail on this trading economy, see R. Hassig, *Trade, Tribute, and Transportation. The Sixteenth-Century Political Economy of the Valley of Mexico* (Norman, OK, 1985).

12. Hassig, ibid., pp. 56, 161.

13. Thomas, *Conquest*, pp. 442–43, 456–57, 488–89.

14. Thomas, ibid., pp. 492–93.

15. J. K. Thornton, *Warfare in Atlantic Africa, 1500–1800* (London and New York, 1999), pp. 47–48.

16. J. K. Thornton, *Africa and Africans in the Making of the Atlantic World, 1400–1800* (Cambridge and New York, 1992), p. 154.

17. Atlantic excursions are cited by Braudel, *The Mediterranean*, vol. II, p. 872.

18. D. S. Landes, *The Wealth and Poverty of Nations* (London, 1999), p. 110. A league varied significantly in length across Europe, from approximately 4.2 to 5.6 kilometres (Hassig, *Trade*, p. 32).

19. F. Braudel, *Civilisation and Capitalism, 15th–18th Century*, Vol. I, *The Structures of Everyday Life* (London, 1985), pp. 421–22.

20. R. J. Barendse, *The Arabian Seas. The Indian Ocean World of the Seventeenth Century* (Armonk, N.Y., 2002), p. 7.

21. For a modern account of the voyage, see G. Williams, *The Prize of All the Oceans* (New York, 2000).

22. For a popular account, see D. Sobel, *Longitude* (London, 1996).

23. "The real revolution, the vital marriage between square-rig and lateen, . . . produced the basic barque, the direct ancestor of all the square-riggers of the Reconnaissance and the later great age of sail"; J. H. Parry *The Age of Reconnaissance* (London, 1973), p. 87.

24. Ibid., p. 92.

25. F. Alves, "Geneaology and archaeology of Portuguese ships at the dawning of the modern world," http://www.abc.se/~pa/publ/gen_port.htm.

26. J. H. Parry, *The Spanish Seaborne Empire* (Harmondsworth, England, 1973), p. 253.

27. If the innate advantage of the galley was the partial capacity to travel against the wind, this attribute was offset by the development of keels in conjunction with the adoption of the lateen rig, thus enhancing the ability to beat to windward by tacking.

28. J. H. Pryor, "The Geographical Conditions of Galley Navigation in the Mediterranean," in *The Age of the Galley—Mediterranean Oared Vessels since Pre-classical Times*, ed. R. Gardiner (London, 1995; reprint, 2000), pp. 206–16, in which he notes the restricted endurance of early modern galleys to about 1,100 miles (1760 kilometres) and their vulnerability in swells of greater than 1 metre.

29. The *Vasa* capsized on her maiden voyage through the flooding of the lower gun deck during a gentle manouevre in Stockholm harbour, which the contemporaneous enquiry ultimately blamed on the vessel's design, with its high centre of gravity; see C. Borgenstam and A. Sandström, *Why* Wasa *Capsized* (Stockholm, [1985]).

30. C. R. Boxer, *The Dutch Seaborne Empire, 1600–1800* (London, 1965; reprint, 1977), pp. 43–44, and p. 20.

31. Parker, *Military Revolution*, pp. 94–95, but see the alternative reading of this situation by N. A. M. Rodger, "Guns and sails in the first phase of English colo-

nization, 1500–1650," in *The Origins of Empire*, ed. N. Canny (Oxford and New York, 2001), p. 93.

32. This preference for fighting sailors may perhaps reflect the deficiencies of the Elizabethan army more than a preference derived from nationalism or calculated advantage.

33. On the impact of Drake's destruction of storage barrels, see the classic comments by G. Mattingley, *The Defeat of the Spanish Armada* (London, 1959), pp. 116–17.

34. A summary account of this action and its significance is given in J. Glete, *Warfare at Sea, 1500–1650* (London and New York, 2000), pp. 181–82.

35. Parker, *Military Revolution*, pp. 99–100.

36. For an account of the growth of English naval power during the seventeenth century, see J. S. Wheeler, *The Making of a World Power* (Thrupp, England, 1999), pp. 43–65.

37. Parker, *Military Revolution*, p. 103.

38. But see also the discussion of different attitudes to naval power amongst societies outside of Europe; Parker, *Military Revolution*, pp. 103–14.

39. D. B. Quinn, *England and the Discovery of America, 1481–1620* (London, 1974), p. 238; the ascription "frigat" reflects the fluidity of terminology in the period; references to tonnage normally referred to cargo capacity rather than displacement.

40. C. R. Phillips, "The Caravel and the Galleon," in *Cogs, Caravels and Galleons: The Sailing Ship, 1000–1650*, ed. R. Gardiner, consulting ed. R. W. Unger (London, 1994), p. 114.

41. Ibid., p. 102.

42. Parker, *Military Revolution*, pp. 91–92, cites vessels with service lives of 60 and 100 years, but these cannot be taken as the norm.

43. For a brief discussion of the seagoing capacities of the first peoples Columbus encountered, see L. J. Ramos Gómez, *Cristóbal Colón y los indios taínos* (Valladolid, Spain, 1993), pp. 9ff.

44. "A female mule, the Arab name for the dhow, the workhorse for the navigation in the Arabian seas"; R. J. Barendse, *Arabian Seas*, p. 13.

45. Parry, *Spanish Seaborne Empire*, pp. 117–18.

46. Dunn, *Sugar and Slaves*, pp. 19–20.

47. Ibid., pp. 210–11; and N. Zahedieh, "Overseas Expansion and Trade in the Seventeenth Century," in *Origins*, ed. Canny, p. 408.

48. Parry, *Spanish Seaborne Empire*, pp. 247–48.

49. For a discussion of changing manning levels in merchant and naval vessels in the eighteenth century and maritime health issues, see Parry, *Trade and Dominion*, pp. 214–19.

50. The forts, castles, and garrisons were built by Europeans as much if not more to protect their interests from other European interlopers than from indigenous threats.

51. On the profit motive for African traders, see the classic P. D. Curtin, *Economic Change in Pre-colonial Africa* (Madison, WI, 1975).

52. For an introduction to this topic, see Thornton, *Warfare in Atlantic Africa*.

53. In the 1560s, the Arsenal "was the biggest industrial establishment in all Christendom, perhaps the biggest in the world"; F. C. Lane, *Venice: A Maritime*

Republic (Baltimore, MD, 1973), p. 362; on the assembly line in operation, see pp. 363–64.

54. J. Brewer *Sinews of Power: War, Money and the English State, 1688–1783* (London and Boston, 1989), pp. 35–36.

55. For a fascinating case study of the creation and maintenance of an indigenous maritime society, see M. J. Jarvis, "Maritime masters and seafaring slaves in Bermuda, 1680–1783," *William & Mary Quarterly*, ser. 3, vol. LIX, no. 3 (July 2002): pp. 585–622.

56. About which I say more in the next chapter.

57. In this discussion, I have conflated the distinction between *navigation* as guiding a ship out of sight of land (essentially by calculation), and *pilotage* as the task in sight of land (essentially by observation); *pace* Parry, *Age of Reconnaissance*, p. 112, although not seeking to deny the importance of the distinction from the later 1500s, as described by Parry.

58. Barendse, *Arabian Seas*, p. 70, n. 10.

59. See the Introduction to this volume, including n. 3.

60. Parry, *Spanish Seaborne Empire*, p. 120.

61. For a convenient introduction to these and further bibliography, see the entry "Sailing Directions," in *Christopher Columbus and the Age of Exploration: An Encyclopedia*, ed. S. A. Bedini (New York, 1992; abridged and reprinted, 1998), pp. 595–97.

62. On the techniques for navigation out of sight of land before the adoption of the magnetic compass, see Cunliffe, *Facing the Ocean*, pp. 79–88.

63. Giovanni Caboto and his son may have extrapolated the existence of a western landmass from the stories of Bristol fishermen who salted their catches on the coast of Labrador; for a convenient summary of the proposition of a pre-discovery as the context for the Caboto voyages, see D. B. Quinn, *England and the Discovery of America, 1481–1620* (London, 1974), pp. 5–23, 47–87. For a recent re-evaluation of the technical competence of English mariners at this time, see S. Rose, "English seamanship and the Atlantic crossing, c. 1480–1500," in the e-journal *Journal for Maritime Research*, hosted by the Maritime Museum, Greenwich, England, http://www.jmr.nmm.ac.uk.

64. See, for example, the sponsorship of mapmaking in Elizabethan colonial Ireland: J. H. Ohlmeyer, " 'Civilizinge of those rude partes': Colonization within Britain and Ireland" in *Origins*, Canny, p. 140; or the 1676–81 mapping of France for Louis XIV: L. Jardine, *Ingenious Pursuits* (London, 1999), pp. 137–38.

65. See the entry for 25 September in the journal of the first voyage, J. Cummins, *The Voyage of Christopher Columbus* (New York, 1992), p. 89.

66. For an introduction to this, see Jardine, *Ingenious Pursuits*, pp. 133–76.

67. For a brief history, see M. A. Mullett, *The Counter Reformation* (London and New York, 1984), pp. 43–44.

68. For further discussion of the meaning of *Spain* in the early modern period, see chapter 7, "A 'Spanish' Empire?"

69. Diego de Landa, *Relación de las Cosas de Yucatan*, 1566; published in English as *Yucatan before and after the Conquest*, trans. and annotated by W. Gates (Baltimore, Md., 1937; reprint, London, 1978), p. 2.

70. Thomas, *Conquest*, p. xix.

71. See, for example, the meeting with local chiefs in Quiahuitzlan as described

by Bernal Díaz in his *Historia verdadera de la conquista de la nueva España;* published in English as *The Conquest of New Spain,* trans. and ed. J. M. Cohen (Harmondsworth, England, 1963), pp. 110–11.

72. On first use of the term, see Thomas, *Conquest,* pp. 366, 441, and 723, nn. 56 and 57.

73. For brief comment on the imposition of *castellano* in Iberia and in the New World, see, for example, C. Mar-Molinero, *The Politics of Language in the Spanish-Speaking World: From Colonisation to Globalisation* (London and New York, 2000), esp. pp. 18–29.

74. Landes, *Wealth and Poverty of Nations,* p. 118.

75. A convenient discussion of the interplay between the economic motive and slave mortality on the Middle Passage is offered by J. A. Rawley, *The Transatlantic Slave Trade: A History* (New York and London, 1981).

76. Citing other sources, Rawley, *Transatlantic Slave Trade,* pp. 289, 290.

77. Rawley, *Transatlantic Slave Trade,* p. 292; N. A. M. Rodger, *The Wooden World: An Anatomy of the Georgian Navy* (London, 1986), p. 99; Rodger also quotes catastrophic mortality in the fleet led by Admiral Hosier to the Caribbean in 1726 (p. 98).

78. See n. 9.

79. For a classic account of the craft, see K. Kilby, *The Cooper and His Trade,* London (1971; reprint, 1990).

80. Rodger, *Wooden World,* p. 85, notes that in his researches on the British navy, between 1750 and 1757, with the exception of stockfish, "there was no item of which as much as 1 per cent was condemned [as unfit to eat], an astonishing fact considering the limitations of technology and the hazards to which the full casks were exposed after issue."

81. P. Russell, *Prince Henry "the Navigator"* (New Haven, CT, 2001).

82. The phrase is used by C. A. Fury, "Training and Education in the Elizabethan Maritime Community, 1585–1603," *The Mariner's Mirror* 85, no. 2 (May 1999): p. 148.

83. The vessel used in the modern reconstruction of the Caboto transatlantic voyages, the *Matthew,* has sails operated from the deck by pulleys, rather than standing rigging to be climbed by the crew; P. Firstbrook, *The Voyage of the "Matthew." John Cabot and the Discovery of North America* (San Francisco, 1997).

84. Sometimes, however, economies could have disastrous consequences, as when the laid-up English fleet was attacked in its Chatham home base by the Dutch (1667).

85. For a concise account of the disease in European experience, see C. Quétel, *History of Syphilis,* trans. J. Braddock and B. Pike (Cambridge, 1990), pp. 9–105, and for its purported American origins, see pp. 34–44.

CHAPTER 3: CONQUEST AND COERCION

1. For further consideration of this theme, see, for example, V. G. Kiernan, *The Duel in European History* (Oxford and New York, 1986).

2. That such warfare was not predominantly ritualistic is cogently propounded by R. Hassig, *Aztec Warfare: Imperial Expansion and Political Control* (Norman, Okla. and London, 1988).

3. For a summary of the issues in the interplay of wars and slavery in West Africa, see J. K. Thornton, *Warfare in Atlantic Africa, 1500–1800* (London and New York, 1999), pp. 127–39.

4. For definitions of and distinctions between these two terms, see the beginning of chapter 2.

5. Notwithstanding the growth in size of armies on the European mainland, however, there was perhaps only one example during this period in which war provoked lasting change in the political geography of Europe: the victory for the Dutch republic in its 80-year war of liberation from the Habsburg empire, finally acknowledged at the Peace of Westfalen (1648).

6. The summary account of her contribution was given by Bernal Díaz (*Historia verdadera de la conquista de la nueva España*, published in English as *The Conquest of New Spain*, trans. and ed. J. M. Cohen [Harmondsworth, England, 1963], pp. 85–87), but for a recent and uncharacteristically sympathetic portrayal of this woman, see A. Lenyon, *Malinche's Conquest* (Melbourne, 1999; London, 2000).

7. This theme is explored by J. R. Hale, *War and Society in Renaissance Europe 1450–1620* (London, 1985).

8. For further discussion of this point, see chapter 5.

9. Although originally employed as a battlefield weapon in its own right (see T. Arnold, *The Renaissance at War* [London, 2001], pp. 85–87), the principal task of pikemen became to give physical protection to the comrades with firearms whilst they were reloading.

10. F. Bacon, "Of the true greatness of kingdoms," in *Essays*.

11. Machiavelli argued that Christianity had undermined civic virtue and accounted for the poor performance of Italian soldiers (*Discorsi*), and Montaigne, for example, commented on reports of the considerable physical courage of Amerindians ("On the cannibals," in *Essais*).

12. Just such an accident led to the death of one of Cortés's most vicious captains, Pedro de Alvarado, in 1541.

13. Díaz, *Conquest of New Spain*, p. 23.

14. Díaz talks of the ritual humiliation, torture, and murder of the Iberians captured in the *noche triste*, amongst other stories.

15. As recounted by English sources, see J. Wilson, *The Earth Shall Weep. A History of Native America* (London, 1998), p. 71.

16. As recounted by French sources, see Wilson, *Earth Shall Weep*, p. 111.

17. On this view amongst indigenous peoples of North America, see ibid., p. 27.

18. Ibid., pp. 201, 203.

19. Díaz, *Conquest of New Spain*, p. 75.

20. Ibid., p. 76.

21. Arnold, *Renaissance at War*, p. 78, illustrates this by describing the complement of a *tercio* in Alba's army in the early 1570s.

22. For a recent brief discussion of this point, see ibid., pp. 39–43. Arnold also notes how prodigiously expensive artillery trains were to operate in the field (pp. 42–43).

23. Burgundian-made in 1449, it is of the bombard type and weighs some 5,000 kilograms.

24. For an illustration of the ideal artillery train, as described by an author in the mid–sixteenth century, see Arnold, *Renaissance at War,* pp. 42–43.

25. The chief proponents of the coordinated use of infantry firepower on the battlefield were Willem Louis, Mauritz, and Jan, nobles of the house of Nassau and military leaders in the Dutch war of liberation. These developments were greatly encouraged by the interpretation late-sixteenth-century military theorists placed on the lessons to be applied from ancient Roman examples (see ibid., pp. 74–76).

26. According to Arnold, conquistadores in Mexico improvised to make gunpowder, collecting sulphur from a live volcano, and constructed artillery from local iron ore deposits; ibid., p. 32.

27. An interpretation implied by the observations of D. Landes, *The Wealth and Poverty of Nations* (New York and London, 1999), pp. 111–12, that, for example, Inca culture deprived people of individuality and initiative.

CHAPTER 4: EXPLOITATION

1. For convenient definitions, and noting the distinction between *technological* and *technical* capacities, see the beginning of chapter 2.

2. As sketched by K. Wrightson's essay "Class" in D. Armitage and M. J. Braddick, eds., *The British Atlantic World, 1500–1800* (Basingstoke, England, and New York, 2002), pp. 140–41, contrasting the plurality of opportunities giving migrants a choice—for example, between economic enrichment in Virginia and spiritual enlargement in New England.

3. Whilst it should be acknowledged that El Cid served several masters, Christian and Moor, he nevertheless remained a model of faithfulness to concepts of duty, as well as valour in battle.

4. Pedro de Cieza de Léon, quoted at http://www.bbc.co.uk/history/discovery/exploration/conquistadors_05.shtml.

5. Bernal Díaz's account, in *The Conquest of New Spain,* trans. and ed. J. M. Cohen (Harmondsworth, England, 1963), p. 413.

6. Bartolomé de Las Casas, Introduction to *A Short Account of the Destruction of the Indies* (1542), quoted in BBC's Web site, http://www.bbc.co.uk/history/discovery/exploration/conquistadors_01.shtml.

7. R. Hakluyt, *The Principal Navigations, Voyages, Traffiques and Discoveries of the English Nation* (London, 1600).

8. J. Burckhardt, *The Civilisation of the Renaissance in Italy,* trans. S. G. C. Middlemore, 2 vols. (New York, 1958; reprint, 1976), vol. 1, ch. 3, "The Modern Idea of Fame," pp. 151–62.

9. We should note that Machiavelli condemned Christianity because it undermined civic virtue by putting a premium on peace and love.

10. Composed from the 1450s.

11. Cited, for example, by J. H. Parry, *The Age of Reconnaissance* (London, 1973), pp. 49–50, and by H. Thomas, *Conquest: Montezuma, Cortés, and the Fall of Old Mexico* (New York, 1995), p. 441.

12. See the summary account offered in Thomas, ibid., pp. 131–35, noting the turbulent but dependent relationship with governor Velázquez.

13. Thomas, ibid., on the question of Cortés's wealth (p. 135) and the extent of his borrowings to finance the expedition (pp. 139–40).

14. According to Díaz's account, Cortés sought command of the expedition to relieve his desperate indebtedness (Díaz, *Conquest of New Spain*, p. 47), which may in fact have been the consequence, rather than the cause, of Cortés's seeking command.

15. Thomas, *Conquest*, p. 135 (citing Las Casas) and p. 140.

16. Díaz, *Conquest of New Spain*, pp. 16ff, 27ff; Thomas, ibid., proposes Alvarado as reporting to Cortés the extent of riches to be had in the western lands (p. 140).

17. Díaz, ibid., pp. 44–45.

18. Thomas, *Conquest*, p. 136.

19. For further detail, see H. Cortés, *Letters from Mexico*, trans. and ed. A. Pagden (New Haven, CT, rev. ed. 1986; reprint, 2001).

20. See chapter 2, n. 72.

21. Smith published extensively between *A True Relation* (1608) and his death in 1631; Dampier's *New Voyage around the World* first appeared in 1697.

22. See J. Robertson, "Re-writing the English conquest of Jamaica in the late seventeenth century," in *English Historical Review* cxvii, 473 (September 2002): pp. 813–39.

23. Such persons lived also in the Anglophone colonies across the Atlantic, even though they were not officially distinguished as a group; J. E. Chaplin, "Race," in *British Atlantic*, eds. Armitage and Braddick, p. 168.

24. Although migration was a common feature of early modern life, much of the historiography on early Anglo-America, for example, focuses on the stability of populations; for further comment, see A. Games, "Migration," in *British Atlantic*, eds. Armitage and Braddick, pp. 43–46.

25. Perhaps the most well-known example, Cortés retired to Castilla in 1540, but this in part reflected the lack of trust in which the crown held him. For examples of returnees from Iberian colonies in the west, see references in I. Altman, *Transatlantic Ties in the Spanish Empire* (Stanford, Calif., 2000). Captain Smith, likewise, retired to his homeland rather than the New World, similarly distrusted by the sponsors of colonial settlement; amongst more celebrated migrants from the Anglophone colonies to Britain, see those who returned to participate in the English Civil Wars, such as the preacher Hugh Peter, the soldier-politician George Downing, and the sometime governor of Massachusetts, Sir Henry Vane the younger.

26. For an illuminating discussion of the complexities of recruitment and service of Europeans around the Indian Ocean, see R. J. Barendse, *The Arabian Seas* (Armonk, NY, and London, 2002) p. 110 and pp. 113–15.

27. Outlined by M. Rediker, *Between the Devil and the Deep Blue Sea* (Cambridge and New York, 1989), pp. 46–48.

28. Outlined, whilst noting the problems of evidence, by R. S. Dunn, *Sugar and Slaves* (New York, 1973), pp. 300–301 and the chapter there following.

29. H. Kamen, *Spain, 1469–1714* (Harlow, England, and New York, 1983), p. 13 and p. 171. Clearly, Sevilla's growth was a function in part of the importance of its role in transatlantic and other international commerce, but the population of the Castilian heartlands was in measurable decline in the later 1500s, so that the rate of growth of Sevilla slowed but did not halt, in the early 1600s.

30. A. Games, *Migration and the Origins of the English Atlantic World* (Cambridge, Mass., and London, 1999), provides a detailed study of migration through

London, derived initially from the port books entries for 1635; the quotation about London immigration is from P. Clark and P. Slack, *English Towns in Transition, 1500–1700* (Oxford and New York, 1976), p. 64. Note, however, the significantly better rates of population reproduction and sustained growth amongst New England settlers than elsewhere in the North Atlantic world.

31. The offices of admiral, viceroy, and governor, whether or not hereditary, were essentially functional and profitable, rather than honorific, unlike a dukedom.

32. For the origins of the Boyle dynasty, see N. Canny, *The Upstart Earl: A Study of the Social and Mental World of Richard Boyle, First Earl of Cork, 1566–1643* (Cambridge, 1982); for a more revealing account of a family's fortunes across our period, see on the Carrolls, R. Hoffman and S. D. Mason, *Princes of Ireland, Planters of Maryland: A Carroll Saga, 1500–1782* (Chapel Hill, NC, and London, 2000).

33. Although the baronetcy was formally extended to Nova Scotia at the same time as it was extended to Scotland, in 1625.

34. M. Rediker, *Between the Devil and the Deep Blue Sea: Merchant Seamen, Pirates, and the Anglo-American Maritime World, 1700–1750* (Cambridge and New York, 1987), p. 261.

35. Ibid., p. 286; note, however, Rediker's discussion of piracy at its eighteenth-century peak as a form of social banditry in which revenge for harsh treatment at the hands of merchant captains was an important core value.

36. Cited by D. Landes, *The Wealth and Poverty of Nations* (New York, and London, 1999), p. 77.

37. Beginning with the classic account by E. J. Hamilton, *American Treasure and the Price Revolution in Spain, 1501–1650* (Cambridge, MA, 1934).

38. P. Bakewell, *A History of Latin America* (Oxford and Malden, MA, 1997), pp. 180, 181.

39. In addition to the extraordinarily productive mines of Potosí, in the viceroyalty of Peru, from the late 1540s.

40. J. H. Parry, *The Spanish Seaborne Empire* (Harmondsworth, England, 1973), p. 90.

41. See, for example, Columbus's account of his efforts in this regard in his journal entries for early November 1492; J. Cummins, *The Voyage of Christopher Columbus: Columbus's Own Journal of Discovery Newly Restored and Translated* (New York, 1992), pp. 112, 115.

42. Although it should be noted how well European weeds fared in the west; A. Taylor, *American Colonies* (New York, and London, 2001), pp. 47–49.

43. See chapter 6 for some consideration of environmental impact.

44. Domestic slavery existed in Iberia, particularly in Lisboa, Andalusía, and later around the court in Madrid.

45. These two latter islands were, of course, part of the Portuguese Empire.

46. For which see Cummins, *Voyage of Christopher Columbus*, p. 115, and his helpful notes on pp. 216–17.

47. Dutch projects comprehended not only large-scale drainage of marginal land, but also the development of specialist, high-value commodities, most spectacularly in the tulip craze, for a summary of which, see S. Schama, *The Embarrassment of Riches: An Interpretation of Dutch Culture in the Golden Age* (New York, 1988), pp. 350–66.

48. See chapter 2.

49. F. Braudel, *Civilisation and Capitalism, 15th–18th Century*, trans. S. Reynolds, vol. 1 (London, 1985), p. 412.

50. I. Wallerstein, *The Modern World-System*, vol. 1, *Capitalist Agriculture and the Origins of the European World-Economy in the Sixteenth Century* (New York, 1974).

51. See chapter 3.

52. See chapter 8.

CHAPTER 5: THE AVAILABILITY OR ABSENCE OF ALTERNATIVES TO NORTH ATLANTIC EXPANSION

1. The alliance between France and the Ottoman sultan became publicly known in 1542.

2. See chapter 3, n. 10.

3. For example, Professor G. Parker, but see the debate on the military revolution for which introductory references are given in chapter 3, "Further Reading."

4. It is perhaps worth noting that experiences in the British isles ran contrary to this trajectory: despite the politicoreligious upheavals of the mid–sixteenth century, the Elizabethan state managed to live in peace with its Scottish neighbour, and likewise with its Irish adventure, until the 1590s. Rebellions against the monarch of the three kingdoms, beginning in 1642, were eventually followed by the ruthless military conquest of Scotland and Ireland and their enforced incorporation into a republic. Although short-lived and undermined by internal divisions, the English republican regimes of the 1650s demonstrated proof of concept for the creation by war of an empire in Europe.

5. The classic account of this is K. R. Andrews, *Elizabethan Privateering: English Privateering during the Spanish War, 1585–1603* (Cambridge, 1964).

6. For a summary account of this episode and its significance for the development of Brasilian society, see P. Bakewell, *A History of Latin America: Empire and Sequels, 1450–1930* (Oxford, 1997), pp. 315–18.

7. For further comment on the islands and outposts claimed by Madrid but not effectively occupied or colonised, particularly in the Lesser Antilles, see chapter 8.

8. For further comment on this, see chapter 6.

9. "Yield Ratios" in ch. 2 of E. E. Rich and C. H. Wilson, eds., *The Cambridge Economic History of Europe*, Vol. 5 (Cambridge and New York, 1977), pp. 79–82.

10. In the early modern period, within the Habsburg duchy of Crain.

11. For an analytical account of the projects, see K. Lindley, *Fenland Riots and the English Revolution* (London, 1982), pp. 23–107.

12. Despite the costs, the Cromwellian settlement of Ireland has been described as the real colonial success, repeated after 1690; E. H. Gould, "Revolution and Counter-revolution," in D. Armitage and M. J. Braddick, eds., *The British Atlantic World, 1500–1800* (Basingstoke, England, and New York, 2002), pp. 201, 203.

13. Perhaps the one notable exception to this proposition was Scotland, in the aftermath of the failure of the Darién project.

14. A. C. Hess, *The Forgotten Frontier. A History of the Sixteenth-Century Ibero-African Frontier* (Chicago and London, 1978), p. 26.

15. See the table of the Portuguese crown's income in the early sixteenth century, reproduced by Hess, *Forgotten Frontier*, p. 33.

16. These products were also obtainable, of course, from sources closer to the European homelands, in the North, Arctic, and Baltic seas and in the Scandinavian lands.

17. Notwithstanding the observation that African and Asian pathogens were more deadly to Europeans than those they encountered in the New World (D. Landes, *The Wealth and Poverty of Nations* [London, 1999], pp. 169–70).

18. Alexander VI was born in Valencia.

19. Note, however, the summary consideration of the relative profitability of seventeenth-century English overseas ventures offered by E. Mancke, "Empire and State," in *British Atlantic World*, ed. Armitage and Braddick (Basingstoke and New York, 2002), p. 190, although Mancke's points are made in the context of the English state's expectations of the implications for its policies and governance of overseas endeavour, rather than the choices of individual migrants.

CHAPTER 6: THE PUSH AND PULL OF ENVIRONMENTAL FACTORS

1. For a recent restatement of a form of this proposition in terms of geography, see D. Landes, *The Wealth and Poverty of Nations* (London, 1999), pp. 3–16.

2. G. Parker, *Europe in Crisis, 1598–1648* (Glasgow, 1979), p. 22.

3. Bulk transport by ox wagon, for example, put a ceiling on the volume and speed of movement of large volumes of foodstuffs—the closer the agricultural areas were to the town, the more frequent the journeys and greater the volume moved by smaller numbers of vehicles (e.g., Paris sits in the centre of a rich farming area); whereas accessibility to waterborne transport could sustain urban communities beyond the food resources of their immediate hinterland (a situation that sustained imperial Rome's bloated urban population).

4. For a convenient summary, see B. Fagan, *The Little Ice Age: How Climate Made History, 1300–1850* (2000; reprint, New York, 2002), pp. 66–69.

5. Ibid., p. 52.

6. Ibid., p. 55.

7. Ibid., p. 113.

8. Consider, for example, the impact of short-term climatic variables and disasters in the 1590s, 1630s, and 1650s.

9. See, Fagan, *Little Ice Age*, pp. 23–28, for a summary of the presumed workings of the North Atlantic Oscillation effect.

10. Cited by F. Fernandez-Armesto, *Civilisations* (London, 2000), p. 186.

11. Ibid., pp. 151–52.

12. Cited by A. Taylor, *American Colonies* (New York and London, 2001), pp. 13–14.

13. For an examination of this question, see K. O. Kupperman, "The Puzzle of the American Climate in the Early Colonial Period," in *American Historical Review* 87 (December 1982): pp. 1262–89.

14. Fagan, *Little Ice Age*, p. 96, citing an unpublished source, David Anderson (1999).

15. The convoy routes are summarised by J. H. Elliott, *Imperial Spain, 1469–1716* (Harmondsworth, England, 1970; reprint, 1983), pp. 185–86; for a concise account of climate factors, see the entry "Weather and Wind," in S. A. Bedini, ed. *Christopher Columbus and the Age of Exploration: An Encyclopedia* (New York, 1992; abridged and reprinted, 1998), pp. 731–34.

16. For an introduction, see the entry "Sailing Directions," in Bedini, *Encyclopedia*, especially p. 597.

17. Fagan, *Little Ice Age*, p. 91.

18. For a further discussion of these elements, see chapter 2.

19. This is necessarily a problematic proposition: in addition to the limited data sets on prices, we must acknowledge that plant pestilence, soil exhaustion and poor farming practice were also relevant, as well as possible problems arising from decisions to import or export foodstuffs in response to commercial opportunities and price advantages elsewhere, both regionally and between sovereign states.

20. A. G. R. Smith, *The Emergence of a Nation State. The Commonwealth of England, 1529–1660* (London and New York, 1984), pp. 433–34, conveniently quotes the scholarly sources, particularly W. G. Hoskins, on grain prices to 1660; in the later period, prices were more likely to have been affected also by improvements in yields and the value of grain exports; C. Wilson, *England's Apprenticeship, 1603–1763* (London, 1965), pp. 249–50.

21. G. Parker, *Europe in Crisis, 1598–1648* (Glasgow, 1979), p. 21, and see also pp. 19–28 for a brief discussion of interrelationships between climate, agriculture, population, disease, and politics.

22. This point, along with the impact of disease that often accompanied famine, is made by H. Kamen, *European Society 1500–1700* (London, 1986), pp. 35–40.

23. And also a concern of the ordinary people.

24. Fagan, *Little Ice Age*, pp. 106–11; for a more subtle and detailed introduction to the issues, see E. L. Jones, "Agriculture, 1700–80," in *The Economic History of Britain Since 1700*, vol. 1, ed. R. Floud and D. McCloskey (Cambridge and New York, 1981), pp. 66–86.

25. See the examples quoted by E. N. Williams, *The Ancien Régime in Europe* (Harmondsworth, England, 1972; reprint, 1984), p. 219.

26. Fagan, *Little Ice Age*, pp. 106–11.

27. J. H. Parry, *The Spanish Seaborne Empire* (Harmondsworth, England, 1973), p. 215.

28. A. Rowlands, "The Conditions of Life for the Masses," in *Early Modern Europe*, ed. E. Cameron (Oxford and New York, 1999), pp. 47–48, describing the period to 1600. The pace of population growth quickened substantially only from the eighteenth century; J. C. Riley, "A Widening Market in Consumer Goods," ibid., p. 233.

29. Quoted by S. G. Payne, *A History of Spain and Portugal*, vol. 1 (Madison, Wisc., 1973), p. 233.

30. Quoted by A. H. de Oliveira Marques, *História de Portugal*, vol. 2 (Lisboa, 1997) p. 99.

31. Taylor, *American Colonies*, p. 210.

32. Kamen, *European Society*, p. 34.

CHAPTER 7: 1492–1607

1. Francisco Xerez (Pizarro's secretary) in his *Report on the Discovery of Peru*, quoted at http://www.bbc.co.uk/history/discovery/exploration/conquistadors_05.shtml.

2. Although the marriage of King Fernando and Queen Isabel is by convention a union of the crowns of Castilla and Aragón, only genealogical chance preserved it, so that to speak of "Spain" as a united political entity is misleading. The term "Catholic Monarchy"—*la Monarquía Católica*—may more properly refer to the royal government of the Hispanic states of Iberia. Similarly, the peoples of the Hispanic homelands were (and to some extent remain) diverse in language and culture, and so perhaps may best be collectively referred to as Iberians, a geographical term, or by reference to the constituent polities of the Catholic Monarchy—for example, Catalunya, Aragón. In addition, from 1580, the constituent polities of the peninsula recognised a common (Habsburg) sovereign.

3. I. Wallerstein, *The Modern World-System*, vol. 1, *Capitalist Agriculture and the Origins of the European World-Economy in the Sixteenth Century* (New York, 1974).

4. The conquest completed by Nicolás de Ovando, in 1503–5.

5. By Juan Ponce de León, who led the exploitation of the gold—and peoples—of the island in 1508; quotation from P. Bakewell, *A History of Latin America: Empire and Sequels, 1450–1930* (Oxford, 1997), p. 73.

6. In 1511, "The occupation of Cuba was a work of violence and terrorism, designed to intimidate the local population into submission," Bakewell, *History of Latin America*, p. 74.

7. Bakewell, ibid., p. 79, notes that terrorism was also effective in encouraging indigenous peoples to ally with the incomers to fight against their neighbours.

8. The laws of Burgos (1512) expressed the contradictions between declaring the indigenous peoples free whilst requiring their conversion to Christianity and their labour to be expropriated.

9. For example, the revolt led by Francisco Roldán in the west of Hispaniola (1497–99).

10. Bakewell, *History of Latin America*, p. 156.

11. For a convenient introduction to this topic, see J. Thornton, "Resistance, Runaways, and Rebels," in *Africa and Africans in the Making of the Atlantic World, 1400–1680* (Cambridge and New York, 1992), pp. 272–303.

12. The term used in seventeenth-century Brasil to refer specifically to a community of escaped slaves, itself derived from the term used by Kimbundu (a people in the territory of modern-day Angola).

13. Bakewell, *History of Latin America*, pp. 327–28.

14. Called *zambos* in the Hispanic empire.

15. Described by Bakewell, *History of Latin America*, pp. 73–74.

16. Friar Diego de Landa, *Relación de las Cosas de Yucatan*, 1566, published in English as *Yucatan before and after the Conquest*, trans and notes by W. Gates (Baltimore, MD, 1937; reprint, London, 1978), pp. 4–6.

17. Ibid., pp. 6–7.

18. Also described by Landa, *Yucatan*, p. 22, "SEC.XIII The Admiral Montejo did not carry out his settlement as he planned. . . . The Indians feeling it a hardship to serve strangers where they had been the lords, began to be hostile on all sides, although he defended himself with his horses and men, and killed many."

19. Ibid., pp. 8–9. It should be noted that Marina was by no means the only person to serve the invaders as an interpreter, but there remains considerable debate about the particular and unique contribution she made to the achievements of the Cortes expedition.

20. F. Fernández-Armesto, *Civilisations* (London, 2000), p. 279.

21. Ibid., p. 285.

22. J. H. Parry, *The Spanish Seaborne Empire* (Harmondsworth, England, 1973), pp. 210, 214, 215, and 218.

23. James Scott, quoted by P. Wearne, *Return of the Indian: Conquest and Revival in the Americas* (London, 1996), p. 94.

24. Wearne, *Return of the Indian*, p. 95.

25. Landa, *Yucatan*, p. 19.

26. See, in detail, P. Boyd-Bowman, *Indice geobiográfico de cincuenta y seis mil pobladores de la América hispánica* (Ciudad Mexico, 1985).

27. Parry, *Spanish Seaborne Empire*, p. 42.

28. Ibid., p. 187.

29. Like other royal widowers amongst his contemporaries—Henry VII of England, Louis XII of France—Fernando knew his own value in the international market for alliances sealed by marriage, and he may even have hoped that his Aragonese inheritance would pass to a son by a second wife. His ambitions in these years remained fixed upon the struggle with France in Italy, although he talked, like so many earlier European kings, of a crusade to Jerusalem.

30. Bakewell, *History of Latin America*, p. 76; the following section on Ovando relies on Bakewell's summary.

31. For an introduction to the variety of the functions of the 10 *audiencias* created in the sixteenth century, see Parry, *Spanish Seaborne Empire*, pp. 190–93.

32. H. Kamen, *Spain 1469–1714* (London, 1986), pp. 91–92.

33. Parry, *Spanish Seaborne Empire*, p. 77.

34. For an entertaining account of the Welser enterprises, see V. W. von Hagen, *The Gold of El Dorado* (London, 1978), ch. 1–5.

35. Kamen, *Spain*, p. 57.

36. G. Parker, *Philip II* (London, 1988), p. 116.

37. Parry, *Spanish Seaborne Empire*, p. 75.

38. Blasco Núñez, killed in the fighting in 1546.

39. See J. F. de La Peña, *Oligarquía y propiedad en Nueva España (1550–1624)* (Ciudad Mexico, 1991).

40. The Mixtón war, in the north of modern Mexico, was perhaps the greatest challenge following the defeat of the Mexica Empire and was concluded with Iberian victory only at great cost and the mobilisation of *encomendero* Indians as the colonists' army.

41. See, for example, the detailed study of humble Castilian migrants by I. Altman, *Transatlantic Ties in the Spanish Empire: Brihuega, Spain & Puebla, Mexico 1560–1620* (Stanford, CA, 2000), esp. ch. 2 and 3.

42. "I obey but do not comply," quoted by Kamen, *Spain*, p. 160.

43. J. H. Elliott, *Imperial Spain, 1469–1716* (1963; reprint, New York, 1977), pp. 272–73.

44. F. Fernández-Armesto, "The Improbable Empire," in *Spain: A History*, ed. R. Carr (Oxford, 2000), pp. 116–17.

CHAPTER 8: 1607–1697

1. Figures quoted by J. Thornton, *Africa and Africans in the Making of the Atlantic World, 1400–1680* (Cambridge and New York, 1992), p. 118.

2. Quoted by A. Taylor, *American Colonies* (New York, 2001), p. 255.

3. For a brief, convenient summary of these efforts, see E. E. Rich, "The European Nations and the Atlantic," in *The Decline of Spain and the Thirty Years War, 1609–48/59*, vol. IV of *The New Cambridge Modern History*, ed. J. P. Cooper (Cambridge, 1970), pp. 672–706.

4. In this study, the ability to perform and repeat complex tasks with reasonable probability of achieving predicted outcomes.

5. "The great 'Atlantic plague' of 1596–1603, which gnawed at the coasts of western Europe, possibly cost one million lives, two-thirds of them in Spain alone"; H. Kamen, *European Society, 1500–1700* (London, 1984), p. 34.

6. A. Rowlands, "The Conditions of Life for the Masses," in *Early Modern Europe*, ed. E. Cameron (Oxford and New York, 1999), p. 53.

7. Ibid., pp. 47–50.

8. The title of one of William Davenant's early London theatrical events was "The Cruelty of the Spaniards in Peru" (1658), and English translations of Las Casas's works were also published at this time.

9. See, for example, the title of vol. IV of the *New Cambridge Modern History*, ed. J. P. Cooper: *The Decline of Spain and the Thirty Years War 1609–48/59* (Cambridge, 1970); or E. N. Williams, *The Ancien Regime in Europe* (Harmondsworth, England, 1984), pp. 76–80.

10. Whilst noting the difficulty in estimating the numbers, for the exodus from Iberia, see H. Kamen, *Spain, 1469–1714* (London and New York, 1983), pp. 224–25; for the possible increases in Nueva España, see J. H. Parry, *The Spanish Seaborne Empire* (Harmondsworth, England, 1973), pp. 232–33.

11. By contrast, Dutch settlers along the Hudson and the Delaware rivers largely accepted their incorporation with the English colonial empire, but their numbers were far smaller.

12. For some further reflections on these groups, see chapter 4.

13. Under which plan, for example, the deposed James II and VII (Stuart) of Britain would have become the new king of Egypt.

CHAPTER 9: 1697–1763

1. Typified by the loss of the English trading convoy from Smyrna (1693), which was estimated to have cost some £2 million, equivalent to perhaps 3 percent of the gross national product, according to T. O. Lloyd, *The British Empire 1558–1983*, Oxford (1984), p. 60.

2. French forces attacked Albany and destroyed Fort William Henry in 1696; English and colonial forces took Port Royal (Nova Scotia) in 1690 and maintained influence there, only for it to be returned to France in the Peace.

3. Incidentally, like Darién, a project led by William Paterson.

CONCLUSION

1. B. Bailyn, Preface to D. Armitage and M. J. Braddick, eds., *The British Atlantic World, 1500–1800* (Basingstoke, England, 2002), p. xix.

Index

About the Author

M. J. SEYMOUR is currently the Postgraduate Administrator at Lancaster University. Educated at Cambridge University and the University of Pennsylvania, Seymour has taught widely on early modern history programs for Cambridge University, University of Florida, Gainsville, University of Texas, Austin, and the University of California, Los Angeles. He has also worked at Boston University.